SIR ALEC CLEGG

SIR ALEC CLEGG
Practical Idealist
1909 – 1986

'I want to stand up and be counted . . . as a teacher.'

Nora J. George, M.Ed., Ph.D.

Lecturer in Education, (Retired)
The University of Hull

First published in 2000 by arrangement with
Wharncliffe Books
47 Church Street, Barnsley,
South Yorkshire S70 2AS

© N. J. George 1999

ISBN 1-871647-99-1

Typeset in Plantin by Phoenix Typesetting, Ilkley, West Yorkshire.
Printed in Great Britain by Redwood Books, Trowbridge, Wilts.

CONTENTS

FOREWORD

*By **Professor V.A. McClelland***

In a recent book ***Why Don't They Believe Us?*** (1993), Philip Fogarty reminds his readers that *'an educational system does not come into existence by itself: it is not a result of blind fate but the result of policy decisions taken by men and women who organize society in a particular way'*. In exemplification of such a truism we cannot do better than read Dr Nora George's analysis of the contribution made by Sir Alec Clegg to the education of the children of the West Riding of Yorkshire.

There were several beacons in Clegg's career that proved illuminating for the development of educational policy at both the macro and micro levels. Clegg began his work as Director of Education in the West Riding in 1945, at the end of the Second World War when, as he tells us, *'central government, local committees and officials were eager to forge ahead'*, emitting a distinct *'élan and zest'* in the process of providing a better educational deal for the children of a generation traumatised by insensitivity and uncertainty. Clegg's later involvement with the Crowther Report (1959) on the education of English boys and girls from 15 to 18 and with the Newsom Report (1963) on the education of children from 13 to 16 of average and less than average ability grew out of his innate concern for young people evincing social and learning needs. He not only wrote extensively about areas of child neglect but he made compensatory education a special characteristic of local authority provision in his county. He strongly advocated the importance of co-operation between the Authority's educational and medical departments and with the social services. In this area of endeavour contemporaries regarded him as a man of vision and rectitude.

It was Clegg's concern for the underprivileged that led him to tackle not only the thorny issue presented by the immigration in the 1960s of a substantial number of Indian and Pakistani children to the Keighley area but also, more extensively, the introduction of comprehensive schooling in the Authority, a policy fuelled by his disillusionment with eleven-plus selection processes. Clegg's concern for pupil welfare also led to major changes in emphasis in the primary school curriculum in the West Riding, with an increased attention being given to the teaching of art, craft, music, drama and physical movement. The establishment of Woolley Hall as an in-service training centre for teachers and Bretton Hall as a focus for the creative arts in education were visible expressions of his determination to change the prevailing ethos of the primary classroom.

Clegg's passion for the reform of primary education led to a desire to delay the transition to second level schooling and he was one of the first

advocates for the establishment of middle schools. The process began in
the Hemsworth area of his jurisdiction. Clegg's conception of the middle
school, however, was essentially that of the extended primary school, associated with more gradual increase in subject specialization and greater
exposure to a range of academic expertise. Predictably its side-effect was
to hold in check the growing size of comprehensive senior schools.

Dr Nora George has written an important and fascinating account of the
pioneering thought and achievement of Sir Alec Clegg, illustrating how
educational policy-making in the West Riding rested upon the visionary
enterprise of a man who never lost his desire to be seen regularly in schools
and to become acquainted at first hand with the varied needs and aspirations of teachers.

V.A. McClelland
Professor Emeritus
University of Hull

NOTES AND REFERENCES

All references and quotations are from Sir Alec Clegg's boxes of papers with the exception of a few items. He ranged across many topics and his remarks reflected the breadth of reading and practical investigation brought to bear through cogent argument on diverse audiences. Additional references, therefore, have been added. Many papers have been given a succession of numbers and in the event the Box Number and Institution have been cited. For the professional historian interested in educational planning and ideas of this period there is much to be found. The papers are at the National Arts Education Archive, Bretton Hall College of the University of Leeds; the Special Collections Section, the Brotherton Library, Leeds University; and at the West Yorkshire Archive Service Headquarters, Newstead Road, Wakefield, West Yorkshire. There is further material at the DES. All references numbered AC/PL/- refer to Bretton Hall, the National Arts Education Archive.

Abbreviations

WYAS   West Yorkshire Archive Service Headquarters, Newstead Road, Wakefield.
WRCC   West Riding County Council.
IAHM   Incorporated Association of Head Masters.
RoSLA   Raising of the School Leaving Age.
NAEA   National Arts Education Archive (Trust), Bretton Hall College of the University of Leeds.
DES   Department of Education & Science.
ACEO   Association of Chief Education Officers.

Italics

Phrases in italics in both text and quotations indicate the writer's emphasis.

ACKNOWLEDGEMENTS

The substance of the book is my own. I served as a teacher in the West Riding in several capacities: teacher, senior mistress and head teacher. I would like to acknowledge in particular the debt I owe to Dr Derek Webster, colleague at the University of Hull, Reader in Religious Education, for much patient supervision and advice, who also served on the academic staff of Bretton Hall University College.

Also to:

Denis Watson, M.A., Principal Lecturer at Bretton Hall University College (retired).

Professor V. Alan McClelland, Professor of Education, the University of Hull, 1974–1998.

Dr Robert Protherough, colleague and Senior Lecturer at the University of Hull, 1973–1987.

The Rev. Alan Loosemore, Adviser in Religious Education for the West Riding (retired).

Miss Enid Webber, member of the West Riding Advisory Staff (retired).

Miss Nancy Smith, formerly Senior Adviser for Wakefield Metropolitan District Education Department..

Dr Partridge, Mrs Anne Farr, and generally the staff of the Brotherton Library, Special Collections Section, the University of Leeds, for much help and advice in tracing papers and on copyright.

Professor P.H.J.H. Gosden, Professor Emeritus, the School of Education, the University of Leeds, and Dr P.R. Sharp, Chair of the School of Education, the University of Leeds, for permission to quote from their book, 'The Development of an Education Service: the West Riding, 1889–1974'.

Bretton Hall College of the University of Leeds:

Professor Ron George, Academic Director of Bretton Hall, and Director of the National Arts Education Archive (Trust), for permission to quote from an extensive archive, and to print the photograph of Sir Alec, and the flower painting.

Mr Leonard Bartle, Centre Administrator NAEA, and Mr Alec Jackson, Archive Assistant, the Bramley Reading Room, Bretton Hall, for time given; also the staff of the Bramley Reading Room, Bretton Hall for their kind reception.

Mrs Ruth Harris, B.A., Principal District Archivist, West Yorkshire Archive Service, Wakefield, and the staff in the Reading Room, for patient help, access to the A. B. Clegg archive, and to print one illustration from Mirfield (Grammar) School in that archive.

Ms Jill Sweeting, the University of Leeds, for initial typing of a lengthy manuscript.

Mrs Rosemary Robins, the University of Hull (retired), for final manuscript preparation and helpful advice.

The writer is indebted to Mr Leonard Bartle for the source of the verse quoted: a translation from Persian, by James Terry White, 1907, 'Not by Bread Alone'.

ALEXANDER BRADSHAW CLEGG

1909–1986

Preface

The opening of the Sir Alec Clegg Library at Bretton Hall College in December 1995

The extensive private papers of Sir Alec Clegg are lodged in the Special Collections Section of the Brotherton Library, the University of Leeds, the Lawrence Batley Centre for the National Arts Education Archive Trust at Bretton Hall College of the University of Leeds; and at the West Yorkshire Archive Service, Newstead Road, Wakefield. West Riding Education Committee records are also at Wakefield.

These sources give a comprehensive background of local and central material of the period; Sir Alec's own papers bring to life the cut and thrust of debate and political argument. It has been the aim in this book, however, to have regard for an achievement which was beyond politics through his own words.

Sir Alec Clegg's service in the West Riding of Yorkshire covering the years 1944 to 1974 was liberal. Early influences affected him and motives for action could be discerned from personal experiences. Since the concern of the book is the span of his life, 1909–1986, the bibliography has been restricted to Sir Alec Clegg's personal writing, books with which he would most probably be acquainted, and a brief list of authoritative texts. Notes of original sources have been made as plainly as possible to indicate where papers may be traced in the hope that these references will be useful to professional historians: the writer is a teacher and has read the papers from the point of view of a trained teacher. Since Sir Alec's death, the educational scene has moved on from that which he experienced and served.

In the period of the West Riding of Yorkshire Local Government and of its Education Department in particular, it is important to have on record some indication of the place Sir Alec held as an administrator and educationist. His archive is accessible and will be evaluated again professionally, but those who follow will not have lived within the context and ambience of the period in which he worked and wrote, and will not apprehend firsthand the unique place he made, or the amount of work he gave himself beyond the remit. He was not a specialist, although with a First in French and German he was biased in his insistence on the centrality of language. His commitment, rather, broadened to a recognition of the educational due and welfare of all children evidenced in his consummate skill in co-ordinating the diverse, essential aspects of educational administration across a very large county.

A library was opened at Bretton Hall College in December 1995 in Sir

Alec Clegg's name. A tribute was paid and presented by staff and students of the college through a selection of readings and performances which illustrated his insistence on a central place for the arts in daily life, as well as their strong contribution to a fair education as the due of every child. This last commitment was at the heart of Sir Alec's practical thinking and was researched by Peter Darvill, directed by Paul Cowan, Head of the School of Dance and Theatre, and produced by Professor Ron George, Professor in Arts Education, first holder of the Sir Alec Clegg Chair. The biography which follows is printed with permission.

A BRIEF BIOGRAPHY

(AC/PL/419, 599)

1909   Alexander Bradshaw Clegg born in Sawley to Mary and Samuel Clegg. His father was Headmaster of Long Eaton Secondary Grammar School which he attended before going on to Bootham Quaker School, York, at the age of fifteen.

1927–30 Modern Languages at Clare College, Cambridge (First Class Honours).

1930–31 London Teaching Diploma at London Day Training College under Nunn, Burt, Dover Wilson.

1932–36 Assistant Master at St Clement Danes Grammar School, London, where he taught languages and football.

1936–39 Appointed Administrative Assistant to the Birmingham Education Committee. Prior to this appointment his experience of this work was limited to several weeks' voluntary service with the Directors of Education for Cambridgeshire and Warwickshire.

1940   Alec Clegg marries Jessie Coverdale Phillips.

1939–42 Appointed Assistant Education Officer to Cheshire County Council.

1942–45 Appointed Deputy Education Officer to Worcestershire County Council.

1945   January to September. Deputy Education Officer to the West Riding.

1952   Britain's first In-Service residential college, Woolley Hall, opens under Clegg's auspices.

1953   'Ten Years of Change', the first of four reports by Sir Alec for the West Riding Education Committee published. To follow were:
'Changes and Delusions in Public Education' 1964
'Education 1954–64. A Report.' 1964
'The Final Ten Years, 1964–74.' 1974

1956–67 Member of Central Advisory Council on Education in England.

1957   Sir Alec visits Australia at the invitation of the New World Education Association. It results in the publication in Australia of five articles during this and the following year.

1958   The first of over a dozen articles for the 'Times Educational Supplement' and the 'Times', spread over the next twenty-five years dealing in a populist manner with issues he also examined in academic journals.

1959   Serves on the Crowther Committee. The 'Crowther Report, 15–18.' Deplored the pressures on pupils to specialise at fourteen or fifteen. It concluded with a demand for a 'firmer educational base than we have today'.

1961   Awarded the 'Chevalier de l'ordre de l'Etoile Noir' by the French Government in recognition of his work for the Yorkshire-Lille Youth Exchange.

1962   Instigates a report on the best means of implementing a Middle School system in the West Riding. In order to facilitate this, enabling legislation was passed by Westminster in 1964.

1963   First appearance of 'The Excitement of Writing', published by the West Riding Education Committee. Published in the subsequent year by Chatto & Windus in London.

1963   Serves on the Newsom Committee. The Newsom Report 'Half our Future' came to the conclusion that the majority of children in secondary modern schools were both undervalued and ill-served.

1965   Elected President of the Association of Chief Education Officers. Awarded Knighthood.

1966   Visits Canada as a Commonwealth Scholar, where his tour of the country was organised by the Ontario Association of Education Administrative Officials, and resulted in the publication of 'Education: Mind stocking or fire kindling?' in Toronto for the Ontario Department of Education.

1967   Addresses the International Curriculum Conference in Oxford. The conference was sponsored jointly by the Schools Council London, the Ontario Institute for Studies in Education, in co-operation with the Centre for the Study of Instruction of the National Educational Association Washington DC. A report was published in the following year.

1968   Addresses the North of England Educational Conference in Liverpool. He reiterated the appeals of the Newsom Report and made clear his opposition to corporal punishment and academic testing. 'Children in Distress' co-written with Megson published. Sir Alec's most academically influential work, in its second edition (1973), exercised a great deal of influence in writings on Social Psychiatry.

1969   Addresses the American Department of Elementary School Principals' Annual Meeting in Las Vegas. His address is later published in revised form in America as: 'Revolution in the British Primary Schools'.

1970   Invited to Australia to give the Seventeenth Frank Tate Memorial Lecture in Victoria. Published in Australia as:

        'Secondary School Reorganisation in England and the Emerging Middle School'.

1970   Invited by the DES to deliver a lecture (Central Hall, Westminster) to commemorate the occasion of a century of State Education. In his lecture he examined the historical resistance to a universal education for the working class.

1972   Awarded honorary Doctor of Laws by Leeds University. Awarded honorary Doctor of Letters by Loughborough University.
Awarded honorary Fellowship by Kings College, London.
'The Changing Primary School' published in the UK and the USA.
'The Excitement of Writing' published in the USA.
'Recipe for Failure' published by the National Children's Home.

1973   'Enjoying Writing' published in the UK.

1974   Delivers the Sir John Adams Lecture, 'Change in Education'.
Retires from his post as Chief Education Officer in March.

1975   Addresses the Plowden Conference on the instigation of the designating of Educational Priority Areas.

1976–79   Chairman of the Centre for Information and Advice on Educational Disadvantage.

1978   Awarded honorary Doctor of Letters by Bradford University.

1980   'About our Schools' published in the UK.

1986   Sir Alec Clegg dies.

Service on:

    The Furniture Development Council
    The Council of Industrial Design
    The Schools Broadcasting Council
    The Central Advisory Committee – Crowther and Newsom
    The Social Science Research Council
    Chair of Yorkshire Television Educational Advisory Committee
    I.T.A. Educational Advisory Council
    The Governing Council of the Open University
    Governor of two independent schools
    UNESCO delegation to Montevideo and the Philippines

THE WORK OF A CHIEF EDUCATION OFFICER

(AC/PL/216)
(Notes of a talk to Leeds University students, 13 February 1958)

1   Chief Officer to the Committee.
2   What does the Committee do? (i.e. what does it spend money on?)

Supply and maintenance of:

		Amount in 1958 £
(1)	Nursery Schools	6,500
(2)	Primary Schools	6,945,600
(3)	Secondary Schools	6,009,600
(4)	Special Schools	190,000
(5)	Evening Institutes }	765,300
(6)	Technical Colleges }	
(7)	Training Colleges	365,500
(8)	Adult College	13,200
(9)	College for Refresher Courses	16,100
(10)	Courses for Teachers	6,500
(11)	Institute of Agriculture & Agricultural Education	31,500
(12)	Youth	46,200
(13)	Medical and Dental Services	468,600
(14)	Meals and Milk	1,908,000
(15)	Recreational facilities	65,200
(16)	Administration	715,400
(17)	Inspection	88,800
(18)	Grants to the Universities	38,300
(19)	Aid to Pupils	922,000
(20)	Library	275,200
(21)	Transport, clothing, board and lodging, etc.	328,800
(22)	Youth Employment Service	61,700
(23)	School Crossing Patrols	32,300

Capital expenditure on building and equipping schools, etc. during 1958–59 will exceed £3,000,000. Annual Loan Charges will be £1,340,300. Committee also contribute £163,400 towards the National Cost of Training Colleges and £290,000 to other Authorities for W.R. residents attending their schools.

3   When he is appointed he takes over a running concern with a staff and his job is a three-fold one:

The day-to-day working of the service, which can be sub-divided into two parts (the Committee routine and office procedure, and the day-to-day work of the outside staff who are concerned with the maintenance of quality in the schools); and the development of the service.

Committee routine and office procedure
He cannot spend one penny without a resolution of the Committee. He will have a lot of committees to attend to, and he has to decide how many he will attend and what he will delegate to his Assistants. He has to put matters to the Committee so that the decision can genuinely be theirs, though his advice will generally be taken. The bulk of the work is done on precedents and previous resolutions and takes place without reference to the Committee, and the Chief Officer will have to decide how he is to handle this work. In a small office the post comes to him and he hands it out to his Sections and they deal with it. In a large office the reverse is the process – the post comes in at the bottom, as it were, to the Sections, and the difficult and intractable problems filter through to the top.

The outside staff
Define responsibility and delegate. Show interest in their work. Consultations. Visit schools with the outside staff. Teachers' courses at Woolley Hall. And so on.

Development of the service
Thorne. Comprehensive Schools. Secondary Technical Schools. Museum Service. Area Courses. Abolition of 11+. Libraries in Schools. Investigation into Arithmetic. Connection with F.E. Swimming Baths in comprehensive schools. Additional amenities for schools in the grimmer areas. Surrounds to schools. Sabbatical year's leave for teachers. Training College for teachers of Crafts. Re-housing of County Library.

4   Contact with Schools
Visit the good, visit the bad, and leave the middling.
Teachers' Associations.
Courses at Woolley Hall to keep contact with teachers.

5   National work
Central Advisory Council for Education.
Schools Television Sub-Committee.

6   Personal relationships
         Relationships with Committee, with teaching staff, with own staff.
         Importance of relationships.
         The classroom revolution of the last ten years. Discipline.
         Failures in personal relationships – Duncan, Moller, Cuthill,
         Manners, Music.

Further References:

National Arts Education Archive, Bretton Hall College of the University of Leeds,
     Sir Alec Clegg papers:
AC/PL/342 'An Education Officer's Job' (Talk at Bretton Hall)
AC/PL/337 'How an Education Officer looks at Education' (Talk at D.E.S. course,
     Durham 1973)
West Yorkshire Archive Service Headquarters, Wakefield: Boxes 1–39, A398, Sir
     Alec Clegg Papers: Box 9 – Notes. Sir Alec Clegg – The man, his ideas, and
     his school: Years at St Clement Danes.

INTRODUCTION

Early experience

The West Riding Development Plan

Parameters for action
Questions concerning the curriculum
Questions concerning selection
The comprehensive debate
The central drive – responsibility

The purpose behind this brief account of Sir Alec Clegg's professional life is his commitment to the possibility of a just system of education in school and beyond school.

His was not the simple progression from an anonymous start through necessary tedious intermediate stages to the isolation of a top appointment and an easily assumed cloak of office, but rather the story of a complex personality who found his vocation through a series of key episodes and who, having arrived at a position of some influence, continued intuitively to add to his appreciation of teaching and learning whilst involved in complexities of local government. Several key experiences made the whetstone on which he sharpened a philosophy of education. In striving to realise beliefs and values into the actuality of positive learning situations, he understood that colleagues of some commitment would be people whom it would not be possible to do without and the schools would have to be known thoroughly and accepted in all their diversity. Egalitarianism would not have to be equated with sameness.

Splendid isolation was not, therefore, a central principle: he did not (literally) sit alone in his eight-storey tower, he went into the highways and byways of the educational landscape as far as physically possible. He needed practical situations to make clear that mental geography which he knew well, the heights and valleys, quicksands and firm ground of educational theory and practice. He accepted all the children and worked to enhance their lives. This is not a tale of a schoolmaster's life lived in the midst of a plethora of local and central edicts, but an account of a teacher's move from an imposed bureaucratic stance which demanded everything filed and taped and docketed to a mellow tolerance of loose ends. Administration became a search for ways and means to achieve a humane educational plan which would work for the entire youth population. It is an adventure in democracy. There was a certain amount of impatience with the nuts and bolts of administration.

Alec Clegg has, luckily, left a substantial, accessible archive which epitomises a more generous-spirited time. A many-faceted mind, which moved intellectually from a detached stance towards those who translated administrative detail into canon law to one where concern for educational values and high standards acknowledged the humanity of those at the receiving end – ends in themselves. His influence spread well beyond his county, to central office, to abroad.

This account follows a time scheme but themes are taken which mark Alec Clegg's concerns; it is not a chronology of Committee Minutes, Reports, White Papers or Acts of Parliament. The shape of the book is determined by thematic divisions which take up some aspects of an informed professional task undertaken within the constraints and balances presented by local interpretation of central authority edict. It was decided, therefore, to make central his own personal response and clearly-stated aims which echo through all his writing.

Period detail is consequently important, and although that day has passed, it has its unique record of progress particularly in view of subsequent events in education. The fact that later social and material developments were only on a distant horizon at his death does not diminish Alec Clegg's stature as an educationist. Bibliography and references have consequently been kept by and large within the dates 1945–1974 and show the climate of educational thought, government edict, and local opinion in which Alec Clegg was obliged to work under the diktat of his official position.

Early Experience

Alec Clegg's own account of his early life tells of the progress of an average boy unconsciously absorbing the supportive, although critical, ambience of a professional family background representative of cultural interests of its period but particularly in art. He was the youngest of a family of five by several years and the only boy. He began his secondary schooling under his father who was Headmaster of Long Eaton Secondary (Grammar) School in Derbyshire and he gives a lively account of his lack of concentration and attention and of his father's dismay. He was given pause for thought when he produced, with aplomb, what he considered to be an adequate sketch of a Christmas rose. This masterpiece occasioned a memorable comment from a shaken father who taught art. Alec Clegg himself neatly summed up the situation: 'The early years of my life were spent in the successful avoidance of all kinds of school work.' There were frequent changes of maths teachers, and he never took to the subject. He liked geography – and the beautiful geography teacher – and eventually gained a satisfactory grade in that subject. Apprenticeship to an ironmonger was suggested but an aunt came to the rescue and recommended Bootham School. He settled down, excellent at games, captained the football, ran a quarter mile record and achieved ninety per cent in School Certificate arithmetic – an advance on his earlier ten per cent. This account of himself was given, clearly with amusement, a little irony, but deliberately conveying a message that the aim to be followed is a search for individual latent abilities. This aim came to be a cornerstone of his professional philosophy.

Alec Clegg's abiding interest became language. Between school and university to follow this commitment he spent a brief period in Weimar, Germany. He 'got to Cambridge on a handful of O levels' and took a First in languages. He went on to train at Borough Road Day Training College under Percy Nunn, Dover Wilson and Cyril Burt, and took the London Teaching Diploma when the majority of graduates were going straight into grammar schools. He built into his philosophy of education a second tenet

– those who teach should train, and first training is only the beginning.

The thirties, as Alec Clegg remarked, were years of unemployment in the teaching profession. He obtained a post at St Clement Danes Grammar School, Holborn, London, teaching French and football. Whilst he was in London, he studied part-time at King's College and took a further degree.

Years later on, in a paper which he titled 'Topics for Aiglon',[1] Alec Clegg wrote in appreciation of the richness of early surroundings which were the source of his commitment to education: he had an extended family group which gave him a background and a base.

'I take courage from the fact that in my wider family there have been individuals who have worked in one way or another in almost every type of educational institution from a nursery school teacher to a vice-chancellor, from a governor of a school for disruptive pupils to a Cambridge Don, from an independent school governor to a technical college lecturer, and I might add that between us, my grandfather, my father, and I have served the public education service in England since it began in 1870, and finally perhaps I should add that as an adolescent I attended a state secondary school, an independent boarding school and for a brief but significant period, a German girls' boarding school in the township of Weimar.'

Such a base made Alec Clegg totally independent in mind and action of the professional and social environments in which he found he had to work. He met colleagues, councillors and caretakers with the same equanimity and grace. He walked alone: consequently, paradoxically, was committed. One turning point came in his association with Robert Logan, Director of Education in Worcestershire. There in particular, the administrative stance was a humane one which in the immediate post-World War II years was in accord with the times. The writer began her teaching experience in the Worcestershire ambience.

After several weeks' voluntary service in the county education departments of Cambridgeshire and Warwickshire, he was appointed Administrative Assistant to the Birmingham Education Committee from 1936 to 1939. From 1939 to 1942 he was Assistant Education Officer to Cheshire County Council, and in 1942 was appointed Deputy Education Officer to Worcestershire County Council. In 1945 he went as Deputy Education Officer to the West Riding County Council. He held this post for nine months and on the sudden departure of A.L. Binns for Lancashire, was appointed Chief Education Officer to the West Riding. At the age of thirty-five he was Head of the largest education authority in Britain. He retired in 1974.

The West Riding Development Plan[2]
The practical situation in 1945 in which Alec Clegg was placed as Director of a large authority was the growth of the West Riding into twenty divisions plus several part III authorities, each with a divisional education officer and

staff. Each division was unique. DEOs ranged in experience from clerks experienced in local administration having progressed through from junior to senior, to teachers with experience in schools. Teaching staffs' professional experience was wide-ranging: from early 'unqualified' status through secondary-grammar/college two year training (later three years), to untrained graduates and trained graduates. Schools ranged from village infant, infant and junior schools, to county grammar, direct grant, grammar/technical/commercial, junior technical schools, secondary modern, middle schools, technical colleges, junior art schools and adult education. The West Riding could produce examples of most types of school and reflected the condition of the country at the end of World War II.

In 1944 the Education Act had provided a Ministry in place of the Board of Education, and a Minister. Sir Cyril Norwood, who was Headmaster of Harrow, had chaired a supplementary committee of the Consultative Committee (chaired by Sir Will Spens) which had been set up by the President of the Board of Education, Mr R.A. Butler, in 1941. His 'Norwood Report'[3] was issued in 1943 and influenced the 1944 Act. Page *v* of the Report defines 'the new secondary education' which would 'cover the whole child population of the country and carry them on to part-time education'. Alec Clegg's training and experience would give him the grounds from which he could evaluate the complex situation in the West Riding and promote considered change in line with the diktat of the Education Committee and the Ministry.

The 1943 Report has roots in the Hadow Committee's Report in 1926,[4] 'The Education of the Adolescent', as well as the 1938[5] Spens Report on 'Secondary Education'.

The Norwood Report was not directly concerned with any one type of school but followed the lead of the earlier Reports in concerning itself with the welfare of the entire 11–16 group. What the Norwood Report effected was the arbitrary division of pupils into 'types' – grammar, technical and practical. Educational psychologists pointed out that the general factor of intelligence was not taken into account and that eleven was too early an age to define a 'type'.

For the people at the chalk face the problem of allocation to the different schools presented itself. Before the end of World War II there was an undertow and an inexorable surge towards comprehensivisation. The year 1944 brought problems over selection and curriculum in its wake. The West Riding County Council Education Committee issued a statement in 1959 on 'Selection at Eleven-Plus' in the West Riding of Yorkshire', which clearly set out fifteen years' sincere attempts to resolve problems in one division.[6]

Parameters for Action
Questions concerning the curriculum
The necessity for legislation concerning secondary education was recognised in the 1902 Act when the curriculum of the older grammar school

was taken as a model. The establishment of School Certificate in 1917 'had the effect of strengthening and intensifying this tendency towards uniformity'. The Spens Report, however, points out the diversity of pupils and their uneven speed of development and the need for a secondary curriculum which would cater for a breadth of needs and interests and 'be thought of in terms of activity and experience rather than of knowledge to be acquired and facts to be stored.' It was recognised that this last essential groundwork is nevertheless open to tick and cross testing. Sixth form work is another matter and was not within Spens' remit.[7] His remit, nevertheless, included a recommendation for secondary technical education, 'a new type of higher school of a technical character, wholly distinct from the traditional academic grammar (secondary) school, . . . a liberal education with science and its applications as the core and inspiration'. It would require a new leaving certificate 'of equal standing with School Certificate as fulfilling the first condition for matriculation' and '. . . the establishment of parity between all types of secondary school is a fundamental requirement'. This was contrary to the general social attitude of mind at the time, 'elementary' attitudes died hard.

Page *v* of Norwood has an outline of the Committee's very broad interpretation of its remit in that it attempted to go beyond Spens' age limit and included a plan which covered 'the main features of a new secondary education which will cover the whole child population of the country and carry them on to part-time education'. In attempting this broad sweep the Committee arbitrarily claimed omnipotence in roughly grouping pupils into three types for ease of administration: grammar, technical and secondary (Norwood, p.2). Administrators are not teachers and arbitrary divisions break down under the sheer presence of pupil diversity: pupils are not easily categorised and tend not to remain quiescent. A system of education which reflected social status would have grammar, technical and modern types in each type of school: public, independent, grammar, technical or modern, depending on parental status and/or money and the parts of town or shire in which they lived irrespective of designated category. Historical, practical, religious and economic conditions had influenced and determined the education system. The arbitrary statement that pupils could be easily divided roughly into three types with ease of transfer between schools was a pipe dream and merely using the three existing types of school for convenience, and did not eliminate social differences. It gave rise to the proposition that classification should be on general intelligence, not type, to find the ablest in spite of school or social class, but one fact on which educationists of the time became agreed was that a final allocation of children at the early age of eleven was not sound psychologically or fair.

Other solutions were put forward, for example the multilateral school where the first two years of a common curriculum were followed by planned courses. In the West Riding, Hebden Royd, Calder High School and Tadcaster School represented this type of planning before and at the end of the Second World War. In 1956 Colne Valley High School had an eight form entry, and the increase in child population produced a sixteen form entry. The first two schools were planned before Alec Clegg became CEO.

Questions concerning selection

'Before 1944 many a deserving child who failed to secure a free place managed somehow or other to get together the money to pay his grammar school fees. After 1944 a line was drawn across a list and the very finality of this line has attracted a mounting crescendo of unwelcome attention to selection practices, with the result that 'the 11+' has become one of the most emotionally charged phrases in current educational jargon, and the strong light of criticism which has been focused on the selection machinery has revealed defects about which little was heard before 1944.'

This quotation from the WREC Report of 1959 serves as an example of administrative problems confronting Alec Clegg daily in his position as Director and the responsibility he had to carry from the end of World War II. Concern surfaced in his careful questioning of the variety of professional and social levels that he encountered: on the rigid use of IQ; the influence and stress of examinations; the 'typing' of children. He went, however, directly to the underlying and crucial implications of theories-made-law which he summarised later on as 'a few things which concern me'.[8] His questioning was directed to make his listeners think, not to live on borrowed ideas, not merely to endorse an existing situation, but at the core 'what are we doing to the children?' From this starting point he set out his priorities.

'. . . The only Plan (that is, the West Riding Development Plan)[9] I know with any intimacy it has been decided to go a long way with multi-lateral schools. This would have been done, I believe, *whatever I thought of the matter*, but I am bound to say that this policy had my support, and indeed I initiated it, as I have already said, by a memorandum to Committee in July last.'[10]

'Again, let me say that I state these views in all humility, knowing that I may be wrong and that the future may prove me wrong. *I am discussing the West Riding Development Plan.*'

'We have had the Hadow, Spens and Norwood Reports, the White Paper, the Act, 'The Nation's Schools' and various circulars. We are told to provide for children according to their age, abilities, and aptitudes, to divide schools into grammar, technical and modern, to put 20% of the children in grammar schools, 10% in technical schools and the rest in modern schools. Educational psychologists whom we have come to respect for their work deny that we can socially do any of these things.'

'. . . the West Riding policy . . . to build multi-lateral and bi-lateral schools in those areas where new buildings will be required to meet the Ministry's needs, to leave existing grammar and technical schools where they are where circumstances make this course desirable, and where modern schools are left in isolation to see that they are not closed at the top and to children whose interests, energies and abilities mature during the school course.'

'I do not believe that the difficulty of selection according to the aptitudes of the child for grammar or technical education at the age of eleven can be overcome either now or in the future.'

'The alternative to selection according to aptitudes is to do as we have done in the past and select the ablest children for grammar schools, the next ablest for technical schools and leave the remainder to the modern schools. Now much as I loathe that infuriating shibboleth 'parity of esteem' I could not happily accept a system of this kind as I have seen the deplorable effects of a double creaming on scholars and staffs and I am sure that such a system is harmful to a properly integrated society.'

Alec Clegg saw that the multi-lateral school did not solve the problem of selection:

'. . . it leaves it to head and staff of the school to solve, and it is my belief that in any school of the kind envisaged the allocation to differential courses by the application of standardised tests within the school supported by the recorded observations made over a period of years by an intelligent member of staff, with any final decision being made by the staff in consultation, must be more efficient than any that could be devised, applied and assessed externally. At any rate, it is the only method which I know which has any chance of taking into account those interests and ambitions which arise at any time during adolescence, which can make all the difference in the world to a child's enthusiasm, application and desire for knowledge, and which can turn the apparent dullard into a great scholar.'

'The Authority has to accept the Ministry's figure (for size of school) in preparing the Development Plan, but I personally do not accept it. I do not know the extent of the borderline and I certainly do not know how any borderline child may develop once his interests have been aroused in any particular direction.'

'Finally, may I say it is the avowed intention of the West Riding Authority once the multi-lateral school is built to leave its organisation and curriculum to the heads and staffs. There will be no rigid inquiry into percentages and the streaming of the school, and heads will, in my view, be given greater scope than they have ever had before. *I must say at this point that it is on this very matter I have my very gravest misgivings.* We have in this county many heads who have an excellent understanding of the grammar school and its needs and a few who are grasping the real signifi-cance of the modern school. It will be difficult to find men with the understanding of both, and as the bulk of the heads are likely to be grammar school men, my fears are not for the grammar schools' streams or for their closely allied technical streams, but for those we call now the modern streams. Our only anxiety at Wakefield will be to see that these are properly provided for.'

'We cannot in the county now provide the differentiation in the sixth form which Manchester Grammar School or Bradford Grammar School can provide and we shall not be able to do so in our multi-lateral schools. *But it is my belief that a number of schools of this kind whose main aim is the university scholarship have little interest in those of their pupils who after a year or two show little promise of this distinction.*'

'. . . there is no doubt whatsoever that in certain directions, in subjects which are most particularly grammar school subjects, the grammar schools have achieved standards which are quite remarkable. In the information subjects – in mathematics, the sciences, history, geography, modern and classical languages – *the achievements of grammar schools have, in my view, at least equalled those of the public schools* if due allowance is made for the enormous advantages in teaching time which the public schools have. There is, however, a group of subjects which I might term the 'expressive subjects' of the curriculum – art, music, poetry, literature . . .'

'. . . it is just not true to say that the acquisition of technical proficiency produces a sensitivity to the beauty of the art in which that proficiency is exercised.'

'. . . it is my belief that whatever School Certificate may have done to the information subjects it has certainly impeded the spread of enlightened education in the expressive subjects.'

'I feel that in these subjects of which I have been talking the desire to be able to mark out of ten has gained a greater hold in the grammar than in the modern schools, and I hope that when the two are combined in a community the greater freedom of the modern school in the teaching of the expressive subjects may benefit the grammar school teaching, and the better scholarship and thoroughness of the grammar school teaching of the information subjects may improve the teaching of these subjects in the modern schools.'

'May I finally mention the fact that we must all have had in mind for some time the fact that by and large these decisions to build multi-lateral schools are based on social and political reasons, and not on educational ones . . . I personally am not too disturbed by this. After all the educational system of this country has always reflected the society of its time.'

The comprehensive debate
Alec Clegg was concerned for children across the IQ range, in that there would be emphasis on examination results. He pointed out unavoidable

high subjectivity in assessing the arts, recognised later developing interests and abilities, and feared that in spite of the abolition of an arbitrary 11+, very little would change. He was not proposing an Alice in Wonderland caucus race, but merely suggesting that the average should be given every chance, and the less able given the care they required in the new organisation. 'My fears are for those we call now the modern streams.' He pointed out again and again across his years of service in the West Riding that those left behind would be neglected only to build up future serious difficulties. Disillusionment would be strong and produce strong reaction.

At the North of England Education Conference in January 1958, on 'The Newsom Report and its Aftermath',[11] educational advances were listed – improved buildings; the curriculum; staffing; Mode Three Certificate of Education; teaching methods; art, drama, music, dance; extra-curricular activities.

> 'But here my optimism, or if you like, complacency, ends. The whole essence of the Newsom Report lies in three words which occur in the introduction. We asked for a *change of heart* toward the children with whom we were concerned. It has not come about . . .'
>
> *'If this change of heart does not come about I personally believe that in the next 50 years we shall run into social difficulties which will make those of the last 50 years trivial.'*

Tripartite reorganisation was unconsciously directed towards keeping the social status quo. He welcomed improvement in access to higher education, and the case presented for special groups – 'but those who are so unfortunate that they don't quite fall into these categories are termed riff-raff, the duds, the blockheads – therefore the delinquents'. He was seriously disturbed and uncompromising in his statements on the implications of failing the pupils surveyed in *Half Our Future*, and in doing so paid tribute to the work of the disappearing modern schools.

> 'All I have to say mirrors the conviction that the task of the secondary modern school is at once the most important and the hardest of the whole field of education today. It is important because our survival as a free and disciplined people matters more than technological expertise and precise standard of living, and that survival depends above all in *what we make of the great mass of ordinary children*, whose worth or worthlessness will determine whether or not we can as a nation sustain the democratic way of life.'[12]

Alec Clegg was obviously worried that at every stage there was a process of elimination which finally left one group branded as completely unsuccessful. He then contrasted the situation of two boys 'identically endowed'—

'one hears good speech, reads good books which are plentiful in the home, hears talk at a discriminating level, is initiated into social conventions which give him ease in meeting people, and lives within the aura of family aesthetic experience; the other is lacking in all this. The first will succeed more easily even if he is only average.'

He was concerned to put his point of view to Alderman Hyman, Chairman of the West Riding County Council and asked him to reflect on whether the comprehensive school would help the boy from a working-class background overcome handicaps any better than the best grammar schools established in the industrial areas. The comprehensive school would not have the social range of the grammar school, would have a wider range of IQ, and it just might in some circumstances be less successful. They were in one sense an advance, but their establishment did not automatically bring about immediate care for all children; they could even preserve class distinction. He could foresee an even wider division of social class than already existing. The dichotomy could be exacerbated also if the comprehensive schools were pressed to attend exclusively to academic attainment and were forced 'to ignore their civilising function'. He deplored 'third rate grammar school courses' in whatever type of academic situation, thinking that children who followed those would only stand out against and not stand with the people from public and independent schools. The bottom half of the ability range would be ignored at the country's peril – they would not only be unemployable, they would be rejected by society. The comprehensive school had a hard task in planning for diversity within a sufficient structure: it had a wide remit.

'Failure to secure work and its consequent sense of being useless in society can be a disastrous effect on youngsters. It can produce apathy, a callous determination to live on the State, or violent aggression. Perhaps the most significant fact about the rioters in the USA is not that they are coloured but that as many of them are teenagers so ill-educated as to be about unemployable.'

By the time comprehensivisation was accomplished there was not the urgency for social change; post-war euphoria had dissolved into a different ambience. The idealism and hope of the immediate post-war years was treated with cynicism as time went on. In 'Children in Distress' he wrote 'over-protected, over exposure – some get tempered and some fall by the wayside'.[13] In this remark he recognised that the final mental move had to be the individual's, nevertheless he need not have the stakes weighted against him totally. He must have necessary and sufficient attention to enable him to take off.

He reviewed the situation at a practical level: children could be 're-organised' in mostly old buildings, cramped and sometimes on two sites. 'Middle Schools' were one solution since the age of transfer differed in several Districts and much correspondence had ensued both at the time of the 1946 Development Plan and later following the 10/65 Ministry Circular.[14] Since the transfer at 11+ had been an administrative ploy, the political concept of a middle school, 9–13, gave thought to a liberal education to the age of thirteen. On 11 May 1965 Alec Clegg presented a Report to the Policy and Finance Committee on the possibility of re-organising schools on a three tier basis. In 1964 an Education Act validated middle schools.

The central drive – responsibility
Post-war problems and later developments had served to concentrate Alec Clegg's mind on what was morally at the heart of the task of planning. He questioned: what is it or what has happened, or what has been deliberately brought about that has produced the immediate situation which is being addressed? Administrators, legislators and teachers were challenged: where did the responsibility lie, and what could be done to plan an education service which would work to the good of the community? Repeatedly across his service he reiterated this constant central drive of his remit which remained through diverse situations, times and groups, and coloured his outlook.

Through Alec Clegg's writing there is erudition worn lightly. In the tradition of the best essayists there is present an irony which delights in obliquely conveying fundamental and abiding concerns. Above all he cared for the pupils in school, was troubled for the average pupils, but also for the entire IQ range – how everyone, from the brilliant, the gifted, to the least able should be piloted towards satisfactory lives.[15] He gave serious thought, therefore, to the places where children were taught, the people who taught them, the people who trained the teachers, and what was taught. He was aware of the diversity of young people. A practical man, he was not an apologist for theory unrelated to practice and consequently interpreted good practice in teachers as knowledge of their subject, plus empathy for their pupils' physical, social and spiritual well-being, as well as their intellectual growth. He talked of 'pot-filling' and 'fire-lighting'. Without making any direct comment he recorded a remark of 'an eminent educationist' who had said to him that he, Clegg, was concerned with the 'deaf, daft and delinquent'.[16] Alec Clegg's stance as an educationist was based on a philosophy of education gained from wide reading across a spectrum of classical writers of educational philosophy plus practical ex-perience rather than from a disparate collection of research ephemera based on little practical knowledge of the classroom. As a linguist he was concerned to get at the meaning of statements spoken and written; as an educationist he was concerned to identify the centre of growth.

Alec Clegg sought to ask those questions which would give an impetus to widely diverse practitioners in equally diverse teaching situations to seek answers true to their particular conditions, then the right challenges would be met each time instead of a search for blanket or cosmetic solutions. 'But we, presumably, are going to have invented for us some miraculous device which will measure the teaching capacity of Mr A, who teaches the children of top professionals, and enables his Authority or some professor to compare him fairly with Mr B who teaches the children of unskilled workers.' Recognising that truth is absolute, he acknowledged attitudes must be balanced: to strive to discover the ingredients which work in each situation, to give intellectual coherence to planning, and then leave people to carry on in the way best for the pupils and themselves. He constantly sought good teaching and said, 'Go and look'. He did *not* say, 'Go thou and do likewise,' but 'look at *your* situation and devise ways and means *which work for you*, justify them.' Giving space in each different circumstance and at each changing time, he allowed for the wide diversity of situations and people which were, and still are, to be found in the West Riding.

He recognised it was grievously wrong and inadmissible to set up a rigid system which precluded movement from one type of school to another, each regimented group condemned to that into which they were allocated at the beginning, 'and the lid put on'. Alec Clegg's care is therefore summarised in 'A few things which concern me'. They are the warp on which the weft of his practical achievement has been woven – as dense as any piece of the finest West Riding worsted.

'A few things which concern me.'[17]

'The disaster of our lost, senior children.'
'Every child should have a measure of success. We need to cater in terms that are meaningful and within which it is possible for him to have a measure of success.'
Many avenues.
Problems which give rise to 'sloppy' situations – not this at all. A *rigorous* plan across a wide IQ range.
Much thought needed: not just 'messing about,' but real care.
The importance of the body and of the person – 'harmony, confidence, and dignity.'
Much more than 'PE', 'drill', and team games, also dance, movement, and individual grace.
Keep the old level of 'standards', but 'relevant to the young adults we teach.'
'The importance of quality and caring.' '(This) largely rests upon the quality and caring of our teachers themselves' and their resources: but always high standards for every action.
'The losers.' 'Less motivation, less interest, less co-ordination, less skill, more self-consciousness, less self-confidence'. 'Never quite make the teams. Never the top, or excel particularly in PE and sport *which is ever at the front. See to it that PE helps and does not instil a sense of failure.*

Of teachers. 'Involvement, of evaluation of steady progression.' 'To think deeply about our work, to question, to read widely, analyse and clarify.'
'What we are up against.'
    'A race for qualifications.'
    'A spate of 'wordery'.'
    'Research which teaches research techniques.'
'Children are not here as guinea pigs to further only your academic work.'
Training.
    'Trainers are also always learning.'
    'To be academic for its own sake is not the point.'
'The task must be thought out and students directed to that learning.'
    'Of aesthetic experience.'
    'Of delight of concentration.'

An apparently plain list of questions masked seriously-held principles[18] based on a humane outlook leaving the unspoken question: how to translate into action? 'Topics for Aiglon'[19] were addressed to himself, as well as to contemporaries, colleagues and in the teaching context. What values lay behind argument and action?

PART ONE

Values

'One cannot deal with people as one deals with invoices.'

'Topics for Aiglon'

Chapter One: 'Something worthwhile out of all children'

Chapter Two: 'Create an environment'

Chapter Three: 'An influence across all lives'

VALUES

Alec Clegg said of himself that it was during his spell of early experience with Worcestershire Education Authority that he came to understand what it meant to be part of a humane education service. Through visiting schools on a regular basis, he began to question how and why things were done. Instead of merely passing plans he agreed with, he looked at matters of which he was critical to discover reasons for success or failure. A critical, negative, judgmental attitude towards those in the thick of affairs was not in his book. He was beginning in those Worcestershire days to go behind the immediate situation, to think about the concept of knowing, and to ask 'How do we get the children to *know?* What do we *mean* by *knowing?*' He had clearly internalised his classical training: what was the difference between possessing knowledge and 'having' it? How do we construct situations in class which cause the pupils to make this mental leap? What was the touchstone? What brings the moment when someone can say, 'I've got it'? He grew interested in all levels of ability, the teachers, teaching methods, and every level of school, open to 'advanced' and 'traditional' attitudes providing they were well grounded. It was the practical teaching situation that counted; what was anathema was cramming to no purpose, or pretentious experiment based on shaky premises which passed as genuine learning.

Three years into retirement Alec Clegg was invited to address a meeting of distinguished educationists. In that year the International Schools Association met at Aigle, Switzerland, near Lake Geneva, in a college based at Aiglon Castle. He had been invited to speak, and with his habitual grasp of the background in which he was required to act, he summarized his own convictions in 'Topics for Aiglon'. He declared a serious decline in his fluency in French which the First at Cambridge and several years of teaching the language disproved, and affirmed his concern for English well used in fact or flights of fancy. Aiglon, the eaglet, would need to learn how to fly; much would depend on the parents' approach to the problem. There had also been a long-running production in London – L'Aiglon – and, appreciative of drama, Alec Clegg would enter into the theme which was concerned with the tragedy of Napoleon's young son. The Greek derivation: Aiglet, Aiglεew, meaning the light of the sun, radiance, daylight, lustre, gleam, paid his audience the silent compliment that he was addressing those whom he knew would share the appreciation of the heart of teaching, the logos, the active principle, which Aiglon must take for himself. Alec Clegg would take for granted that they would recollect the argument in the Meno when the slave boy, in the demonstration of a geometric principle could be led to reason for himself and arrive at true knowledge as distinct from a catalogue of parroted stages. The pot had to be filled, not crammed. For the teacher, the responsibility is heavy: what is taught is the truth, and in that teaching grounds or reasons are realised. On basic principles soundly appreciated rests the slave boy's ability to fly at the height of which he is capable. To reason, to work out together, was another teaching skill. Skills could be measured, but apprehension and appreciation could not. The distinction between what is measurable and what is not leads us to all kinds of difficulties. Knowledge produced by instruction must be a specific account of the grounds of the subject, not mere information. Alec Clegg stated categorically that there must be this grounding: a prepared mind. This skill was not only demanded of his specialist audiences but was clear in the way Alec Clegg himself presented ideas. He wished his hearers to think: in some depth. He had consistently produced a series of apparently innocuous questions around his topics which he considered held active principles at the core He avoided a didactic attitude: he wanted his listeners to go away, think, get annoyed, argue, and arrive at a true belief in *their* solutions and a resolution of their own teaching situation. His classical education was evident in his wish for dialogue and he paid his listeners the compliment of working with them, rather than dictating. 'Topics for Aiglon' are the measure of the man and he paid his listeners the compliment that they would understand and interpret.

Six points were presented in the summing up. They encompass the central themes on which the many lectures across his service, given to widely diverse audiences, orchestrate variations. Alec Clegg returns again and again to the 'ordinary' pupil who represents children in all their variety. 'Topics for Aiglon' can be read at several levels: concepts for those of all ranks responsible for children and concepts ingrained in their curriculum. True to his classical education he metamorphoses the person, the teacher, and the pupil into more than one semblance. He himself at times is Aiglon. He sought definitions, explanations, and informed commitment:

> 'What I mean by education.
> The effect on society which has been created by the
> education conceived by my generation and my immediate forebears.
> I would like to ask and attempt to answer the question, 'why do we
> teach what we teach?'
> To look briefly at the oddities of the education service.
> Equality of opportunity.
> The pendulum of education.'

Alec Clegg often told the story of an aunt who had a sampler on her wall:

> 'If thou of fortune be bereft
> And of this earthly store hath left
> Two loaves, sell one, and with the dole,
> Buy hyacinths to feed the soul.'

His interpretation was:

> 'The loaves are specifically what the child has to learn.
> Loaves and hyacinths together could equate with learning and speaking poetry.
> If you take hyacinths on their own, this line could be interpreted as representing the child's own feelings and views expressed in a medium in which he has a skill, e.g. words, paint, clay, wood, music, movement.'

> 'One and two can be marked with a tick or a cross.
> Three can only be judged according to the views of those who judge him.
> A distinction between what is measurable and what is not.'

Much of Alec Clegg's writing and active administration can be understood in the light of the brief list which reveals the positively charged centre of growth of his educational remit – to get something worthwhile out of all children, to create an environment, to recognise what is a good influence across all lives.

CHAPTER ONE:
'SOMETHING WORTHWHILE OUT OF ALL CHILDREN'

Ten years into Alec Clegg's tenure, four Reports influenced local and national attitudes.

The Crowther Report of 1959[1] on the education of pupils between the ages of fifteen and eighteen produced incontrovertible evidence demonstrating the waste of ability lost through educational administration operating under a constraint due to the unequal distribution of opportunity. It advocated the school leaving age should be raised to sixteen and proposed county colleges which could provide part-time education to eighteen. Other radical proposals were: less specialisation in sixth forms; extended use of sandwich courses; and a substantial increase in the supply of teachers.

The Beloe Report of 1960[2] recommended the establishment of a Certificate of Secondary Education alongside the established General Certificate of Education of England and Wales.

The Robbins Report of 1963[3] was an influential Report on the provision of higher education which recommended a wide expansion to include all students who could benefit, particularly women, and students from working-class areas which had not an accepted social tradition of an automatic route into advanced studies. This Report recommended the upgrading of training colleges (to be renamed colleges of education) and suggested a B.Ed. degree on completion of a four-year course. The colleges of advanced technology (CATs) should be given the status of technological universities awarding first and higher degrees.

The Newsom Report of 1963[4] from the Central Advisory Council was concerned with the education of less able pupils in secondary schools and in making recommendations made an impression, although response was slow. 'Half our Future' made radical recommendations: extra payments to teachers serving in difficult areas; a revised curriculum with reduced emphasis on public examinations; sexual education; improved buildings; relevant teaching methods and equipment; and to raise the school leaving age which last was finally achieved in 1972.

Alec Clegg was invited to become a member of the Crowther and Newsom Committees. Membership of the Crowther Committee gave an overview of countrywide reactions towards the highly intelligent and average children. West Riding reaction was initiated through the Thorne Selection Scheme; evaluation of examinations and awards and expansion of the sixth forms; the Oxbridge Scheme; and concern expressed for the entire ability range.

The amount of original papers in archives held at the West Yorkshire Archive Service, Bretton Hall College and in the Special Collections section at the Brotherton Library, Leeds University, are evidence of the breadth of remit in the County in remedying inequalities and putting theory into practice apposite to local situations in the light of the four Reports. Circumstances prescribed that progress should be piecemeal, but the task ahead, particularly during the immediate post-war years, was immense, and there were exigencies of money, teacher supply, local predilections. Further Education became the remit of the Deputy Education Officer. Alec Clegg's commitment was to the children: he recognised one common commitment – the upbringing of the next generation. It was essential, he said, if not in Christian charity (which it should be) then from plain common sense and common humanity, that all the children should be educated. Membership of the Crowther and Newsom Committees left an indelible mark, although he had assisted in development schemes within the West Riding 1944 plan and knew what was ahead.

From the optimism of the immediate post Second World War to 1959, the date of the Crowther Report when it was apprehended that inevitable social change would be reflected in educational planning, to 1974 when some consequences of social change had become clear, Alec Clegg quietly worked on behalf of all the children in his Authority from the brilliant to those needing special treatment. In speech after speech professional and lay audiences were addressed, figures and evidence produced to support the argument, and inevitably the questions came. His excursions into history were always from the starting point of personal experience – the social lives he, his immediate forebears, his contemporaries and colleagues had lived, and, centrally, the methods of teaching and curriculum they had experienced. Facts were presented to give their own message, skilfully as though by accident, to be apprehended, and illustrated the progression of educational thinking on childhood and youth.

There is subtlety of technique behind an apparent ordinariness of speech and simplicity of questioning. His was the Socratic method; he asked apparently simple, but ingeniously devised questions which obliged his listeners to work with him in seeking more than cosmetic solutions (which do not affect the status quo) to ongoing problems, and with persistence asked them to face difficult answers which might imply altering structure. Audiences were neither hectored nor lectured – they were talked with. He made his listeners pay attention to his themes – just as he expected his teachers to make pupils think – from transient Ministry politicians, through Civil Service mandarins, to county officials and fellow chief education officers; to headteachers, teachers, parents, and not least the pupils. The problems were difficult, not impossible, since his audiences were being trained as he talked with them. Aiglon came in many guises.

The Crowther Report of 1959 dealt with pupils from fifteen to eighteen across a wide range of intelligence. Although the Report gave attention to the Sixth Form, one aspect of the evidence which Alec Clegg heard as a member of the Committee was his discovery of misadventures which could happen to those pupils who for diverse reasons did not enter the Sixth. Influence of home and social ambience plus the relationship of home with school became a recurring theme in many of his papers. The testimony of a wide range of teachers' immediate experience and the sum of evidence left a deep mark.

Crowther itself stated that the education of most English boys and girls was not complete, indeed 'most of them are not educated'. The Report pointed out the urgency of a good standard of living which implied 'a firmer educational base'. 'Materially and morally' the conclusion was that the compulsion was 'to go forward' towards some reform.

The Crowther Committee, however, was overtaken by events. By 1959 when the Report was published the birth-rate had increased and the average age of marriage had lowered. Classes were kept within reasonable numbers with difficulty, but class size inevitably increased. In spite of this trend, the Report recommended the school leaving age should be revised to sixteen, with classes of forty in the primary school and thirty in the secondary school. Along with these provisions there should be a complementary Youth Service and an efficient part-time continuing education available.

A distant aim was to have half the pupils at school in full-time attendance until eighteen. A twenty-year programme could be set up to have results by 1980 with this aim in view. The Committee deplored the waste of talent and solid ability where the proportions of those staying on to only seventeen were twelve per cent. They recognised the social structure which influenced early leaving and deplored the effect on the 'second quartile' – those just below the top twenty per cent. Alec Clegg repeatedly pointed out this waste. The emphasis was on more full-time education, and this brought the acceptance of a fixed IQ into question.

The Thorne Shadow Scheme
The 1944 Act introduced the tripartite system which was skewed from the beginning in that technical provisions were quickly ignored, and the divisions into grammar, technical and modern were too arbitrary in spite of a 1943 White Paper on Educational Reconstruction which had stated ' . . . in any case, free interchange of pupils from one type of education to another must be facilitated'. Concern for the above-average pupil lost, or misplaced, in a rigid system led Alec Clegg to query 'the sanctity of the IQ,'[5] and the weight of the Norwood Report behind the setting up of the tripartite system. Termed 'the second quartile' in statistical jargon, there was a 'borderland' in Alec Clegg's language of pupils who could go a long way in their later studies and careers given initial, careful guidance into ways of study and necessary techniques in finding out for themselves as

distinct from being 'left to discover'. On no grounding at all, when 'find out for yourself' was equated with 'discovery learning', this simplification was, in his opinion, misapplication of a very difficult technique. However intelligent, if untaught, some tasks would be impossible. There is the repeated semantic argument where the use of loose terminology could be disastrous if, for example, the word 'difficulty' were substituted for 'impossible'. The example given was pertinent to the examinations – the trained mathematician might solve 'difficult' problems; anyone not trained in mathematics would find them 'impossible'. The ground has to be laid.

Alec Clegg sought opinion on the IQ tests from established education-ists and was concerned that an individual's IQ could vary between a few points and although recognising inclusion of IQ papers in the 11+ tests, he deplored the drawing of an arbitrary line and sought to mitigate the finality of the examination in his experimental 'Thorne Selection Scheme'. This scheme gave an opportunity to review the 'borderland cases'. His sugges-tion was taken up by the County Psychologist, Hugh Armstrong, who organised the scheme for the county.[6]

The cut-off line for transfer to grammar school seemed to Alec Clegg stark and arbitrary. He found the attempt to 'determine the narrowest cate-gories of children' 'alarming'.

'. . . things you see upset the idea that I had acquired about the sanctity and invariability of the Intelligence Quotient. It became obvious that even if the intellect of an individual might be of low horse-power it was possible to apply to it a super-charger of affection or interest which could ensure the procedure of very good results indeed.'

An accumulation of experience and evidence from service in Worcestershire and the West Riding made him question the immutability of the IQ. This influenced his concern for the 'borderline' case, and those pupils immediately above or below.

The 11+ tests which the West Riding used were the Moray House tests. When the test results were listed in order, the line was drawn down the list under the number of available places. The next name could be only one mark less. 'Though it is fair to say we do have a system of special scrutiny in certain cases which appear to be particularly deserving.' 'Whether you set the old 'County Minor' or the National Foundation tests or the Moray House tests, or you rely on the teachers' opinions of the children, you are likely to get about 20% of your children admitted by whatever test you set. What you don't know is which method is effective in dealing with these 'borderland groups,' which was the result of 'arbitrary and mechanical line drawing'. For Alec Clegg it was a 'borderland' area, rather than a 'border-line'.

The Thorne Scheme arrangements attempted to tackle their problem by using the teachers' expertise. The teachers themselves, in the area, were asked to select five practising colleagues in whom they had confidence, one grammar school, one secondary modern, three from primary schools. The four names below the drawn line from each school made a group of about thirty-two children. The children were invited to spend a full day in school with these five teachers who were given a remit: 'You can spend a whole day examining them in whatever way you think fit and at the end of the day we want you to divide them into two halves'.

> '. . . Those children were there with this group of expert teachers and indeed there were some very good teachers on that Panel, and they spent a whole day with them, examining them, talking to them, testing them this way and that.'

The standards that obtained in all the schools would be plain . . .

> 'They would be all-round standards, because the Panel would not examine necessarily only in arithmetic and English; they would probably ask for a composition. They might find out what the boy was able to do, what sort of initiative he had, what sort of verbal expression he had . . .'

The problem of transfer of a child to the grammar school who ought not to be there was solved as far as possible. If one school's four below the line did not meet the criteria, then the four above were interviewed.

It was also suggested that the children's progress in the grammar school should be noted, particularly which junior school's pupils were successful and which less so; then support could be given to some schools. The Panel in its professional capacity could be drawn upon.

The writer is witness to this scheme, since her school was host to the first two years' groups of pupils in one Division – to the care taken in assessing them, and the care in receiving the parents and children, the midday domestic arrangements, and the calm atmosphere prevailing. Although facing tests, these were not made alarming; the pupils had a happy day as far as testing days can be happy.

Examinations, awards, home influence.
Since the curriculum of earlier grammar schools was taken as a model, the curriculum of the secondary grammar school became orientated towards the grammar school examinations system. Oxford and Cambridge locals date from the 1850s; in 1884 a lower certificate was introduced; in 1905 this became the School Certificate which in time became an accepted leaving certificate. Matriculation, accepted in its original status as an introduction to a degree course, became in its turn a leaving examination sought by business and local government for clerking and intermediate levels. Concern was expressed that pressures and cramming would become heavy. Finally two standard examinations resulted, the school certificate which tested the general curriculum at sixteen and the higher school certificate testing specialist studies across a narrower range at eighteen. This had the

effect of excluding other examinations at a technical level and served to widen the gap between 'secondary' higher education and 'further education'. The practice of granting loans to selected students was deplored on the grounds that repayment would be a heavy burden.

When Beloe was introduced ('Secondary School Examinations other than the GCE'), Alec Clegg wrote:

'Beloe is going to be frightful and such evidence as I have seen myself shows an appalling similarity between the papers in many subjects and GCE 'O' Level which we all know to be a preposterous examination. And one could weep when one thinks that this has been brought on largely by teachers. The very people who have now climbed on the bandwagon and denounced the 11+ are themselves seeking to impose a 16+ which, in the end, will be far more deleterious.'

In 1960 at a course held at Woolley Hall, Alec Clegg said:[7]

'One of the great changes that we are in the middle of is that caused by the demand for more higher education, the expansion of the universities, the growth of colleges of advanced technology, the increase in sixth forms, the problems there of literacy and numeracy and the use of minority time, the throwing up of potential sixth formers by the 'A' forms of big modern schools, the petrification of sixth form teaching by the inexorable external examination, the advent into the sixth forms of those who have no intention of going further, the battle of the general sixth against the demand for 'A' level by the training colleges, the influence of 'Oxbridge', the effect of home background, and so on. *This is a list which the days spent with the Crowther Committee have fixed in my memory.*'

Crowther was firm in its support of the 'O' level examination and disliked any suggestion of examinations at national standards being below that level, but suggested regional or local examinations for 15+ pupils in the modern school. These, however, would be suitable for only two-thirds of the modern school population. Alec Clegg, following Beloe, at the annual meeting of the Association of Chief Education Officers in 1957 when there was a discussion on 'Secondary School Examinations at the ages of 15 and 16' faced the fact that examinations would be a feature of modern schools, but was seriously opposed to centralised modern school examinations for lower than sixteen. He commented on the heavy weight of grammar school examinations and stated that 'the grammar schools have shown the least progress in the last thirty years, due to the external pressure of the examination.' He also thought that the same tests were being set for far too wide an ability range. He had concern for the rejected group: '. . .we shall create a group that has been doubly rejected, and from the rejected group we shall get more and more lethargy, aggressiveness, apathy, indifference and shoddy work'.

When Crowther turned attention to the sixth form, the Committee was adamant that 'we are agreed in accepting and endorsing the English principle of specialisation or intensive study, as it would be better described . . . the best line of advance, in our opinion, is to reaffirm the principle and reform its application'. Alec Clegg suggested that with the growth of larger sixth forms in the comprehensive schools, the breadth of IQ and perhaps required commitment to a subject as a means to an end rather than becoming a pleasure in itself, would produce different responses and attitudes. The curriculum could become less of a liberating agent and the average pupil would end being little more than crammed which would leave him at a serious disadvantage at university discourse level. He visited several grammar schools on their Speech Days, and was aware, particularly in the early days before widely spread comprehensivisation, that he would be talking to people who would take it for granted that their children would enter professions or equivalent status in business life. He always included remarks addressed to pupils and very plainly took their academic ability for granted:

'I believe that you ought to organise your opinion (on these things), not leave it to be done by catchpenny magazines or even by critics who have to write down to the standards of the people who read the papers they write for. You ought to organise your opinion and let it be known through the Press and amongst the producers. If an organised body of young people had some means of making known an opinion which would either bring the whole of their fellows to the cinema or keep them away, film producers would very soon have a healthy respect for such a body.

A similar body of youthful opinion ought to be organised to criticise certain of the worst of our newspapers. You ought to go out of your way to find out what constitutes a good newspaper and also to see whether its opinions can be relied on. You ought to find out why one paper gives an inch and another a whole column to a particular item of news.

I would like to see you concern yourselves with the building programmes of your local authorities, and if they are putting up badly designed and badly planned buildings I should like to see you organise protests against this sort of thing and if need be get your views expressed indirectly or even directly on local councils.'

They would become leaders of opinion, therefore they should have standards. Without endorsing privileges, he emphasised responsibility and what they could do:

'First of all, it has been decided that the type of education best suited for you is the education produced in this famous old West Riding Grammar School (Ilkley Grammar School),[8] and from a personal point of view you ought to take full advantage of it. But there is another side of this problem which interests me very much indeed. It is that in the interests of the community you ought to take full advantage of the education that is being provided for you.'[8]

'All these (modern) developments require highly trained personnel, and if the industries themselves cannot recruit people who are sufficiently highly trained this country is going to suffer and suffer badly. You all know that we rely for our standard of living on what we can export. In order to buy what we need we have got to be able to sell, and we cannot compete with the bigger countries like America and Russia on mass-produced goods. So we have to rely on quality, and we cannot achieve quality without highly trained people to man our industries. It is essential, therefore, that schools such as this one (Otley Prince Henry's Grammar School)[9] should turn out people as well trained as possible, some of them to go on to the universities for still further training, and others to enter industry with the training they have achieved here. I would, therefore, say in your own interests and in the interests of the community you should take the fullest possible advantage of what this school has to offer you.'[9]

Alec Clegg interviewed for the old County University Awards and was dismayed to find from time to time that the examinations were looked upon as a final goal, not the passage to higher education. He was concerned at the specialisation in some sixth forms, which seemed to produce narrowness of interest and little curiosity. He wrote to his headteachers on a central belief of his philosophy of education – that pupils should develop an enquiring mind. 'Questions for Aiglon' were of vital, central importance: what was the quality of communication with the pupils?

He particularly expressed the hope for a common element where scientists and arts specialists could come together:

'We attach great value to the English practice of specialisation. Equally, we attach great importance to those complementary elements in the sixth form curriculum which are designed to develop the literacy of science specialists and the numeracy of arts specialists . . .'

The people pupils would become was of paramount concern to Alec Clegg:[10]

'For five or seven very important years of your lives you are going to be dominated by the fact that you have got to do well at your work . . . But I think it is important that even at this stage when you are so wholly absorbed in your school work that you should face the fact that there are other things which are going to matter in your life, and matter just as much to you and to what you become as the success in your school work will matter; . . . when you are finished with all of these, when you take up a job, *you will find out immediately that what you are is more important than what you know.*'

'Don't be in too much of a hurry to leave the school. The education that is being provided here for you is very costly, and it is important in your own interests and in the interests of the country that you take the fullest possible advantage of it. The country needs people trained in the way they are trained at this school. But there are other things in life that matter a great deal. It matters, for instance, whether people like you or not, whether you can take an unpleasant decision and stand by it, whether people trust you, whether you are careful about your personal habits and your personal appearance, whether you speak well. All these and many other similar things will in the aggregate and eventually be just as important, if not more important than, the success that you may achieve in your work.'

The importance of home was never underestimated and he never hesitated to address parents:

'. . . what is going to matter to them in the future is *what sort of people they are rather than how much they know,* and what sort of people they are will depend very much on the influence that they are meeting with in the 16 or 17 hours daily they spend with you . . . The school masters and school mistresses, it is true, can work wonders, but they can do it so much more easily if they are working with the home background rather than against it. *I am quite satisfied in my own mind* and from my experience that the fundamentals of good behaviour, of decent living, of consideration for others, of respect for property, *begin in the home training.*'

'The point I want to make to parents is that in the first fifteen years of his life the child spends a year and a half or so in school and the rest of it is spent at home. Now what Mr Simmens and his staff have to do at this school is not just to teach the children to read, write, and do sums, important as this is. *They are concerned with everything that makes a child worth living,* and they are concerned to oppose everything that's bad about it, and you and your homes either help them or provide them with some of their worst difficulties. For obvious reasons it wouldn't be a good thing for me to outline the worst things that a home can do for a child, but I can mention one or two things even before the children. For instance, every time you tell a child not to do something when there's really no need to tell him that, it's a bad thing. Every time you tell a child not to do something and then let him get away with it, it's a very much worse thing, and you have done some damage to that child which the school is going to find it very difficult to undo. If you are one of those parents who gives the child too much pocket money and doesn't watch what he does with it you are doing him a disservice and a serious disservice. Any bad examples of any kind which is set in the home is something the school has got to correct. Your children will talk as you talk, they will govern their tempers as you govern yours, they'll admire what you admire, and if your standards are low theirs will also tend to be low, and the lower they are the bigger job the school has in trying to raise them. *On the other hand, the home can assist the school and assist the educational process as nothing else possibly can.* That a child should be busy and not idle, kind and not cruel, courageous and not cowardly, eager and not bored, straightforward and not shifty, are at least as important and certainly as much a part of education as the multiplication table and they can, in my view, all be dealt with at least as well in the home, and probably better, than they can at school. And for this reason I am very strongly in favour of the child from a very early age taking a sound and wholesome part in the running of the home, and I think it's a good thing that every child should be required to do a fair share of what has to be done in the home.'

'*I cannot over-emphasise the importance to the parents of the part which they play in the educational process*, and, as I have hinted once before, I think a school will be very lucky if it is able to overcome the worst obstacles which some parents put in its way.'

'. . . Their health, their energy, their enthusiasm, their determination, their respect for others and for themselves, their standards and values – in short, all the things that really matter in life – are at least (I repeat, at least) as much your job as the school's.'

The Oxbridge Scheme [11]

Alec Clegg's concern for school/home links carried weight when he looked into scholarships to university. The West Riding was successful in sending students to university, but it was noted that few gained places at Oxbridge. Grammar school headteachers were consulted and their response was that some students, although academically of a high standard, appeared to be lacking special skills and that experience which came from membership of the special Oxbridge classes which public and direct grant schools could provide from their extra resources. Several Oxbridge colleges fell in with his suggestion whereby, in place of the usual entrance examination which followed public and direct grant school teaching, he himself would interview selected pupils.

In a talk given on the Third Programme in 1962,[12] Alec Clegg asked what could the schools themselves do?

'I myself believe that the problem of the right selection of pupils for academic studies is well on the way to being solved. Comprehensive schools, overlapping courses in grammar and modern schools with the grammar school sixth form available to both, the concentration of all those pursuing their education between 16 and 18 in a junior college, and something I met with the other day for the first time, cross-setting for academic subjects between a grammar school and its neighbouring modern school, all mean that in future few children able to reach the sixth form will fail to do so.'

'The ladder that was built in 1902 didn't reach down as far as Huxley intended.'

'. . . the fact which emerges . . . is that nearly all the (working class) successful children came from the topmost layer of the working class . . .'

'. . . they are the sons and daughters of local office holders, of foremen, of self-educated men, children of parents who had come down in the world from the middle class or had themselves been unable to take the scholarships they'd won as children. Most of the families were of one or two children only. They lived in mixed social areas and their children attended primary schools used mainly by the middle class.'

He had realised that there was a section of the child population that 'resented the symbols of dominance that the grammar schools imposed' . . . 'the (scholarship) children didn't come from the heart of the working class'. Coming into the West Riding from Worcestershire, he had found in certain districts a totally different social ambience – and committed himself to the welfare of their children. People do not operate in a vacuum: attitudes are one property of social groups and it is essential to view the individual in relation to his group in order to evaluate cultural pressure. A person's creative achievement is balanced with what he sees as his role in the group. Solidly working-class group pressures, particularly those dependent on one industry as the urban population expanded, became a heavy weight on the individual, his personal group laid a heavy obligation on him. Alec Clegg grasped the fact that one section of the adult population would not be responsive towards scholarships and had settled into its own vernacular. It indulged its children through their childhood, but on maturity tied them to the family group with hoops of steel, their only approved way of escape being light entertainment or sport. The working man who loved literature and music and the countryside was a very lonely person indeed; his forebears had, usually, been well-based country-bred people and a few links remained. The Public Schools' ethic of loyalty to its caste is the mirror-image of a work-force encapsulated in its own vernacular.

In this BBC talk on 'Education and the Working Class', Alec Clegg stated two requirements:

'The deficiencies from which the genuine working class youngsters suffer aren't superficial, they are very real, and they can only be remedied if our wisest and most gifted and most venturesome headmasters and headmistresses can in some way be enabled to educate their pupils in their last three years at school in a way which is *right for them*.'

He therefore, in selecting for the Oxbridge experiment, sought heads of certain 'accredited schools', enabled them to nominate suitable candidates for a university – 'candidates whom they would select and to whom they would then give a course of study and experience designed not only to prepare them for the university but to remedy deficiencies arising from their background.'

He was concerned for the successful pupils during their university careers. The headmaster of a school near Leeds wrote in 1995:

'Before, during and after our stays at Oxbridge, Alec Clegg made a point of organising a number of social gatherings for us, usually at Grantley Hall, Bramley Grange or Woolley Hall. I attended two of these, and I have a vivid memory of a small, grey-haired but bright-eyed and dynamic man who seemed to derive great energy and pride from being surrounded by the young men who had been part of his experiment. A person for whom *education*, in its widest sense, was a lifelong process, and frequently said as much. The last time I saw him was in the summer of 1971. I remember him saying then that the Oxbridge scheme was now in danger of folding, because many of the colleges had said that Clegg had now made his point and it was time for the West Riding to put working-class students back through the entrance examinations.'

This remark gives insight into the approach to selection the universities had at that time, and some attitudes: 'Faculties which provide adequate tutorial arrangements and those which do not depend less on finances than on whether the professors and lecturers see their job as one of pearl casting or pastoral concern'.

The Scheme was started in 1963 and was due for review within five years. In a Report to the Policy and Finance Sub-Committee in March 1969, Alec Clegg recorded visits to all three Oxford colleges, Merton, St Catherine's and University College. Time had passed and with the growing popularity of the new universities and availability of places, heads of schools had queried whether the Scheme still met a need. Also the Scheme demanded a 'third year' between school and university. The schools themselves had to provide those educational situations normally given in a home where education to eighteen is the norm, in addition to bringing them to A-Level standard, including, where required, the necessary Latin qualification. They should feel at no academic disadvantage. King's, Churchill, and Fitzwilliam, Cambridge, withdrew in 1969, having considered that the Scheme had fulfilled its purpose. The Scheme finally came to an end in 1970. There had been a special mention in the Report of the Franks Committee:

'There might be the development of special relationships with schools in particular areas along similar lines to the existing West Riding of Yorkshire Scheme.'[13]

Out of this scheme came more thought and some thinking aloud on the quality of teaching/lecturing relationships. Alec Clegg agreed a high standard of assessment of performance from the brightest pupils, but not a pared-down curriculum for the rest, that is, the close second quartile and those 'as far down the pyramid as possible'. He did not advocate a change in kind but of degree. Pupils' stages of comprehension would be of import-ance, therefore the teacher in Aiglon's guise would regard methods of teaching the less able and retarded as a totally different and separate problem. The 'second quartile' pupils in their turn and on their own momentum would benefit and be as successful as some of the brightest. They needed skilled, professional patience. He was adamant that the over-riding aim of teaching must be the personal development and social competence of the recipient. He argued that real learning begins when words are about experiences, ideas, and interests, then the language is not sophistry; 'and, I would add, any other medium of communication (used)'.

The heart of Alec Clegg's philosophy of teaching was the centrality of language – precision, exactness, well considered sentences. 'Modern' methods, as called, were not easy; he was scathing about the list of clichés which proliferated, and he has been seriously maligned in that respect. Both 'modern' and 'traditional' methods alike were successful if the eureka connection had been made and the pupil could reason 'what if . . .' 'why . . .'. Of 'modern' methods a colleague had remarked to him that 'some had climbed the bandwagon and could not play the tune'. He felt science specialists should be literate, and arts specialists numerate. In this last respect he tells a joke against himself – that he was not, at school, numerate, and in his first School Certificate arithmetic paper, he gained ten per cent. The next time round he gained ninety per cent.

He had faith that, given good circumstances, a great deal could be brought out of many more young people, leaving behind cramming dreari-ness or, infinitely worse, a 'you can't give *that to those children*' attitude. They deserved more than 'O-Level porridge or Nuffield cornflakes'.

The range of ability
The reader of Alec Clegg's papers is left in no doubt of his concern for the brightest people across all social levels, and for the close second quartile. His concern was that at *every* stage 'it is always the top groups which get the attention: the Oxbridge group, the stayers on, the scholar-ship class, the near-normals of the ESN school'. He said 'What are the dangers of this?'

On reading many of his papers it becomes plain that Alec Clegg's serious concern was for the total youth population and *which teaching approach would be appropriate for which pupils in their widest diversity at which stage.* How to teach? How can the approach be the same for all pupils at the same time, which seemed to be the main aim of most pre-scribed syllabuses?

This aspect of school life he referred to as the 'Code Tradition': the checking of 'standards' defined by Lowe and 'monitoring' required of the first inspectors. This was 'pot-filling'. Perhaps his sympathy with the average pupil lay in his admission that 'the early years of my life were spent in the successful avoidance of all kinds of school work'.

He referred to another tradition of education as the 'Hoole' tradition, from the writing of Charles Hoole, Headmaster of Rotherham Grammar School, educated at Wakefield Grammar School, whose methods were centred on teaching pupils as individuals. This, Alec Clegg considered, was 'fire-lighting'. *'Both are equally discernible in the schools of the West Riding at the present time; there is no doubt at all that both are intermingled in all schools, one tends to predominate in the secondary schools and the other in the primary schools, and there may be sound reasons for this.'* He argued that this was a reasonable division:

> 'Homogenous groups are unattainable; if they are homogenous one week they are heterogenous the next. Stream your school and you are likely to get a 'C' performance from a 'C' form child. All the paraphernalia of external examinations are used by those whose teaching is so poor that it does not carry its own incentive to learn. Work prepared to someone else's syllabus is likely to be impersonal and sterile. Only the form and letter of education can be tested; *the substance and the spirit cannot.* We can test a child's ability to read, but not *his desire* to do so; we can test his ability to play an instrument, *but not his love of music*; we can form a numerical assessment of his draughtsmanship and precision, *but not of his growth in creative power and imagination*; we can mark out of ten his knowledge of a tree, but not his love of nature. Moreover, we know that if you teach a technique *there is no guarantee that the understanding of spirit and substance will come from it.* If you teach a child to play the piano or draw or write, he may well play, draw, or write rubbish.
>
> And yet most would agree that the desire to read, the love of music, the development of imagination and creative power and the inculcation of really high standards of aesthetic enjoyment *are things that matter supremely in the field of education.'*

Alec Clegg very decisively came down on the side of 'fire-lighting'.[14] He did not, however, totally dismiss the 'pot-fillers' – it would depend how they set about the task. Those of whom he did express the strongest disapproval were the crammers, when 'the kettle was held under the tap while the lid was still on'. 'The child, unready to learn, did not learn.' 'By mental process, I mean the ability to master and learn the multiplication table. By spiritual force, I mean the force that makes a child want to do this. By mental process I mean the process of translating print into the spoken word – the reading process. By spiritual force I mean the desire to read.'

He also voiced doubt, having identified overlap of intelligence between grammar, technical and modern schools, influenced by his discovery of a considerable breadth of personal inclination in each type of school in addition to the social ambience of districts where schools are sited. He stated clearly that he had seen both teaching approaches used in the schools and: 'I do not know which ought to preponderate at which stage and with which children,' but:

> 'the kind of questions I would like to have answered are these:
> Should the balance of fire-lighting and pot-filling be the same for both the able and the less able children?
> Are they both equally effective or is one better than the other for young or for old children?
> Do fire-lighting methods and specialisation clash?'

The present and future needs of pupils he indicated, had to be balanced, academic achievement plus self-belief and self-confidence; they would be expected to think, perceive, calculate, weigh evidence, decide on courses of action, so develop that their capacity to feel grew stretched, not shrunken. Employment competence on its own was not enough, life competence was the essential element. Teaching and schools were there to create an environment that pot-filling and fire-lighting could be in the right balance: for individuals to be tailored to an end result suited to the demands of bureaucracy stifled and blocked development. A budget alone plus 'we-have-always-done-it-like-this' (pseudo-tradition) would not help pupils meet changes in living. Orthodox methods and innovation both had their place.

It was a matter of knowing when to fill the pot to some purpose. The present and future needs of the pupils, he indicated, had to be balanced, academic achievement plus self-belief. He asked: 'What are our conclusions about these children? What do they mean in terms of what we do in the classroom?' In other words, how do *we* accept them? What are *our* attitudes towards the bright? the average? the less able? He reiterated: 'The basis of learning *is the child's own experience, but none could be left to themselves.*'

Again, the reader of Alec Clegg's papers is left in no doubt of his concern for average pupils; indeed it could be said that he related to them, that he had a fellow feeling. Time and again in beginning his papers he told his audience, 'You are the experts, or professionals in this (or the other) field: I am the man asking the questions.' A clever move: and at two levels he put his questions for Aiglon. Compassion was reserved for those hastily branded failures because they go through their studies at a slower pace yet sustain a consistently good level: not retarded or euphemistically 'less able', but committed scholars *if interest is caught*. At the Conservative and Unionist Teachers' Association Annual Conference in London in 1966, he hoped that 'the purpose of Working Paper No. 2 is not to act as a force which is to make a change-over from O Level porridge to Nuffield cornflakes'.[15]

At this conference he followed his habitual method of asking questions which demanded thought and which challenged entrenched judgements or bland sophistry. He pointed out that (at that moment) the 'second quartile', and the 'average' were practically the remaining eighty per cent of pupils, after grammar school selection. They would not all be 'mentally sub-normal,' or 'very slow,' or 'less able,' so what held many back? The writer at Woolley Hall heard him say, 'We have made indifferent use of the intel-lectually average'. They are the people who just miss and continue doing so. They keep daily life ticking over, quietly carry appointed tasks through to the end, step by step. They are a pleasure to teach and deserve the widest and most sustaining menu since they will never scale the heights. They are the observers of sports, not participants. They need as many mental and spiritual resources as possible to draw upon and build upon to give breadth and margin in what most probably are looked upon as pedestrian lives. They are the so-called 'B' stream; some 'second quartile' who had missed 'A' stream, some 'average', and a few 'below average', and comprise the widest band catered for by the technical colleges which deserve every support possible, and every enhancement culturally.

Alec Clegg's questions at the Annual Conference of South East Lindsey Secondary Schools at Horncastle in 1964 [16] were pertinent:

'I want to discuss what makes these children of average and less-than-average ability, to what extent are they born this way and to what extent do circumstances create them.'

'What are the facts that the Newsom Committee revealed about the way this country treats its children who are considered to be of average or less-than-average ability?'

'I want to look at what Newsom says about examinations and what are the risks that we run of ignoring the Newsom children over the next 20 years?'

Membership of the Newsom Committee was a salutary experience. This Report was published by the Minister of Education's Central Advisory Committee in 1963, chaired by John Newsom, who was knighted in 1964, Chief Education Officer for Hertfordshire from 1940 to 1957. This Committee was charged to investigate the education of children of 'lower average' ability and the 'less able'. The Report immediately followed the Crowther Report which had been concerned for that broad band of more able children who were still nevertheless termed 'average' or 'the second quartile'.

The Committee followed Crowther recommendations, aimed to raise the school leaving age to sixteen, and looked for an enriched school day which would incorporate into the curriculum those activities which were regarded as voluntary by many schools. Much was required of teachers and pupils and it was suggested that the school day should be longer. A great deal was being attempted with too little time at disposal, and when home-work was only compulsory in the grammar schools.

Recommendations at the heart of the Newsom Report demanded an evaluation of other services impinging on the lives of the pupils in school social services and teacher training sectors. With an omission regarding training the trainers, the emphasis was on an exacting, satisfying programme which, since it would fall on the teachers, implied the retention of 'concurrent' academic and professional sectors.

The vast amount of factual information gathered by this Report covered all aspects of the pupils' lives and left a permanent mark on Alec Clegg. His family life and extended links had been strict but happy, his professional links in later life gave a reservoir of advice and information which never suffered a drought. The fact that children could suffer hardship, disadvantage, ill-treatment, indifference, encapsulation in social situations from which there was no remit, came as a distinct shock. Use had been made of the Social Survey and National Service statistics. It was discovered that nearly eight per cent of school buildings in which these pupils were being taught were seriously below a reasonable level. Any reference to 'secondary modern' or the new comprehensive schools was avoided in the Report. The educational needs of an entire band of pupils were the central problem irrespective of the type of school.

Telling information gleaned from statistics was of treatment received and attitudes towards these pupils and that a good proportion in this group were shackled by social factors and not innate mental inferiority. Limitations of home background resulting in less fluency in speaking and writing scarred unrealised talent.

The pejorative tone in the use of the words 'average' and 'below average' was deplored in that these groups were often . . . 'described as being regarded as *generally inferior and in* some *ways less worth educating than their* 'above average' brothers and sisters'. The Newsom Report continued to point out that the 'average' or standard of achievement had risen quite markedly and questioned could many people, in the light of this success so far, go further? The final comment was that extended provision should be given from the point of view of common justice and 'in economic self-interest'.

That common justice and economic self-interest could be regarded as inseparable the Report suggested in the light of the country's needs. Its people were its wealth. Additional talent would be required, the duty and problem would be care for the average and below average. The demands of the second half of the twentieth century would be for skilled workers, but more 'better educated and intelligently adaptable' people. Speaking at the National Froebel Foundation at the College of Preceptors in 1965[17] Alec Clegg outlined the Newsom recommendations:

'. . . better buildings, better staffing ratios . . . we asked that more *attention should be paid to speech*, that the child's environment and his experience should be made to contribute more to his education – in this way the curriculum should be revitalised. The less able children should have more, not less, choice than the abler ones, and we ask for a generous use of arts and crafts. Homework of a new kind should be introduced, the lines between curricular and outside activities should be blurred, and experiments tried with a three session day. We asked for a revision of RI syllabuses with a view to basing them on what a child can be expected to understand, rather than what adults think he ought to know. *The status of older pupils should be stressed and group responsibilities in the service of the community used to emphasise the moral responsibility that each adult owes to it.*'

With uncanny prescience Alec Clegg predicted difficulties if the pupil labelled 'less able', 'less motivated', was subjected to continued indifference, the chill factor. He even went to the extent of outlining probable future behaviour citing present behaviour as an early sign.

'. . . the more pupils there are who get certificated the greater the *responsibility for those who don't.*' 'Perhaps it wouldn't be quite so bad if we know that all the Newsom children were in this category because of mental frailty. *But we don't know this.*'[18]

He went on vividly to recount the home and school background of the 'Newsom' child, and in 1965 this was dismal. He quoted Dr Douglas's Report *Home and School* (1966):

'He (Dr Douglas) takes the view that amongst working class children there is a lot of wastage of ability that could be prevented, and he is of the opinion that it is likely that in the pre-school years the mental development of many children is stunted by the intellectual poverty of their surroundings. I am bound to say I have not yet heard this factor quoted as a reason for abandoning nursery schools.'

Almost all Dr Douglas's sample, four out of five, came from the slums, housing estates, mining, or rural areas.

'The main point I am making in all this is that there is a good deal besides lack of native wit which can put a child into the Newsom category where he tends to be so inappropriately dealt with.'

Alec Clegg pointed out in the West Riding the brighter side appeared to be that records showed there was progress, especially in reading, across 1945, 1952, 1956, and 1961, and that also in some schools situated in the most deprived areas results were achieved well above the national average. He was, however, alarmed at a possible reaction of the losers, and warned what could happen:

'The Report (Newsom) is about the way we deal with the less able half of the pupils in our schools. The reactions of despised groups, which believe themselves to be despised, are the cause of most of the world's troubles and much private misery. Hitler was himself a failure in his youth and believed Germany to be held in contempt at Versailles. The racial problems of Africa and the USA derive from the fact that the Negro races believe themselves to be despised by the whites. Lack of respect by management will cause workers to contrive reasons for a strike. If nothing commendable can be found in the dim-witted group on the back row of the class they will make nuisances of themselves one way or another.'

'. . . one of the most unpleasant facts of the Newsom Report is that we just don't know how the less able children would behave if they had the degree of attention that the ablest children (1965) now have. *What we do know* is that the less able resent, and sometimes resent bitterly, not having this kind of treatment. They *know* they are less able and accept it; what they do not accept is being treated as second-rate.'

He had strong views on attitudes towards pupils, and indeed between professional colleagues. He put it as either co-operating, giving pastoral care if needed, or 'casting pearls'. He was concerned to have pupils and adults alike see themselves in relation to their contemporaries. He was dismayed at evidence in the Newsom Report which revealed a disparaging attitude towards pupils who are considered to be 'less than bright'. With the raising of the school leaving age he foresaw that the schools would have a broad middle group which has a wide IQ range from 'second quartile' through HE technological level, to Further Education, to those with learning difficulties. *They could not be taught en masse.* He wrote with some feeling that 'we have to change our attitude to the less bright'. Thorough respect and appreciation for the British tradition of grammar schools did not give him that myopic vision which saw the remaining eighty per cent of pupils through a mist. The tunnel vision which produced a remark: 'What will happen to us as a nation if we don't look after our brightest? They must be given everything and more, and what is *left* must be spread as far as it will go,' gave him grave doubts when he heard it.

'When Russia put up the sputnik the USA developed a pedagogical panic and started to talk heavily in terms of schools for the real intellectual elite. I am bound to say that the possibility of doing this in this country, *which I predict will be upon us before long*, horrifies me. The thought of selecting a group of youngsters who are selected not because they are equally honest, or equally compassionate, or equally athletic, or equally mature socially, but because they have an equality of high measurable intelligence would, I think, be educationally futile and socially dangerous.'

'It is, I think, true, and probably inevitable, that every educational institution except the infant school expends its care and concern mainly on its brightest youngsters.'

'I have the gravest doubts about express courses which sometimes, though not always, deprive a child of his childhood. I suspect that many such children who had been cooped up together during their school life would turn out insufferable little prigs who might well claim from society more than their right and would almost certainly get their values wrong by rating their particular gift higher than, say, compassion or selflessness or honesty, or many others, which we as a Christian nation should deem the more worthy. I suspect we should make it very difficult for Divine Grace to reach them, and in any case I cannot see why we should deem it a great virtue *to deprive the mass of children of their pace setters* or why we should think it an achievement if we can force a child under pressure to do in seven years what he would normally do in eight. But there are more serious social considerations still . . .

. . . The (Newsom) Report is about the way we deal with the less able half of the pupils in our schools. The able half we treat well; the less able we treat badly. *These proportions are going to change.* Those we treat well are going to increase in number, those we treat badly are going to decrease; and *I believe that unless we take steps to prevent it this process is going to create one of the gravest social problems which our children and their children will have to face.*'[19]

Alec Clegg was indirectly pointing out that these pupils were a charge and a responsibility. As the educational success rate moved lower down the pyramid, in the end there would be a group that would need compassion and some kind of oversight all their lives. He asked 'what happens to those whose future is bleak?' 'How *do* they fail?'

'He can fail at 11+. *Many* do and he will get over it.
He will go to the Modern School and miss the CE group.
He may also fail the CSE group.
When he leaves and gets a job he may not be good enough for the group who qualify for day release, and this means of course that he has no chance of an apprenticeship.
The youngster (who) cannot make the apprentice grade, cannot be employed (through regulations) on shift work, *what happens to him?*'

He did not attach a label to them. He pointed out that in a group of thirty:

'We take children who vary from the very bright to the very dim, children from stable homes and children from disturbed homes, children of the deaf and dumb and children of the highly articulate, children of the virtuous and children of the immoral and criminal, children from the literate and numerate and children from those who can barely read or count, *and we put them together in groups of 30.* We either stipulate the ground that they must have covered by a certain age when they will have to face . . .'

He valued teachers' skill in identifying mental and emotional responses in the pupils they met daily – immaturity, maladjustment; 'educationally below normal' (low IQ, 65–70) and working to the limits of their capacity which would be much lower than the rest; the linguistically handicapped who had little cultural influence in the home. There had to be motivation to learn before the pots could be filled, for by secondary school they had long acquired a history of failure and had lost the desire to be taught. Older pupils' interests could be used as a springboard, a source of conversation. Remedial reading on its own from 'Janet & John' type books or their later equivalent could be of little value.

He again sounded a warning: sentimentality, plus lack of stimulation, compounds the attitude; contempt plus inaction could not be tolerated:

> 'I hope that (at this course) some consideration will be given to the many aspects of the human mind and soul in which a child may be normal though he be intellectually backward, and that we do not become either morbid or sentimental about backwardness.'[20]

He seriously pointed out many times that we do not know how to get the best out of average pupils, and particularly out of those of below average ability. Without comment, Alec Clegg recorded that a 'highly eminent educationist' accused him of putting 'the deaf, daft and delinquent' first.

Alec Clegg died in 1986. He did not live to see the decline of heavy industry in the Riding although he witnessed the County's arbitrary division into fourteen disparate segments; he did not see the world-wide computer social revolution. His was, nevertheless, a forward-looking informed imagination and he saw vast unemployment on the horizon and insidious social trends which would incline towards a less caring society. On hearing a headmistress describe the background of the major proportion of her school's intake and her vehement protest that we as a society were responsible, he wrote: '. . . I couldn't agree (with some aspects of the talk) but I have seldom felt more uncomfortable about any accusation against the service in which we work'. Home and school were unavoidably linked.

Home and School

> 'Few things cause more trouble in the world than one person or group of persons holding another person or group of persons in slight regard.'[21]

> 'The child that is driven to disaster by circumstances in which it is reared . . . these are the circumstances in which we know that appalling damage can be done to a child which we are powerless to prevent.'[22]

> 'And we are heading for an age when the simplest amongst us will have no job to do because the machines will do all that they are capable of doing.'

'. . . what we have to do is to change the nation's attitude to a whole section of our community and if we fail to do so the difficulties we create for young people will be very great indeed.'[23]

As a member of the Crowther and Newsom Committees Alec Clegg's awareness of ills and accidents as well as the difficulties some children experience was increased. Together with the evidence of Douglas's 'Home and School' Report, he had substantial local grounds for serious concern. He saw distress amongst children as a social problem. '. . . *we are dealing with a major problem, not a side issue.'*[24] He turned to heads of schools,[25] inviting information 'in strictest confidence' on the circumstances of some children – 'a matter which is giving me great concern at the moment':

'Many heads tell me that from time to time they come across a child who is living under great stress at home but not of the kind that could be solved by court action or indeed by the intervention of any outside agency. Sometimes the stress is so great that it is likely to mark the child for life one way or another. Often it is the heads of schools who are among the first to be aware of the child's circumstances.'

Full assurance of confidentiality was given and the response was quite matter of fact, without sentimentality, but heartrending, and could not be retailed. There were five sections which covered specific difficulties. It was recognised, nevertheless, that children could not fall exclusively into one category. Causes were noted as far as possible and the most important ringed:

'Children from problem families, living in bad conditions from squalid homes, with feckless parents, dirty and therefore ostracised, badly fed, clad, lacking adequate sleep.
Rejected or neglected children subjected to deliberate cruelty by a parent or guardian or is neglected by parents.
Children from homes under stress – a broad category: where perpetual strife reigned, or strain resulting from the fact that one parent is left to bring up a family, or divided loyalties are present, or one member of the family is seriously ill, or the parents are anti-social.
Children who, in themselves, have lost ground through illness or strain.
Children recognised as mildly ESN on whom ordinary school work makes a heavy demand.'

Included also are those children who are violent or depressed for no apparent reason, whose behaviour cannot be explained.

Alec Clegg was sufficiently disturbed by the response to his enquiry that he sought information from other local authorities on their adopted measures. All recognised the existence of intractable cases, and one officer remarked 'I am glad, like you, we do not shrug our shoulders'. Various

methods were reported – from liaison with other departments, occasionally 'bending the rules' where possible, and recognising 'all these problems
need more than one agency's help', to making use of existing laws and
agencies and comments from the County Medical Officer.

Alec Clegg himself looked at the social causes. At a UDC Association
Annual Conference in 1966[26] he had given a paper on 'Problems Solved
and Unsolved'; he asked his audience to look back on the kind of society
in which they were born, and to think about 'the problems which beset and
are besetting the education service of this country'.

'The crucial problems against which the teachers had to do battle were
poverty in the home and unemployment, or employment which made
child labour cheap to the employer and source of income to the parent.
The log books of the day reveal that the sort of things which disrupted
schools were death, bad weather and temptations of casual child labour.'

'I would like to turn now to what has always seemed to me to be an
extremely difficult problem, and that is the extent to which the schools
are helped or hindered by the adult society of the day whom they are
expected to serve.'

'. . . in other ways in those days society helped the schoolmaster. The
Church and Sunday School were a force . . . and there were defects in our
society which were to be condemned and against which the young had to
be protected. Duty was considered a good thing, as was service. Charity
got a bad name, but at least it bore testimony to a good intention.'

'But bad as are the mistakes and illusions under which our education
system labours, they are insignificant, in my view, beside the handicaps
which modern adult society, our society, the society which you and I have
built up, imposes on the schools . . . When my father and grandfather were
schoolmasters they had to cope with poverty, physical dirt and disease.'

'The disintegrating factors in our society take little heed of class distinction . . . I do *not* believe that the abolition of poverty has reduced the
number of homes in which distress, and I mean real crippling distress
based on cruelty and unhappiness, occurs. When I say crippled I mean
the kind of thing that can mark a child for life. . .'

'. . . There is in our society a thin stratum of youngsters who are spiritu-
ally undernourished and we can do little to help any of them unless we
get a conviction . . . And it is this distressed or discarded group coming
from homes under pressure of some kind or another who, I believe,
produce something like one-half to three-quarters of our maladjusted
and ESN children. In other words, this proportion of these children
would not be so labelled and would not need this kind of treatment if they
came from different kinds of homes. In their case distress and rejection
are the disease, maladjustment and educational subnormality are but the
symptoms . . .'

'. . . We have many distressed children in our community. We know many of them and we can identify them in our secondary schools, our junior schools and even in our infant schools. Our schools can in fact name the group of children from which most of the next generation of adult criminals and social misfits will be drawn. We do nothing about them until they are so far advanced in their distress that they have to be taken into care or custody. We are concerned with only the tip of the iceberg – with about one out of ten. We ignore prevention . . . We wait until the cure is very difficult and very expensive. We have lulled ourselves into the belief that the reduction of poverty will reduce child distress. *My belief is that other factors may cause it to increase.* The child, we say, should not be separated from his parents, and I would agree with this . . . but not when the child is unwanted or terrified or even hated, and these conditions are the real recipes for crime.'

'Deprivation is relative . . . I am not concerned exclusively with any one social class or group in our society . . . in simple terms . . . (those) who are miserable, distressed and often so much so that their school life, and indeed their success in life generally can be grossly impaired.'[27]

'And let us be quite clear at the outset that the distressed child who cannot be reached by any existing service may suffer more and more grievously than the child who is fortunate enough to do something which gets him taken into care or custody. The outcast in a large family who is picked out as the family drudge and told by her parents that they wished she were dead may be at least as severely damaged . . . but she will be far more difficult to help.'[28]

'Distress is dependent not only on the severity of the adverse pressures which are exerted on the child but on the stamina – a spiritual resource which he can call upon to help him resist these pressures.'

'. . . I am also aware that there is much that we could do now in the present limited state of our knowledge and if we do nothing more than continue to measure and diagnose, generations will go on suffering while we do it.'

'We delude ourselves in thinking that, because we have greatly reduced the poverty and under-nourishment which was such a grievous feature in society in the early years of this century, the child distress which was thought to result from dirt and hunger must be on the decline. Distress . . . probably far less severe in most cases than distress caused by lack of love and to the production of unloved children.'

He pointed out the diverse ways in which life at home can be under stress, the most vicious being covert severe cruelty. Children also could be caught up in parental sickness and death, gross immorality, mental disorder, or separation. If separation occurs they might go with the less preferred parent. The child may be the drudge if the mother gives up trying to cope, or they could be members of a neglected family. He had read case histories of unacceptable situations and heavy afflictions:

'If the resistance of the child is low, he may by such afflictions be permanently damaged and marked more seriously than many who take route through Borstal, the approved schools, probation, psychiatric treatment, or schools for the maladjusted.'

'For most children afflicted in these ways their only hope is the school. The other services are as overworked dealing with children who have fallen over the precipice that they have neither the time nor the staff to deal with those who are moving at various rates towards it.'

He concluded:

'And what I am fearful of is that just as we are doing far too little for the developing countries and far too little for the needy industrial towns of the north, we are doing far too little for the child whose fault may be not that he is less honest or less considerate or less courageous than others, but because machines can do the only work he is capable of; he no longer matters to us and we care little about what happens to him. If we want to see the consequences of this kind of attitude, and you will notice that all the time I have been concerned not about technical development but about the attitudes that technical development engenders, we should do well to look at the gap between rich and the poor as it is growing in the United States. We can see the effect of it in the big schools in the cities of that country, which have to be policed daily while they are in session, and we are beginning to find out in this country that Tom, Dick and Harry who may be limited in ability can nevertheless create destruction . . . and disruption on an ever increasing scale. And I doubt very much whether severe sentences, however needy they may be, will be found to alter the course of events unless we can provide more concern, more care, more attention, for the youngsters who do not succeed in the knowledge scramble, but are nevertheless capable of becoming worthwhile citizens.'[29]

'There is no doubt that here are born a number of potential firsts whose qualities are such that they win through whatever their environmental disadvantages, and another, considerably larger number who if trained by the most famous teachers in history would still fail their examinations, but in between there is a vast mass whose performance at both entry to higher education and beyond depends greatly upon how they have lived and been taught beforehand . . . *the difference between children of the same potential but different backgrounds widens progressively.*'

'I think we are facing a grave danger of creating a most grievous problem. We are creating an under-valued, even a despised sector in our society, and we under-value them because they cannot make what we regard as minimal academic grades. When they are under-valued and discarded they become anti-social and we blame them for becoming what we have made them. We give them money but not status. Our treatment of them corrupts and then we punish them for corruption. We are widening the gap between the acceptable academic or trainee or apprentice and the youngster who falls into none of these categories, and in my view we are deliberately creating a social problem of the utmost gravity. There have been riots in the USA where there have been thousands of vacancies for trained men and women and many more thousands of untrained people unable to take them; we in this country have created a dissident group of teenage malcontents who cause us from time to time most serious trouble; and recently we have seen vicious troubles in Amsterdam. *I expect to see more of this and we shall blame it all on original sin*, using this as an excuse for our own educational incompetence.'[30]

'Above all, we shall have to avoid the danger of thinking that all these grievous problems will be solved by the change of organisation which we are about to face. I think I can claim to have been a convinced comprehensivist since long before many of the present-day converts even began to think of such a system, but I am under no illusions as to the limitations of comprehensive schools, and some of the dangers of the slow learner may be increased rather than diminished by the change. They will have to be positively guarded against.'

At the North of England Conference in 1972 Alec Clegg spoke on 'Disadvantage in Education' and quoted Plowden's recommendation of 'educational priority areas which would need far more than equalisation of resources'.

As a matter of urgency a learning environment had to be set up for all children. Change of organisation would not in itself be sufficient, dangers would lurk should 'organisation' become an end in itself. Children's personal gifts, within common resources provided for all, could only be released if those resources gave the stimulation for self-authentication. Realisation of this living principle came through teaching and the ethos of a school. Alec Clegg was seeking to create an environment where every child would learn how to live and have skills to live by.

Chapter Two: 'Create an Environment'

'How to live. . .'

One implied question pervading Alec Clegg's lectures was how aware his listeners were of a necessary balance between drives and values in the pupils' social environment. Cultural differences and social differences produced variety in pitch and volume of interests, motives, and efforts towards individual ambition or a common goal. Whether an individual's goal came first or the group's solidarity depended very largely on social bias in the district where the school was built. With the passing of grammar schools social background became less broad and schools became largely community schools. He was emphatic that school stands at that critical point where drives and values meet. Western European society expects a product which can compete in a sophisticated, informed, competitive world and remain a human being capable of responsibility, decency, and moral courage. His shorthand – 'pot-filling and fire-lighting' – identified the problem: sufficient didactic teaching to sustain the individual in the system was a primary remit; but also to awaken enthusiasm, intuitively catch the imagination to make a human being. He looked for rigour in teaching, whether orthodox or 'modern' in approach. He said: 'Create an environment', 'the pupils must have skills to live by, *but learn how to live*'.

Alec Clegg sought a philosophical base on which to construct an education plan adaptable to different conditions. People are not paper strings of cut out figures. A single, rigid structure into which the entire youth population could be pressed, which refused to recognise diversity in predilection and development would leave many losers, marked as permanent non-starters. Alec Clegg insisted on a balance between 'pot-filling' (instruction), and 'fire-lighting' (guidance). This, he said, is the teacher's skill, and not open to a tick and cross method of evaluation. He sought the development of the complete, rounded person, living within his culture, and this implied individual attention.

In promoting these values his practical application fell broadly into five fields: first in his general work as Chief Education Officer, and following logically within his work for the West Riding County Council where this had relevance within each school. Crucially nursery and primary schools must be well funded and in such a way that lively, thoughtful, active, open-minded children moved on to the next stage. In his concern for the exclusion of many through a rigid examination system he sought ways to make technical and further education a liberating experience. There followed inevitably concern for the 'Newsom' pupil.

He reiterated these values many times, to varied audiences in different situations, quoting Thring, his representative Headmaster. A common sense approach to organisation was an attempt to translate theory into practice, to turn government edict into workable situations in multilateral schools, comprehensive schools, sixth form colleges and community schools.

> 'As a result of his beliefs and determination, West Riding schools and classrooms were touched with a sense of beauty, compassion and the human spirit.' (Obituary)[1]

> 'There is no getting away from the sense of excitement that prevailed in his schools.' (Obituary)

> 'We should obviously not give all children the same educational treatment, but they should all receive a generous share of our concern, or, if it is called for, our compassion.'[2]

Alec Clegg also said to Australian teachers:

> 'The country which gets the richest and most healthy secondary education *will in the long run* be the one which most readily trusts its teachers.'[3]

He was concerned that in the rush and anxiety to get the pupils literate and numerate 'we tend to overvalue what can be measured and undervalue what cannot'. He was concerned that the schools should be sympathetic towards social conditions which impede progress and to make the most of influences that complemented their task. For crucial learning he listed: happiness, security, enlivening experiences, recognition of achievement and the ability to shoulder responsibility. 'These problems affect every class on earth. *It is the solution of these problems which is the professional job of the teacher while his imparting of skills and of knowledge is his technical task.*' He also made the point that every group of pupils produced its own social climate and although there was a set syllabus, each class needed a specific approach towards 'pot-filling' technique plus 'fire-lighting' professionalism. Gone were the days when:

> '. . . a teacher having prepared his notes could use them year in and year out with successive generations of pupils – each year they got more and more stale, each year the same old joke got more and more wry as it was introduced into the same old lesson, and of course the teacher virtually laid claim to infallibility.'[4]

> 'We overvalue what can be measured and undervalue what cannot.'[5]

Theory on its own was not enough. At two Bingley vacation courses in 1950 and 1952 he stated his position clearly. At the same time Alec Clegg was not careless, untidy, or mawkishly sentimental, in spite of the fact that he said 'on the whole I think you can put me down in the 'fluffy' or 'woolly' camp'. He was actually in neither camp, but his own:

'I believe that first and foremost we must give absolutely sound training in the three R's. . .'

'But having said what I have said about reading and writing and arithmetic, I think after that we must give the teachers very considerable freedom for sound and wise experiment. I firmly believe that unless we learn, and learn soon, how to train and educate that part of the child that cannot be labelled intelligence and which undoubtedly accounts for his everyday actions and behaviour and reactions to his fellow men, our civilisation may end in disaster. We cannot go on specialising to an ever higher degree in the training of the intellect at the expense of our emotional and spiritual development.'

'But I do stress with all the urgency at my command, however much we digress from the orthodox, however much we endeavour to evolve methods of education which we believe have an effect on the emotions and the temperament, our approach to this difficult problem should be strictly intellectual. *Let us know what we are doing, let us know very clearly what we are doing*, and let us avoid everything which might be considered stunting or quackery or window-dressing in our education. If we are to depart from the orthodox, let us be wise, and *above all let us be sincere in what we do*.'[6]

'The teacher must know for any particular group the kind of experience to provide and when and how to provide it. He must know for each individual when to encourage and when not to do so. He must know when to manipulate the experience of each individual child so that the different skills are practised and different areas of knowledge explored. He must know when an experience has outlived its pedagogical usefulness. He must know when a distaste is arising in an individual and how to thwart it. He must know when the interest is so intense that rigorous but necessary drills will be readily accepted. All these, and many more, are the very essence of the professional teacher's skill.'[7]

Although he said one could put him on the 'woolly' side, his approach to teaching and methods was the opposite of 'fluffy' or 'woolly'. He did not advocate that children should be left to themselves 'to discover' unless they had been thoroughly prepared. Key words were 'approach' and 'method'; that is, the degree of instruction. 'If and when you show the child 'how?', the method is the way the child is shown.' Method goes from freedom of expression in the extreme to minute detailed outlines, both of which could lead to irritating frustration. 'Obviously the extent to which you show a child how will vary from subject to subject, from child to child, and from teacher to teacher.' One teacher may excel in stimulating a child's interest so that it develops the impetus to go ahead on its own. Another's whole training and outlook may make him excel in putting information and technical information before a child in easily assimilable doses that the child never really loses interest but may never engender enough to carry him on under his own steam. He subtly implied judgement, otherwise teaching would be reduced to instruction.

> 'My own view is that where tricks have to be learnt a fairly formal method of approach will do no harm and for many teachers it may be good, and I would place class reading and writing and certainly arithmetic in its early stages as subjects where the tricks and facts have to be known.'

> 'I know that what I say about reading and arithmetic and the skills generally may not be acceptable to advocates of modern methods, but I do think that a great deal of time might be wasted if you leave a child to find out too much for itself. I agree that there is a time in the development of a normally able child when he will learn to read much more quickly than if he had been made to do so earlier in his life. On the other hand, *I am extremely suspicious* of those who say that a child should not learn to read until his interest in reading has been stimulated or aroused.'[8]

> 'I believe there is a great deal of nonsense talked about formal and informal methods of teaching. The fundamental fallacy about it, or so it appears to me, is that it gives the impression that in any given school all children are taught in all subjects by all members of the staff either by one method or by another, that formal and informal methods cannot exist side by side in the same school, that all subjects are equally susceptible either to one method or another, and that no teacher will use either one method or another at all times and in all subjects.'[9]

On the three Rs Alec Clegg was adamant that every pupil should be able to 'surmount . . . problems of his daily life accurately and without tiresome concern'.

> '. . . Let me say that in my view these ends are so important that I am not bothered much about the means used to achieve them provided always that the child is not made miserable by them. Thousands and thousands of teachers have for a hundred years taught these subjects (the three Rs) successfully by antediluvian methods and despite the shocked admonitions of Mr Armstrong (Educational Psychologist) or anyone else I don't really care how long this continues provided always that the ends I have mentioned are achieved and that the depths of the individual child's ability to do these things are completely plumbed.'

> '. . . Nature study, painting, music (in the junior school), craftwork, things which are markedly distinguished from the three Rs in that the ends are without social significance . . . I don't care about a child's achievement in these things as I think it is unimportant, *but I care more than I can adequately say about the way these subjects are presented to him, the way he tackles them, and the satisfaction he gets out of them . . . for the ordinary child the very practising of the subject is the end in itself for children other than those who later in life use the subject vocationally.*'

'Everyone in this room knows that if a child becomes enthralled in a school activity which draws out his own power to produce something, all kinds of desirable things happen to help along his development, some of which we can name, others which we may not yet have got to the bottom of. He gains confidence from the sheer satisfaction of producing something, he probably gains an entitlement of the esteem of his fellows, he becomes interested and alive, and he becomes happy, and, as Earl Russell says, he will tend to be good because he is happy. Most important of all perhaps is that his whole attitude to his work tends to become quickened and vitalised.'

'Then again, it seems to me that the pressure of our economic existence demands that in these formal subjects a child shall be made to learn – willy-nilly as soon as he is intellectually able to do so. It's all very well talking of the development of the child in theory as if we were all Jean Jacques Rousseau each educating his little Emile *in vacuo* and regardless so to speak, but that is not our situation and some regard must be had to the exigent and clamant demand of contemporary society . . . *It does, however, seem to me that a very considerable amount of harm can be done if one uses similar methods in subjects which are designed for the exercise of the child's expressive powers and for his particular enjoyment.'*[10]

'My own belief, therefore, is that where the *skills and information subjects of the curriculum are concerned there has got to be a good deal of direct instruction by the teacher.* Where the expressive subjects are concerned I think that that direction is something that is much more subtle and should take the form of careful guidance if the child's spontaneity and vitality are not to be inhibited by it. What matters in these subjects is endeavour and interest and sincerity – things you can't easily *mark* – and I doubt whether in fact the artistic subjects are really examinable in the way that the skills and the information subjects are.'

'On the question of method, there is very little indeed that I would venture to say other than that I am really not bothered. What matters to me as an education officer is results, good standards, *at the appropriate age.* If a child learns effectively and without strain how to read and to write and to do its arithmetic, I really do not care what methods are employed.'

'I hope you will forgive my cynicism, therefore, if I say that I don't think that we shall increase our efficiency a great deal in the teaching of the formal subjects, but I do believe that in our approach to the expressive subjects we have got a very long way to go indeed and the art people are showing us that way. And I would include in the expressive subjects movement, music, gardening, woodwork, metalwork, domestic subjects, and all the crafts . . . and I would remind you that these expressive subjects are not only amongst the most important in our curriculum but occupy a very great deal of time, so that if the time is wasted, and I think it often is, in our schools, we have a good deal to answer for . . . I think that a good deal of confusion and bad pedagogy has resulted from the discoveries of practical teachers being built into an elaborate theory by the less practical, *and then pushed to extreme.*'

'The danger is, I think, having discovered a better and more effective way of teaching the expressive subjects, they claim this as the only way and promptly apply it to those where formal methods have in the past been not unsuccessful.'

Alec Clegg had faith in his teachers. He expected the syllabus to be well designed and lessons formulated to the best advantage of the children in their variety in the different classes. These expectations were the teachers' remit. They were expected to find out what worked with their classes and what did not and habitually to evaluate teaching situations: there was ongoing process always and therefore development through time, and refreshment and reappraisal threaded through from start to end. He was emphatic that a teacher should work out what he/she could do. This eliminated the search for 'the latest tricks' or repetition until a plan had lost its usefulness. A practical man, practice was intelligently applied theory: informed ideas, far removed from gimmickry. A technique could be sharpened, they were not 'naïve' artists. High expectations and concern for individual abilities informed the progress of all pupils, and created the environment – which produced a liberating influence whether the school ran on 'traditional' or progressive lines.

He regarded the teachers as the experts who could judge what was going on in the schools, not the 'social scientists'. On organisational matters, however, he consulted in scrupulous detail with heads and practitioners 'whose experience entitled them to pronounce a measured opinion'.[11]

Alec Clegg was an inveterate visitor of schools. A senior clerk's complaint on one occasion was that 'he'd slipped t'leash'. The daily round of administration made him impatient as he grew more focused on the schools and teaching method.

'. . . for 30 years I was the Executive Officer of an education authority, charged with the care of some 300,000 children and 1,200 schools, which meant that on any day of a working week I could leave my desk and go out and see teaching genius at work. To do this was a delight and an inspiration and a refreshment in which I had to indulge at least once a week. So I shall describe what I was interested in *but any cures or recipes or methods will be those of practising teachers* whom I know personally, some of them as friends.'[12]

He looked primarily for quality but accepted variety in teaching methods as well as innovation, but gave credit to quiet application. There had to be commitment. In 1974 the Times Educational Supplement recorded his remark that 'the highly gifted folk who have the power of changing teachers and schools are rare'.[13]

At Bingley vacation course, 1950: [14]

> 'The danger arises perhaps in the sort of thing which I heard a
> Correspondent to the Managers say to the headmistress the other day at
> the school sports. 'Have you been on a course recently to get any new
> stunts?' This made me ponder for a moment on the fairly easily recog-
> nisable categories of teachers. There are a few who are the geniuses of
> their profession and they show us what can be done with new methods
> and new enthusiasm. They are very, very few, and they are the standard
> geniuses. There are those, unfortunately a somewhat larger category, who
> seek to emulate the genius and imitate without any real understanding.
> They are the group who were, as the Correspondent said, *ready* to learn
> 'new stunts'. Then there is the vast mass of the teaching profession, for
> whom I have the greatest possible respect, who rely on tried ways but who
> are constantly on the lookout for new ideas and who are prepared to
> modify and adapt and experiment right up to the last years of their pro-
> fession. And there are those who have never excelled in their profession
> who tend to seek kudos in other walks of life and who are ready on any
> occasion to damn a new method because they themselves cannot master
> it. And I think there is also the final, devastating category . . .'

He was particularly hard on those who used jargon without thought, clichés
used as ends:

> 'Primary school education has, in the last few years, thrown up a number
> of clichés, such as learning by experience, finding out rather than being
> told, the integrated day, family grouping, lack of structure, free choice,
> integration of subjects, relevance, and others. These clichés were the *short-
> hand* of teachers who knew what they were talking about, have become
> the jargon, so glibly used by those who, as a former colleague of mine put
> it, 'have jumped on the band-wagon but can't play the instrument'.'[15]

The Newsom Pupil: [16]

> '. . . what we wanted is the teacher who follows the normal training college
> course rather than the trained graduate and certainly rather than the
> untrained graduate. We expressed the wish that all teachers in their
> teaching practice period should have some experience of teaching slow
> learners. There should be some in-service training.'

> 'It is my personal and deep conviction that only the bright child can learn
> what is irrelevant and I doubt very much whether such learning adds to
> his mental stature. But the less able the child the less he is able (to gain)
> from what to him is irrelevant or unenjoyable or uninteresting. The idea
> that a child must first face adversity by learning what is repugnant is, to

my mind, as idiotic as transferring seedlings into a box of ashes on the grounds that they will eventually have to grow in poor soil.'

'. . . what you in fact do is exploit the child's way of living or *give to him a way of living* which will develop in him those *powers and abilities* which we know he is going to need as an adult.'

'We ask for the Newsom children that they should have an education which is practical, realistic, vocational and offers choice. Practical work must lead outwards and must accept the fact that even with the lower ability groups some children are better with words than with things. *Realistic is to the classroom subjects* what practical is to subjects which take place in other rooms, utilisable is a word we use – what is taught must make sense to those who learn. *Vocational* is a dangerous word, and by it *we did not mean that a child should learn mechanical skills* – what we did mean was that *if a vocational bias gives a study relevance in the eyes of the child it should be fully exploited.*'

'The important thing is that every teacher should know why he is teaching what he is teaching and every headmaster and every teacher should know what his subject should be doing to and for each child.'[17]

'. . . The teacher must realise that however quickly it may be possible to push a child from short to long division, in the world of the creative arts the child must take his own time.'

'I think that your first job as schoolmasters and schoolmistresses is to produce normal happy children, and I believe that that is a task of world significance at the present state of our civilisation.'[18]

'The Newsom Report is a fairly straightforward account of the way we neglect not the least, but the less, able child. He needs the best teachers, we give him the poorest; he will benefit most from a rich choice of subjects, in fact he gets far less than his brighter fellows; he needs the stimulus of varied and specialist equipment, not only does he not get this but he is all too often conscious of the fact that his needs are being sacrificed to those of his abler brothers and sisters.'[19]

'. . . we console ourselves with the idea that we must give the best to those who have the best brains. But we are in fact creating for ourselves a major social problem, which I believe is now causing difficulties of immense magnitude. We say to these boys, 'You are clever, you can do A-Level', to these 'You can do O-Level', to a third group 'You can do CSE', to others 'You can leave and take an apprenticeship', to others 'You will receive industrial training' and to a group which is ever more intensively compressed and depressed 'You get nothing'. So the boy gets his motor-bike and his drink and his girl and his pocket-money, he grows his hair long and he says 'I'll show 'em', and he does.'

'*Now the more you care for by education and training the harder to bear will be the plight of those whom we reject.*'

'. . . skills to live by . . .'

Alec Clegg's personal commitment to the total child-student population as well as his professional responsibility gave him a sharp awareness of a school's ambience. On his unofficial visits around schools he countered teachers' general response to their remit with questioning: Where are we going? What are we teaching? Why? How? For what end? An environment is created whether consciously or unconsciously. We give skills, hopefully, to build towards a worthwhile life, so he asked: What are we giving? What are we testing? What means are being used to what ends? In 1954 at a weekend in Woolley Hall organised by Leeds University Institute of Education on 'Modern Educational Problems':

> 'The real questions at issue are what ought schools to aim at producing, and for what kind of social order in the future ought they to prepare the rising generation.'

The Schools Council was established in 1964 and ceased in 1996. This Committee was given a remit to promote ideas in curriculum planning. Teachers were included in the Council's central committee. During its life it gave attention to specific topics and modes of teaching rather than surveying an overall scheme. It adhered to the principle that each school had responsibility for planning its curriculum relating to contemporary life, work, and teaching methods.

> 'In England new knowledge spreads amongst the universities and technical colleges and it also comes into them from the five great research councils: the Agricultural Research Council; the Science Research Council; the Medical Research Council; and the Social Research Council. This knowledge flows from these sources into the scientific journals and it is also disseminated by ever-interchanging university staffs. Furthermore we have a National Foundation for Educational Research which carries out its own investigations and promulgates its findings. *But this new knowledge needs to be made appropriate for school use* and we have recently established a Schools' Council to do just this. It is beginning to look at new methods as well as new material and make them available.'[20]

> 'The most important task of all is that of introducing new materials and new information to the teaching force. To do this successfully there has to be some careful system of in-service training. Such a system will be futile and may do more harm than good if it merely dispenses tips for teachers . . .'

There were two attitudes of mind: one that the 'bright', the 'able' and the 'capable' should be given every chance according to their innate ability; the second, that environment held the key to success. The first overlooked the fact that after each creaming there would always be a group left, a 'fail' group, and the other contained the belief that children could educate themselves. Alec Clegg stood mid-way: he deplored the tiered creaming-off strategy, pointing out the potential danger that in the final analysis a disaffected group of permanent failures would be produced; at the same time he recognised that all pupils should have a sufficiently literate grounding as of right so that they could pick up threads at any time later on in search of advancement or for personal satisfaction. Home and school acted upon each other – a two-way process. His compassion went to those pupils who suffered deprivation or distress. He asked how did delinquency come about? He did not condone it. He stated quite categorically that problems should be resolved with coolness and intelligence – but with compassion. Excuses were not enough. In an educative democracy he said that opportunity must be given to every child to go as far as that individual child is capable. That meant diversity, not pseudo-egalitarianism but opportunity for suitable transfer *for all*, hopefully at any period in a person's life. There should be more than one shared rationale, however detailed: there is more than the immediate goal; the teachers are more than instructors. A curriculum for all should be more than mere holding, but 'contain' in the true sense of the word that which is necessary for all pupils in their particular schools, no group disregarded.

There was during Alec Clegg's time a contrasting content and method which still separated those going on to the professions and those going into articles, apprenticeship or employment at sixteen or eighteen. 'Integrated courses' developed which, since they began well down the school, made it difficult for movement across to traditional subjects on the part of a suddenly-motivated late academic. The grammar schools continued serene in their responsibilities to work with GCE; the comprehensive schools, when they came, continued with their grammar schools sector, also with CSE, Mode III, adapted to the interests and environment of the pupils. There was emphasis, generally, on method rather than content, and the act of raising the school leaving age masked the question 'Is it possible in the true sense *to educate* all children?' The élitists were sceptical, considering the direction of popular culture. Alec Clegg himself said we could and should give breadth and vision, but sadly listed what popular culture could produce:

'Since the war the changes in our society have been as rapid as they have been disturbing. To take one example only. We have created a new kind of teenage society which is highly paid and very self-conscious, and for this we as adults are responsible. They are courted, cosseted and grossly exploited by the fashion houses and other commercial interests and the huge pop music industry is parasitic on them and extracts millions from them. The less intelligent section of this group . . . one suspects . . . behaviour arises from the fact that these youngsters . . . are nevertheless dissatisfied because they feel themselves to be contributing little to society and to be valued accordingly.'[21]

'. . . The gutter press, tawdry novels, bad films, litter, gambling and all the other dubious advantages of education and relative wealth will not outweigh the enormous steps that have been made in health, material comfort, and indeed in the growth of humanity generally in sympathy for the afflicted and the underprivileged and in abhorrence of much that happened 50 years ago which was a daily affront to human dignity. But I must dwell on the gutter press, and the bad film and the money spent on stimulants as forming a very real part of the background against which Further Education has to be carried out in the future.'

The Schools Council's extensive remit produced planned examples of teaching projects assisted by the Nuffield Foundation. The final product masked years of planning, from initial feasibility studies to finding directors for pilot schemes who could co-ordinate activities with some skill taking people from different educational sectors to work with teachers in school, and inviting people external to the educational system in addition. The Schools Council's Working Paper No.2 took a positive approach in quoting the experience of those schools which up to the time of writing that paper had kept 'appreciable numbers' of average pupils for a fifth year and had found these pupils able to 'acquire insights into abstract ideas'. Emphasis was laid on method – oral work, and starting with pupils' experience, introducing crucial new experience which helped them take pleasure in attempting harder work which they had thought they could not do.

These projects were constructed not solely as preparation for work but as an attempt to meet social, moral, recreational as well as vocational needs. Alec Clegg referred to 'O-Level porridge and Nuffield cornflakes'. With his experience of the raising of the school leaving age to fifteen at the end of World War II, he knew the raising of the school leaving age in 1974 to sixteen would produce more problems. He pointed out that the final year should not be a year of 'courses' tacked on. The entire curriculum must be re-planned.

'We need these things to enable us to get new knowledge on to the school menu:

1   Ways of ensuring that new knowledge enters the education system.
2   A way of ensuring that it is made ready for school use.
3   A way of ensuring that teachers who want to use it can do so,
     not mechanically but with understanding.'[22]

He was pessimistic that the major problem of ensuring new concepts would be learned, would be recognised. 'It has been for centuries – in fact since the Renaissance – a major defect in our education that we have identified it with the acquisition of knowledge.' Inert knowledge. We are back to Aiglon:

'Great men throughout the ages have deplored this. Socrates, of course, would have none of it; his whole method was based on so stinging his pupils into active thought that they reasoned from their own experience. I have no doubt, however, that his inferior contemporaries were content with finding out what their pupils knew.'[23]

How new knowledge is made available in schools:

'. . . there is a more sinister danger and that is programmed learning. Do not think for one moment that I under-estimate the power of this new technique. The ironmongery associated with it is largely a nonsense, I think, but a *well constructed programme* which will impart an essential drill or knowledge which a child must obtain at a given time is tremendously valuable. Moreover, the fact that a child can learn at his own pace and have his errors corrected at once and on the spot is an entirely admirable development.'

'But the educative force in learning through science is the wonder and romance which derives from pursuing one's own disciplines, the value of artistic training is the ability to express oneself in one's own way in a chosen medium and the value of literature or music lies in the love one has for it. These essentials – the joy in hearing or seeing, the romance of curiosity and speculation, the ferment which can arise in expressing one's own ideas – do not lend themselves to cultivation by a programme.'

There was a place for 'pot-filling':

'What the well-constructed programme does is enable facts and skills to be learned more quickly and perhaps more effectively. The danger is, therefore, that we are learning what can be programmed and neglect what can't; that we absorb more inert ideas and do so quickly that we have even more time available to learn more inert ideas.'

But

'Programmed learning, team teaching, the initial teaching alphabet, closed circuit television, language laboratories and a host of other devices, gimmicks, theories and fads, some good and some bad, will be thrust upon the teaching profession. All of them will be treated with caution by, and will contribute something to, the powers of the good teacher; many of them will be seized by the bad teacher in the quite illusory forlorn hope that they will make his teaching less bad.'[24]

He felt that teaching methods to some extent had lost flexibility, had suffered from pundits' labelling 'acceptable' or 'unacceptable' and intro-ducing ideological rigidity. Methods of teaching are methods only, and what proves successful should not be elevated to a philosophy or constructed into a set of values. 'The basis of learning is the child's own experience.'

> 'Rarely in my view is anything well taught unless the teacher knows precisely why he is teaching what he is teaching to the children whom he is teaching. Success springs from the depth of the teacher's conviction about the educational wisdom of what he is doing.'[25]
>
> 'Those who teach a body of knowledge – they will be the professionals. Those who peddle 1066 and all that will be the technicians of the service.'

Alec Clegg had a vivid appreciation of educational history particularly from the time of the Taunton Commission, 1868, through to his own period. In many lectures and impromptu sessions with in-service teachers at Woolley and Bingley in particular he gave vivid accounts of early arithmetic and English lessons, the killing influence of Lowe's Code, and of the inclusion of subjects which would be to the advantage of more children as the school leaving age was raised from eleven to thirteen (1902), thirteen to fourteen (1921), fourteen to fifteen (1944) and fifteen to sixteen (1972). It is only when this progress is seen as it is presented in Alec Clegg's historical reviews that the extent of nineteenth-century and early twentieth-century reforming-minded educationists' stamina is appreciated. Alec Clegg had a lively awareness of what had gone before from the evidence in records of his father's and grandfather's schools in Derbyshire. His overview of the different parts of the education service in the West Riding was thorough in that he did not hesitate to seek extensive information central to all parts of the education system.

'Parts of the education system . . .'
The nursery/primary ambience
The Plowden Report of 1967 focused attention on the first years of schooling, and to a certain extent these were the years which attracted Alec Clegg. He very clearly enjoyed visiting primary schools and had a valued collection of young children's art exhibited in his office, and a wider collection which he took with him to show audiences in this country and abroad.

The changes in primary and early junior education in England influenced lesson planning; pupils' learning related to their environment; and a complex attempt at interrelation of the parts of a re-planned curriculum. Teaching methods and therefore testing affected the entire school organisation and the school building. As new schools were built, open spaces were planned for informal activities which accommodated individual and group work. Formal class instruction shared the school day with integrated topics which aimed to have the children use subjects of the curriculum. The content of school curricula had not yet been prescribed, although programmed texts made their appearance. The 11+ examination influenced primary school curriculum planning until the comprehensive system was well established. Criticism of the topic method was that children acquired their individual subject content in a fragmentary and unsystematic manner. It was pointed out that it required very capable teaching and detailed knowledge of each child's stage; the argument for it was the skills acquired in finding out for themselves, sorting out their material and *reasoning with the teacher*, being responsible for their own personal written work and, in addition, having worked through stages and checked with the teacher, like the slave boy they would have made the knowledge their own. They learned to make use of their time; the weaker members would be reliant on the teacher giving an explanation of a basic concept. This method required a vast amount of resource material. Four experimental areas were: the Initial Teaching Alphabet, Nuffield Primary Mathematics, Nuffield Primary Sciences, and the teaching of French.

'The day opens quite frequently with a period during which the children choose what they will do and how they will do it from a range of materials carefully prepared by the teacher . . . The basis of learning is the child's own experience. There is a wide element of choice both of topic and of the medium of expression – points on which, incidentally, the Newsom Report laid such stress. There is stress on the importance of exploration and investigation, a feature of junior school teaching which gives it an affinity with good sixth-form practice . . . There is an absence of competition and a consequent reduction of failure and almost an inevitability of success which, of course, is the most powerful spur to learning.'[26]

'*There is something I would say about this kind of teaching – it is a professional talent of the highest order.*'

But as previously quoted, in his own words he was guarded in uncritical acceptance of any methods and attitudes.

Technical and technological aspects
Alec Clegg had formed a definite point of view on educational priorities. At a meeting of administrators and officials in higher education in 1970 he said he would ask his audience . . .

'. . . to look at the relationships between different parts of the education system. I want to propose a form of further education which is quite different from the one we know in that it accepts its obligations to the whole school system and to society and aspires to create a community in our country and not a hen-run of selfishness, in which pecking power is rewarded and lame ducks despised.'[27]

'. . . Hadow (1931) and Bruner (1965) have a vision of Education as serving democracy, serving a society organised for freedom. That is a definition I prefer . . . *I want to stand up and be counted, as it were, as a teacher.* The issue is sometimes posed as if schools were the enemies of pupils' freedom – there is a large talk of emancipating pupils from the teachers' authority. In fact, for very many of the nation's children *the school is the only glimpse they will ever see* of light, of colour, music, the chance to learn an instrument, to study a foreign culture, to meet decency in talk and personal relationships, not to speak of books. It is no service to these children to knock or worse to patronise the schools they go to and those who teach in them, often in appalling conditions.'

At this meeting of administrators, university and civil servants, he outlined his programme to meet this problem of democratic education for all children. The proposed raising of the school leaving age to sixteen had presented chief education officers with a complex, practical problem. The actuality was that complicated reform measures would have to be dispassionately sorted out which would demand a courageous and original overview of the entire educational service. All children had to be included. Questions of streaming or not streaming, general studies to sixteen or earlier specialisation, arts and/or sciences, larger sixth forms, would of necessity present consideration of a wider remit beginning with university entrance and going on to a requirement to satisfy those diverse ambitions which at a practical level demanded other solutions with equivalent advanced technological and technical qualifications.

Alec Clegg openly stated that he had had little experience of technical education and training. He proposed a deputy education officer to be responsible for this educational priority. James Hogan was appointed. He supplied the chief education office with information and statistics which were used to advantage, yet Alec Clegg never lost sight of his model of a liberal education and the sustaining power of art. At a refresher course for FE teachers at Illminster in 1956, he talked at length on design and popular tastes.

> 'The Council of Industrial Design, of which I have the honour to be a member, is, I think, doing an extraordinarily fine piece of educational work . . . Members of the staff talk to retailers and manufacturers about the importance of design, and the Council has a number of services which are available to schools . . . We ought to be promoting . . . the same sort of interest locally as the Council is trying to disseminate from the Centre . . . We survive on quality, and good design is an absolutely essential ingredient of quality.'[28]

He recognised that fragmentary or unsystematic re-planning of the curriculum was not 'reform' – science and technology were part of a liberal education, there was feedback both ways:

> 'the Technical Branch of the Education Service is becoming more and more the subject of public utterances which, though sometimes vague, ill-

defined and ill-informed, and *often without knowledge of the complexity of the problem*, nevertheless betray a general public anxiety.'[29]

His questioning continued:

'Those who urge the need for more technical education seldom particularise; they usually content themselves with a statement that technical education is something we need more of. They do not answer the questions: Are we to have more atom bombs or more confectionery; more jet engines or more vacuum cleaners? We need more of these things, or better quality, or both? Do we want more applied scientists, more technologists, more technicians, or more skilled craftsmen? Do we know what we mean by these terms? Do we know which group we need more of most urgently? Do we want a large national technical college – a MIT or a Zurich – or do we want to spread technical education at that level over a number of universities and technical colleges? Should the universities absorb the larger technical colleges, or should some of the latter assume university status? Is it the grammar schools – the source of our leading scientists and technologists – which are at fault, or is it our National Technical Certificate courses (with a wastage approaching 90%) that need reforming? When we speak of technical education do we mean all vocational education, and if so, should some of this be a part of the secondary school course, or should industry attend to it – and if industry, why not commerce also? Is there any justification for the secondary technical school? Exactly what should such a school do which a good modern school cannot or should not do?

And, finally, are we to exclude liberal studies from technical courses on the grounds of economy and/or expediency, or are we to increase them on the grounds that sound management (a technique in which we seem not to be as expert as some of our competitor nations) is basically a human problem?'

These fundamental questions, which remain constant, he regarded as of importance, and to that extent he put his teachers into Aiglon's shoes. He sought to have technical and technological work conceived as a possibility in a wider cultural context. The questions remain constant – they are to seek knowledge of the context of education; teachers' and administrators' solutions would have relevant breadth in relation to social conditions and to particular regional educational priorities as well as those of government. A planned national curriculum could not in one sense be seen in exactly the same light in every district or region. Alec Clegg's priority was adequately educated citizens who, in living their lives to their personal fulfilment in their personal context also could meet the industrial, commercial and professional needs of the country, a two-way exchange in a co-operative temper rather than competitive.

'But education is fundamentally a civilising process and the purpose of further education is no longer what it once was, viz., an opportunity to allow the person born before the age of compulsory education to make up for what he had missed. It is, or should be, as much as any other branch a part of the civilising process and it should concern itself as much as any other branch with the great human values, standards and principles.'[30]

'. . . we have all been through the same mill – we still do the Stuarts, we do A Midsummer Night's Dream, we do the trade winds and quadratic equations . . .'[31]

'We select at 11 and we put the ablest 20–25% of our youngsters into schools which are not only dominated by but geared to the universities by means of a very rigid examination system . . . The sixth former all too often will go to a technical college only if he has failed to get into a university and doesn't want to go to a training college. Now fortunately our selection methods are faulty. I don't know the precise extent of the fault, but it is probable that of the ablest 30% of the 11 year old age group more than one-third is wrongly placed. Another way of saying that is that of every 30 children admitted to a grammar school 7 are admitted who should not be and 7 are not admitted who should be. Partly as a result of this fault a considerable number of able youngsters escape the grammar school route and are able to follow a part-time day-release or evening institute route to an Ordinary National Certificate.'

'You know in this country we go out of our way to create failure, to wreck the morale of a child by branding him as a failure. We create failures at 11, 16 and 18, *and at every year in the 15 to 22 FE Course*. We know full well that hundreds of youngsters who embark on an ONC Course and fail to make the grade are so disheartened that they never tackle the City and Guilds course which they could manage. Is this *sound* morally, socially, industrially, or in whichever way you care to look at it?'

'. . . this matter of inefficiency. One in ten makes the grade to HNC and a somewhat larger proportion to ONC, and the same in the City and Guilds courses. *What would happen if selection in these courses were really effective* – as effective, say, as the 11+ selection or the university entrance?'

At the Textile Institute, Manchester, in 1959, Alec Clegg evaluated trends in technical education and firmly voiced his stance. He had an invigorating approach to what were continuing problems at the heart of educational planning which remained, whatever surface rearrangement or re-planning was done. His concern was for all pupils and students from 'the top five per cent of the intelligence range' to the less able. Arguing for an enriched curriculum for all children he said we imply: 'You are less able, therefore we shall spend less effort on the refining and civilising processes of your education,' and continued: 'How wise is this I wonder in a democratic age when we have come to rely less and less on authority and coercion and more and more on negotiation, co-operation and a right understanding between management and men?'

Alec Clegg was concerned that under the tripartite system pupils should be placed where they could profit most. Some pupils either by strong inclination or family bias could and would choose a technical school, and therefore '. . . we have got to get some local Panel to go into those cases for us, see the children and interview the children with the parents present'.[32] He had a strong faith in the professionalism and expertise of the teachers. He cited the Crowther Report, Chapter 12, in regarding the fifth year as a transitional year from school either to work or to the sixth form. There was an abrupt transition from school to work, occasionally wounding, occasionally damaging, or an intellectually taxing step forward to advanced studies. The school had a responsibility. With the raising of the school leaving age the schools had pupils who were no longer children and they faced either longer working hours, or a longer day of study.

Crowther pointed out an attitude which looked for school conditions being brought nearer to working conditions. This would only apply to the length of the working day, and hours actually spent in school. If homework was done adequately, the school day was already extended considerably, but only where homework was part of the school remit. Comprehensive and modern schools it was suggested could profit by including homework. It was clear that staff and children could make use of this extra margin given by homework, and would 'raise the educational yield'. More demands were being made by developments and changes in many occupations, some changes being 'out of all recognition'.

> '. . . It is a society which can show little or no spiritual development to compare with its material progress, a society in which there are predatory forces seeking to exploit the greeds and lusts within each individual on a wholesale scale never known before, a society in which money holds a supreme position, in which intellectual gifts no longer have the prestige they once had. It is a society by which men can earn their living by monotonous repetitive processes in which they see little purpose and can take but little pride, and their reward is to be bombarded with a variety of spectacular entertainments which demand nothing of them and add nothing to their stature.'[33]

He reviewed the change in manufacturing and commercial life which demanded different aims and results from the educational system and compared the state of those studies in further education with their opposite numbers in the USA and USSR. He accepted and pointed out that to keep up with the larger nations the British aim must necessarily be for quality and that 'we would expect our technical education to be of the best 'quality''.

'Now when I make these strictures I refer to the training of technicians and craftsmen rather than to the training of our technologists who more and more in the future are going to be drawn from those who have achieved an 'A' level result in the G.C.E., go either to take a degree at a university or to full-time study or a sandwich course at a college of advanced technology. I am less concerned with these in that I am much more happy about them.'[34]

'. . . there is little doubt in my mind that by comparison with all other branches of the service, for example the education of infants, juniors, adolescents and university students, FE is inferior, inefficient, illiberal and inadequate.'

'May I make one further point which to my mind leads to inefficiency? The City and Guilds courses evolved in the 1879s in the days of whiskey money and the Technical Instruction Act. *They drew on the whole ability range of the nation.* Even the course system, which was a development with which I was concerned in my early years in administration, was begun as early as 1890 *in this* City (Manchester) by the Sanitary Engineering Department of the Manchester Technical School. At the time when the regional bodies such as the Union of Lancashire and Cheshire Institutes came into the field there were very few youngsters going to the Grammar Schools and there must then have been thousands of men now in their late 50s and 60s following a City and Guilds course *who were perfectly capable of taking a good Honours degree.* The realisation of this fact, together with the growing need in industry for a body of well-trained technicians, led to the invention and the development of the National Certificate courses after World War I. But these examinations are tending less and less to be aimed at the young men *of the ability of those for whom they were originally devised.* When I came to the West Riding fifteen years ago (in 1945) we offered about 70 Major Awards each year to the University – we now offer about 700 and there is no doubt whatsoever that we are drafting into the University *in large numbers* young men who previously would have followed a National Certificate course.'

Industry is making a wholly different claim on education from that which it used to make. High intellectual ability is being demanded. Unskilled work is disappearing. Such unskilled work as there is today is even less interesting than it used to be because it is totally purposeless to the operator who cannot see the end. Alec Clegg saw the problems:

'1   to make silk purses out of sows' ears,
2   to compensate for the deadliness of most routine jobs.'

As always, his concern was for pupils and students. He was alert to the lower social status of FE and knew this was due to the structure of end-on courses for earlier elementary and central schools. He pointed out emphatically that times had changed drastically. We were now looking at a total youth population whether an acceptable fact or not, irrespective of social layers, and attempting to match education and training to abilities and predilections. Class structure in England was the added factor. He pointed out that few people would, if able to choose, send their children to a college of advanced technology as a first choice. He added, then, uncomfortable questions: How many grammar school/college principals, and education officers, would do so? He concluded: 'What hope has technology which is clearly non-U?' Further, he suspected, few grammar school heads 'know nearly as much about the way our technicians are trained to a standard which is after all well above that of 'O' level in G.C.E. Neither do our modern school heads who are educating our future craftsmen know nearly as much about their teaching as the average grammar school head does of the university teacher training routes.' It was a question of status and snobbery.

'. . . But we are entering on a stage now when secondary schools are going to be so reorganised that substantially all the able children will be funnelled through into the sixth form. This will be done either by comprehensive schools or by the 'Leicestershire Plan' or by overlapping courses in modern or grammar schools. If therefore we have to continue to rely on our 15 year old leavers to produce a high proportion of our technicians, the outlook will be pretty poor.'

'I said that the system was inefficient, and by an inefficient system I mean one that produces meagre results after prodigious effort. Let us remind ourselves that of 100 pupils who embark on a Higher National Certificate course, 10 are likely to gain the certificate. I remember once talking to a grammar school headmistress about selection at 11+ and she said, 'If only you will give us enough they will include the ones we want'. I was profoundly shocked at this statement as it implied to me – give us ninety a year and forty-five will probably turn out to be good G.C.E. material, and it doesn't much matter what we do with those who don't, they'll manage somehow. The same plan is put forward by the universities who would like to say to the LEAs 'You pay, let us pick out students, and those who can't make the grade at the end of the year will be pitched out'. Here again, what shocks me is the *callousness* of people who are, let us face it, in the top 5% of the intelligence range.

But all this is nothing compared with the fall-out in the training of our technicians and craftsmen . . .'

'Do you demand that the brilliant line up with the maimed and the halt and all attempt the same course?'

Alec Clegg deplored an examination system which wasted so many:

'When I turn to my further education colleagues and point out this iniquity, they round on me and say 'Ah, but it is the wicked industrialists who do this. They say let them all have a shot, if they don't they'll blame us instead of their own incompetence'.'

Before he retired, Alec Clegg saw the beginning of more developments in technical education. What comments he would have made on the computer age is a delightful conjecture. He saw the beginning of proposals for city technical colleges, the broadened sixth form, and some sixth form colleges. Technological universities were on the horizon. He said:

> '. . . the real truth of the matter is that technical education is not an integrated part of our educational system *based securely in a philosophy of further education.*'

A philosophy that would be concerned with more than instruction.

'Pace setters. . .'

Alec Clegg was the first to acknowledge that the task of educating a school population in a large county of widely varying districts would present each school with a set of unique problems in addition to the general remit. One of his reference points was the aim defined by Thring of Uppingham School which he compared with his grandfather's teaching at his school in Derbyshire. Thring's concern was for the minds of his pupils who came from a social background which produced teachers and scholars. He commented also on the advantages Uppingham had in having the boys for a long school day and for several years. His grandfather, head of a school with four assistants, had the children for three brief years. His concern was for minds and welfare in a different social situation, and 'he did the thing that only could be done, they reduced the content of what had to be taught to the barest minimum and insisted on much of it being learned by rote.'

Alec Clegg contrasts two men, Matthew Arnold and Robert Lowe. He understood that Matthew Arnold's letters indicate a personal response[35] as well as his other writing, and 'did much to relieve this emphasis on rote learning of facts'. Lowe, Alec Clegg pointed out, brought disaster, 'payment by results', wherein Lowe pointedly defined a diminished status for the children of the entire working population of the country – the vast majority of whom it was recognised by committed educationists had to be educated to meet growing economic needs and conceded also, for their own sakes:

> 'The great inspectors of these early years, of whom Matthew Arnold was, of course, the greatest, saw where this system was leading, and they did much to try and relieve the emphasis on rote learning of facts; but then came the disaster of payment by results . . . Robert Lowe, the Vice-President of the Department (of Education), devised the system whereby grants were paid to managers provided that pupils put in a certain number of attendances at schools and passed successfully a 2 or 3 minute examination conducted by HM Inspectors, most of whom bitterly resented the triviality of the job.'[36]

'The author of the Revised Code obviously believed that the school-master's job was to teach children to read, write and cipher and instil into them as many facts as possible culled from such fields as learning of history, geography and particularly the scriptures; and it was those who believed these things that prevailed. They are the direct ancestors of the 11+, the 'O' and 'A' Level, the UCLI, the RSA, the College of Preceptors and all the rest of them.'

Alec Clegg quoted Thring again:

' "Does the carting into the mind of a few bushels of facts to be peddled out again make the owner more of a man? Does any amount of accumu-lated brain-store, *if that's all*, make the man more of a man or anything better than an animated knowledge shop?" '

When Robert Lowe's dead period of 'payment by results' passed, the task became one of questioning ways and means of assessment and evaluation and again Alec Clegg quotes Thring:

' ". . . enough has probably been said to show that examinations are very efficient for judging neglect or idleness; are also efficient in a very few well-defined instances in determining a certain kind of merit, but that they break down utterly for many reasons over a wider field. They are also most fascinating exercises of power to those who believe in them. If memory rules, and neatly packed knowledge makes men, up with the flag, enlist our workers under the banner of Examinations. But if education and training are the true aim of mankind, and power in a man's self the prize of life, then no superstition ever ate into a healthy national organism more fatal than the cult of the Examiner . . . The civilised mumbo-jumboism which thinks it can award over a whole kingdom the power of mind. Examinations in that case are but another name for death to originality, and all improvement that is original." '

Alec Clegg's firm conviction that the 'pot-filling' applied exclusively was a means to an end, not an end in itself, material to be used, thought about, worked upon, applied to ideas and situations:

'. . . But the teacher must make the taught do the work. The teacher's work is to direct, suggest, question and inspire; he adapts himself in every possible way to the individual minds, never resting till he has made them master of the skill required and seen them become capable of working on their own account.'

With Aiglon in mind he had, therefore, a firm concept of what he thought was a good head teacher and a good class/subject teacher. He was concerned that 'we have constructed a public system that brands the unsuccessful'. His search was for a solution, the construction of a scheme in which there was room for wide skills and predilections where a 'fire-lighting' technique could be used to balance the 'pot-filling'. It was, he recognised, a hard-headed intellectual task which exercised compassion not sentimentality.

Again he questioned: 'What is the solution? How do we make a strong mind rather than a full one?'

> 'We are frightened by the absence of knowledge. We still teach under the shadow of the polymath. All children must have a smattering of a lot of subjects. And yet how absurd this is' . . . 'Knowledge, in my view, does nothing to the mind unless it works on it as yeast works on dough.'

He went on to remind his audience that the Education Act of 1944 enjoined us 'to concern ourselves with the spiritual, moral, mental and physical well-being of our children; so what do we do?' He defined what he would do in the classroom, and from accounts of his own pupils in school, they learned by doing, and also on his own admission were successful sometimes and not on other occasions. He looked for an 'eager and enquiring mind', interested in the natural and human world; and a strong imagination not in retreat into a world of fantasy but with the power of creating a sustaining inner world, able to act imaginatively towards people and the environment, to think and act in several fields. This would include the enjoyment of art and craft, active discrimination to understand people and one's heritage. 'I would want my pupils to have visions of human greatness in a variety of spheres.' The ability to take on personal responsibility implied self-respect and respect for others. It was a tall order.

Alec Clegg viewed headteachers from the starting point of these aims which he thought were the real subjects of the curriculum. A classical ideal, Alec Clegg was true to his own upbringing, education and training. What sets him apart from the average is that he wanted a schooling of quality given to all children. He never said, as the writer heard one educationist say, 'You can't give *that* to *those* children'. Alec Clegg asked the question: 'What happens if you do not?' and answered it himself through his personal distress for the children of his Authority whom he knew from reports were held back by deprivation, ill-treatment or sheer indifference.

His ideal school ignored economics:

> 'I should have at my disposal a great array of material; and the pupils should have – games and history, excursions and mathematics, religious instruction and the dance, science and drama, geography and pictures, language and gymnastics, school dinners and field studies, art and crafts, and the personal bearing and demeanour of myself and my staff . . . if I had specialists I would present them with my few aims and would exact from them a fairly precise statement of which aims their particular

specialism was going to contribute to and how . . . I would want to know that the atmosphere for doing it was right.'

Alec Clegg went into schools in a spirit of inquiry and was alert to social climate and social areas. In 1960 he was already discussing 'Problems of the Final Year', how the subjects of the curriculum could encourage sixteen-year-old pupils to be resourceful, enquiring and thoughtful. He felt this was clearly a base on which to begin discussions although the actual raising of the school leaving age could be ten years ahead. In reviewing all the subjects he asked 'Why are you teaching this subject to these children in this way? The great sin is to teach without an aim or with a mere examination syllabus in view.'[37] In 1960 he said:

'Many modern schools, as if dissatisfied with the old methods, are constantly groping for new and better ones. Sometimes a method is pursued with conviction, projects, centres of interest, job cards and the like: or it may be a new subject is introduced which is to be the salvation of our schools – social studies, modern dance, rural studies and so on. And when they succeed we don't quite know whether it is because of their intrinsic educational worth, or because of the faith with which they are handled at a given time by an individual teacher.'

'Even the grammar schools themselves, as if knowing the utter dullness of much that they are required to dispense in the classroom, provide the vitality which carried over into the classroom work by the excellence of their out-of-school activities – clubs, hobbies, sports, excursions, choirs, and the like – and from my experience of many schools I can affirm that the schools in which these things are done well are in fact the schools which achieve academic excellence.'

'Before the war (WWII) those wishing to visit schools which provided a really civilising environment, and where behaviour, activities and values were of the highest, would have had to visit a grammar school. This is no longer true – not, of course, because grammar schools have deteriorated, but because modern schools have equalled and in some cases surpassed them in this respect.'

'The plea I make is for a period of peace for the modern schools. Their building and staffing difficulties have been severe enough, but they have been grossly misrepresented by fiction writers and the Press, who have deliberately exploited the fringe behaviour problems which no doubt exist in a few schools in a few areas.'

'The modern schools should be allowed quietly to develop so that the best of them by teaching the child rather than the subject will show the way to producing eager, resourceful and sensitive children with a respect for themselves and others and for the things around them.'

He acknowledged the work the modern schools had done and the skill of staff. When Alec Clegg joined the West Riding Educational Service, he joined a committee which already had opted for multilateral schools. The first head of a multilateral school was appointed before the end of World War II at Tadcaster. The school was a four-hundred-year-old school whose governors were presided over by the Bishop of Selby. In July 1946, the West Riding Education Committee recommended:

'. . . that the Authority should continue wherever possible the policy they have already adopted at Otley and Tadcaster of building community schools large enough to take all types of children in the area but not sufficiently large to become unwieldy.'[38]

'Then came World War II and a new idea. Everyone was to have secondary education and the meaning behind this was that we had to get the best out of every child. But we didn't mean it of course. We still aimed at getting the best out of the best. We were then prepared to do what we could for the average. We offered compassion and support to the really weak, but it was the devil take the next to hindmost, and this after all was merely a reflection of society.'[39]

'We had now reached the stage when the public school product mattered, the new grammar school product mattered, but the rest didn't. As one grammar school headmaster said to me, 'Give to the bright the money they need and spread what remains as thinly as possible over the rest'. But already society was racing ahead of this kind of conception. We could not get enough professionals and technicians and machines began to do the simple jobs of life . . . And in the United States there began to be indications that those who were only educated up to the simple jobs were likely to be out of work . . . So it looks as if perhaps we ought if not as a matter of Christian principle then as a matter of social expediency to be equally concerned about all our youngsters.'

Reorganisation

The West Riding Post-war Development Plan committed the county to comprehensive schools.[40] Alec Clegg, as its Chief Education Officer, took responsibility. He himself was welcoming, but sanguine about some outcomes. As usual, he asked questions and pointed out 'current dangers and anxieties' at a conference in Buxton in 1966.[41]

'. . . I believe that comprehensive education with all its faults is bound to come and I believe that it is right that it should . . .'

His fears were:

'(1) That we construct bad and makeshift comprehensive schools;
(2) That ignorant or politically biased people assume that

comprehensive education is going to solve all our difficulties.'

'And I certainly reject selection with its massive 40% or so error.'

The first comprehensive school in the West Riding was Calder High School at Mytholmroyd. A new secondary modern school had been started before the war, and this site was completed for the accommodation of an 'upper school' for pupils aged thirteen to eighteen. The old Hebden Bridge Grammar School buildings took the pupils from eleven to thirteen. The use of two sites was unavoidable in this instance, but it was pointed out that 'we are avoiding as far as possible 'botched' schemes of one school in several separated buildings, or schools with a very narrow age range, say 11–13'.[42]

The next comprehensive school to be opened was in 1955, at Colne Valley; Penistone and Tadcaster followed.

The comprehensive plans were not followed through uneventfully. The Conservatives won the 1955 local elections with a small majority, but this balance enabled them to declare they were not favourably inclined to a general policy of comprehensivisation, and the 'wiping out' of existing grammar schools was viewed with apprehension. Nevertheless, Alec Clegg saw that the delayed move towards comprehensive schools gave pause for thought and avoided hasty schemes. By 1964, when the Education Act was passed, discussion with several Divisions on the age of transfer – 11–18; 11–13; 13–18 – could take place.

'The pioneering of the three-tier form of comprehensive reorganisation was probably the West Riding's greatest single contribution to national education in the post-war period. Without this innovation the un-suitability of existing buildings and the weakening economic position of the nation would, in combination, almost certainly have provided an insuperable barrier to comprehensive reorganisation in many areas in the later 1960s and 1970s.'[43]

In *The Development of an Education Service: The West Riding, 1889–1974,* Gosden and Sharp give a detailed analysis of administrative arrangements in their complexity under Conservative and Labour, and the part played by the last Chief Education Officer. The planning and administration of the Thorne Selection Scheme referred to earlier is one example, assisted by G. Peaker HMI, of Alec Clegg's attempts to give every child its opportunity. He disliked the finality of the 11+ examination. Following the coming of comprehensivisation in 1964 and Circular 10/65, he summarised:

'The county has favoured three kinds of comprehensive school:

(1) The all through 11–18 school as in the Colne Valley.
(2) A number of small junior schools (5–9 years) contributing to a few middle schools (9–13) contributing to one large secondary school (13–18). This was not legal when we first made the proposal in 1962

but was made legal on a limited scale by the 1964 Education Act and is now being widely adopted.

(3) The 11–16 school followed by a centralised sixth form. We have a very big example of this in Mexborough and a smaller one in the Wetherby/Sherburn/Tadcaster areas. The advantage of this scheme is that additional sixth forms can develop as soon as the numbers staying on warrant such a step.

(4) We abolished the kind of 11+ examination which damaged the junior schools as early as 1955 when we introduced the Thorne Scheme. This is a scheme based on school assessments but with a special device for making sure that the borderline in one school is the same as the borderline in another.'[44]

The sixth form at Mexborough Grammar School grew rapidly in size. The new building became available in September 1964. The Crowther Report had outlined a 'case for Junior College' which had a sixth form curriculum, but could be widened to include practical courses such as commerce, pre-nursing, but necessitating a full complement of staff contributing to academic and personal development in an adult atmosphere.[45]

'. . . in the West Riding the sixth forms in the last five years have been increasing at a rate above the national average but we have the national swing away from science to arts and social studies even in the south of the county.'[46]

The widened sixth form college as set up by Mexborough gave heavy responsibilities towards a broader IQ band than that catered for by the traditional sixth. This presented problems. A major one was the provision of courses other than the traditional A-level patterns, but at an acceptable intellectual level. This was solved by providing for advanced and scholarship levels but also 'cultural level' (non-examinable), vocational level and ordinary level. The timetable was permanent and each student had an individual timetable. A general studies course, not set against the other courses, was available for a number of students. Socially the students became responsible through the 'College Society' for their own organisation. The premises were open during the evening. The load of decision-taking was tempered. Academic discipline stayed in the hands of headmaster and staff.

The sense of community was evident, and due to a certain extent to the fact that

'Mexborough and its surrounding townships retain to a larger extent a sense of community which may be lacking in the larger cities, so that students entering the college are not readily distinguished from those coming from the lower school, and many of them have in fact been friends and acquaintances for much of their lives.' . . . 'Social freedom has been granted on a much more extensive scale than is usual. It has been obvious for many years that some change was necessary. Early maturation, much greater affluence and a rapidly changing public opinion was making it necessary to treat the sixth form as an adult group, which indeed it is.'[47]

The sixth form college could be either an integral part of a huge comprehensive school or an academic institution on its own. Another 'pace setter' was the concept of a 'community college' which furnished special centres for older pupils in secondary schools. This type of centre was the brain child of Mr and Mrs Medd of the Ministry's Architects' Branch. Their buildings or extensions were so designed to meet the need for informal activities of many kinds of leisure activities and on school premises which would contribute to an extended school day and take in leisure activities. To a certain extent these activities would be used by the older pupils along youth club lines. Alec Clegg thought this would be an excellent proposition for the proposed new school in a mining area at South Kirby / Moorthorpe. The Carnegie Trust gave a grant towards the cost. In February 1969 the building of Minsthorpe High School was completed and opened, and incorporated the community centre.[48]

CHAPTER THREE:
'AN INFLUENCE ACROSS ALL LIVES'

Love of the arts was a unifying theme at the centre of Alec Clegg's concern for children. This perceptive recognition of quality was extended in discourse, informal situations, developed through his speeches, visits, and at the many meetings of private and public committees he sat on. He said the arts were 'an influence across all lives'.

> '. . . a word about the arts generally, and I include all that are readily capable of being taught as arts, i.e. drama, art, music, domestic subjects, craftwork, gardening, and I would also include games and spoken and written English.'[1]

These subjects contributed towards 'a humanising curriculum'. Alec Clegg took office at a point in time in educational planning which had caused a review of educational principles and practice. Subjects which had been set on the fringe became incorporated into the timetable, for example, domestic science, art, music and drama were included in general principles and philosophy of education and within the wider cultural context. Alec Clegg appreciated the contribution of art, music, movement, and their part in drama, together with their influence on speech and creative writing. He consequently valued the place of art and the teaching of art; and the influence of movement on physical education to give 'harmony, confidence and dignity'. Always there was consideration of the centrality of language.

The place of art and the teaching of art
Children should be encouraged to look at and think about things around them; it was unkind and impractical to select one or two gifted pupils. The rest need different care, but take off when richness is put before them. The teachers in school were professionally obliged to encourage all the class. He asked 'What really happens? What really matters? What is art? What is an artistically educated person?' He was saying 'Look at Aiglon, how are you going to see that a discerning, receptive attitude of mind is inbuilt, how to be habitually observant and thoughtful.' As with the 'two Rs', he did not dismiss technical skills which were necessary to make effective statements, but was sceptical about transfer of skills. At appropriate times it was possible to teach principles, and thus build up a teaching scheme catering for skill to apply these principles analytically and creatively. This is 'basic'. He quotes Herbert Read's statement that 'art is an agent of education'.

'My father was a grammar school headmaster who once produced a book on art which most of you would now probably condemn every page. But he had a passionate faith in the place of art and craft in the curriculum; . . . The beauty of things mattered more in his school than in any other that I have ever known.'[2]

'. . . The real purpose of art and music in our schools and youth clubs is that more people should learn to like beautiful things and more people learn to love good music. Unfortunately we do not know how to achieve this end, but we do know how to impart technical efficiency, and we like to believe that out of the one the other will develop. Unhappily, the acquisition of a skill is no guarantee whatever of any creative ability in the use of that skill or of any sensitivity to the creative effort of others in the use of that particular skill.'[3]

Art could and does absorb and transform. The child's art is not adult art, he paints what he sees, as he sees it, and his product cannot be judged as adult art. Children unconsciously convey in symbolic form what is in their minds. Effort is learned, and application, selection and invention. They come to look at pictures with recognition of the effort put into them and begin to try to work out what the artist was getting at. So they get beyond the 'I like' or 'I dislike' stages. Painting for them is an expressive activity, and a normal part of the day. They learn control of the medium and ask for help – rules are not cast away. The school experience is individual. They move from play to involvement in planning, and older children's blanks in technical knowledge are filled. They are not left 'free' to the extent that a gale blows through their minds. A good working situation engenders good work habits. The art of teaching, Alec Clegg defined, lies in its subtlety which might look like *laissez faire* but is actually extremely taxing. It gives a base and a continuing feeling for art. Conditions had to be there for 'sensitive work which was more than sensitive copying'.

'. . . I believe that a man who loves beautiful things is likely to be more tolerant, more kindly, more understanding of the troubles of others, and more pleasant to live with than one who is not, and I am convinced that until we can secure a large reservoir of young, purposeful people who do care about beautiful things, we shall not restore to this generation the ability to build beautiful buildings and plan beautiful cities which has been lost to us since the onset of the Industrial Revolution . . . If, however, we can persuade more and more people to paint for the *fun* of the thing, we shall have taken a step in the right direction and shall begin to produce a generation which will no longer tolerate ugliness and squalor in their country.'

Bretton Hall College was set up particularly to foster excellence in art, drama and music. From the beginning, at an early foundation meeting[4] in

1949, Alec Clegg emphasised that he was not as worried about the exceptional child – the incurably musical or the incurably artistic child. Optimistically he thought they would get where they wanted to go. He wanted teachers who would go out from Bretton to give their classes experience and space in which to exercise creative ability. He emphasised that this kind of experience was not only good for the child at the time but it also contributed to his development. He wanted children to enjoy good music, art and drama, to recognise accepted civilised values and taste, to be able to distinguish between what is spurious and what is genuine. He did not believe that creative experience would necessarily produce this love of beautiful things, but young people would have been placed in an environment which contributed to discrimination in buildings, furniture, dress, fabrics, personal relationships:

'(a) not by factual knowledge,
 (b) not necessarily being competent in this or that branch of an art,
 (c) not by the history of art,
 (d) not by School Certificate art papers,
 (e) not by the lives of the great artists,
 (f) not by lectures on appreciation.

Mainly by exposure to beautiful things in doses appropriate to their age. The child brought up amongst tawdry things will want tawdry things, and a child brought up with what is good will love what is good if he has an *intelligent* interest in it.'

His key word is 'intelligent'. It would be a question of informed response to an environment in which the pupils could mature. He recognised that the 'innocent eye' is a mental construct. Rather, present insights or intuition gained from perceiving cannot be separated from past impressions and experiences. The art adviser, Basil Rocke, was reluctant to interfere with children's initial efforts: what they painted gave insight into their vision of things around them. We put meaning into what we see using past experience: 'Create an environment'. Alec Clegg's deep compassion was given to the able blocked by circumstances. In ill-treatment, isolating, scapegoating, and maladjustment he identified plainly the origins of delinquency. He questioned time and again what was the best for those people *left behind at each stage* of the examination ladder; he warned repeatedly that if they were ignored a social price would be paid.

Children's paintings do not disclose all the invisible effects of the teaching, but trained, sympathetic teachers and advisers who know the district learn to identify pupils' mental set. Starting with the pupils' planning, when to introduce technique can result in not only a wide range of subjects but also responses which promote individual skill. As the pupils mature and skills and techniques are gained, a few take off, but all the pupils will have had a worthwhile, enjoyable experience and have gone some way down the road towards valuing creative work when they habitually use a 'seeing eye' in the daily round. They are ready to seize opportunities for living at a more observant mental level, and grow disciplined in their own planning. Art becomes a source of inspiration and consolation. At their later stage in school they grow into habits of observation and study since earlier spontaneity has not been crushed. They go through required examinations more calmly because these do not come to be the end but a means to an end – the cultural experience has been deeper and broader. Each pupil is different and their end products are not mere representation.

'. . . see to it that his pupil paints as a child, acts as a child, and sings and dances as a child. What one must look for, or so it seems to me, is not something that is right or wrong and can be marked out of ten, but a sincere expression of a child's creative powers and not an insincere imitation of an adult conception. Finally, the teacher must encourage and bring out rather than instruct and instil. He must learn to recognise the demand for technique when it comes (i.e. then instruct) and must not dam up the child's exuberance by inflicting it on him prematurely, and he must also learn that the developing techniques in a child are to be seen when he (the child) first becomes *consciously aware* of something that he has done unconsciously for some time. Finally, he (the teacher) must realise that what he understands as technique is a *technique of the adult* and he must avoid it in any considerable measure until the child begins to reach the adult stage, that is until he reaches his early 'teens. The teacher must do this, that is if he is to have any hope of sustaining that spontaneity and vitality which is the essence of all art.'[5]

Child art records a child's inner world, he has his own symbols and can distinguish between make believe and reality in the context of traditional family patterns. His own world is represented in relation to the external world, and the external world in return is represented in relation to his own world: there is a two-way traffic.

Basil Rocke, the senior art adviser, summarised his principles of teaching art at a secondary headteachers' conference on 10th December 1960:

'In art education we have the opportunity to develop ideas and the imagination.'

'In any career . . . the man or woman who has vision and the ability to think and act creatively is surely of enormous importance; without making any extravagant claims, art education can make a very great contribution to this end.'

'The result of good art teaching is visual . . .'

'How I recognise the good art teacher: use of the environment, own ideas, not copying, variety . . . children involved continually in creative thinking

The Flower Painting is by Fourth Year, South Kirkby Primary School, 1953/4
(*Bretton Hall Archive.*)

and feeling . . . extensive use of materials and tools . . . explore with colours, observe closely, interpret character and objects in paint.'[6]

Alec Clegg recognised technical skills – these were needed to make effective statements in art, movement, drama, music, reading and writing. All have their own unique language – communication is difficult and has to be worked at. He wanted an environment for the children that would encourage this working at some concept and insisted that far more pupils were capable of difficult sustained effort. 'You can't give *that* to *those* children' attitude was equivalent to a criminal act. He returned with vehemence often to this theme of the vital role of the arts in all types of schools, in all lives.

Alec Clegg's notes for speeches, 1956,[7] again were summarised in questions, and again sought the central principle which governed thought on the subject, resolutions about how and what to communicate, and consequent actions:

'What, in order of importance, are the purposes of teaching an art?
  Enjoyment of art by the masses,
  Skills as amateurs in the art by the many,
  Skills as professionals by the élite.'

He included all the curriculum subjects which enhanced self-possession and self-respect.

'Harmony, confidence, dignity'
Alec Clegg made his point of departure very clear: children are the central concern, not embryo artists, gymnasts or professional musicians. Teachers do not 'train' in technique or give instruction, but guide children's necessary learning – reading, writing, art, music, drama, talking, dancing and physical education, and development of technique. His own learning experiences in the gymnasium and on the games field as a boy and later as a games teacher led him to establish firm attitudes generally towards teaching and instruction but towards physical education particularly. Respect for every child's potential implied *recognition of diverse responses* including acceptance of those who found PE unattractive. He could reminisce vividly on his own trials and in doing so unconsciously disclosed how he had established his own point of view.

'My life has seen – *Drill* and its military obedience and remedial work.

'*Ring*' on which I was brought up by Heyhoe – its concern was easy flowing synchronised rhythm.

Laban who drew movement out of children rather than imposed it on them and he was aware of *quality* in these children-generated movements.'[8]

(These were) 'the years in which many of us were born. And the practices I have described are practices on which many of us were reared and by which we were trained. But at least in these years physical education achieved respectability.'[9]

He was enthusiastic in his preference for 'the new form of physical education which inculcated a practical approach to the children in all their variety who found PE was a compulsory part of school life'.

'What would I claim for the new form of physical education? The most striking thing is that apparently every child exerts himself. I am not certain what the reasons are for this, but there seems little doubt about it. Under the other ways of teaching physical education children would all perform the same thing at the same time, and their incompetence, if they were incompetent, was manifest to the whole class in a way which does not occur so blatantly in other subjects. With the newer methods children tackle *what they are able to do* and apparently persevere until they can manage it to their own satisfaction, but even so I do not know why they become so engrossed in what they are doing. This is something that the psychologists ought to look into and it is interesting to speculate in it. *Once we manage to call on a child's energy and individual effort and enlist his creative powers* he automatically finds the zest to do what he has to do. The newer methods of PE are the old games coaching methods. If you coach young-sters in, say, football and do it by means of intensive exercises such as may be advocated in the textbooks, you only retain the interest and keenness of those who are adept at the game; the rest drop off quickly. If, however, you do (as most sensible folk do) encourage the child to play with a small ball until he has mastered the technique of that, and then face him with the challenge of a bigger ball, but at all times leaving the child to find his own way and his own enjoyment, you will kindle a much greater interest in the many, though you may conceivably not get such good results from the few. This seems to me to be one of the principles that the newer methods of physical education are based on.'[10]

Alec Clegg asked how 'concern for all youngsters' could be 'realised through physical education'. His remarks did not suggest blind acceptance or worse, blind application without understanding, one fad following another, rather he suggested an informal look at what was best for different teachers in different circumstances – then to think on how success had come about.

'Cisek showed us the creative urge that is in all children and the way in which it can be drawn out of them in art, and then came Rudolf Laban, that kind, gentle and sensitive man who fled from Hitler and who brought us modern dance with its own ballet, time and motion study in industry, and a form of physical education based on natural movement.'[11]

In February 1967 a memo was prepared for the Policy and Finance Committee[12] in which the growth of physical education was outlined from the time of the 1902 Act when many of the schools were built without gymnasia and when there was no teaching expertise on which to draw. 'It is interesting to note that a forward-looking West Riding Committee under its Chairman Alderman Dunn in the first decade of this century entered into an arrangement with the Danish government to share one of their specialists for six months each year. They did not appoint their full-time Adviser until 1914. Physical activities had developed into three categories: sport and recreational facilities for the few, for the unfortunate many military 'drills' which were the forerunners of the rigid 'gym' lessons of between-the-wars, and a third wherein lay hope of progress since this was directed towards physical education in all the schools and not a closed élitist performance.

> 'During and since the war (World War II) two distinguished German refugees, Kurt Hahn and Rudolf Laban have changed the whole philosophy of physical education as it is now practised in this country. The former initiated the Outward Bound movement, and the latter the forms of physical education based on movement training.'

The purpose of physical education moved from the concept of a healthy body, a sound mind and muscle training for the individual to a concept of personal development – 'the idea that sound physical education can exert a powerful influence on the development of the human spirit'.

> 'What else can we claim for these new methods besides this remarkable reliance on individual initiative as against mass response to an instruction? There is the point made that the borderland between physical and mental, or even spiritual education is disappearing. This is probably the most significant thing of all. But I ought perhaps to define my terms, particularly the word 'spiritual'. By mental process, I mean ability to learn and master the multiplication table. By spiritual force, I mean the force that makes a child want to do this. By mental process, I mean the process of translating print into the spoken word – the reading process. By spiritual force, I mean the desire to read. Translating this into terms of physical education as we now understand it, I should say the mental process is the child's ability *to think out a way of overcoming an obstacle placed in front of him.* The spiritual force is *his desire* to do this the second time better than he did it the first time, and it seems to me that if we leave aside the particularly adept child, the newer methods do evoke a much better response than the older ones.'[13]

Alec Clegg's personal experience of lessons from a drill sergeant prior to his success at Bootham School, followed by his own games teaching at St Clement Danes School (he said it contributed towards his success teaching French), plainly influenced his attitude towards physical education. This is made clear in a paper written for the West Riding Education Committee. It is a professional statement acknowledging the expertise of a large group of PE advisers who worked in the West Riding. His service on the Newsom Committee again added to his concern for all children. He emphasised the essential need for worthwhile activities which established interests and attitudes to carry into adult life 'when they may well have more time and money at their disposal than in the past and one of the most important objects of policy should be to give them a taste for worthwhile physical activity'. He quoted five paragraphs from the Newsom Report which summed up his opinion of the place of physical education and which are indications of his own appreciation of the contribution which Laban's conception of movement and dance made.

The paper concluded with a note of principles governing modern physical education suitable for inclusion in an imaginative wide-ranging curriculum which he hoped the committee would endorse for the schools.

Having been at both the receiving and giving end of demanding physical activities made him emphatic in his statement of what physical education should achieve, in sharp contrast with old 'method' when the 1933 syllabus prevailed.

> '. . . what really happened to any class of 30–40 children in those days was seen most clearly in their drill lesson when all were asked to surmount the same obstacle. The gifted dozen or so succeeded with aplomb and were cheerful about it; the second dozen probably improved under teaching and tolerated it; the third dozen, who were clumsy, had to display their incompetence before their fellows and loathed it. The teacher took the credit for the success of the first two groups and blamed the failure of the third group on their native endowment or lack of it. And so it was, though less obviously, in all subjects.'[14]

Alec Clegg was writing and speaking from his own personal experience of the killing 'physical training' inflicted quite impartially on school children from the time of compulsory elementary education to the end of the Second World War. When girls' education was extended during the first heady days of women's emancipation, the move for this freedom came from middle-class women who wanted the same education as their brothers and this was resolved by almost a slavish interpretation of the syllabus, including physical training. Some boys' grammar schools had a 'drill sergeant', an ex-NCO usually, who put them through army drill.

An account of the early progress of PE as a subject in school was given to a conference of Organisers and Lecturers in Physical Education at Harrogate in 1950. He traced stages from instruction given extraneous to the school programme through 'Swedish Drill' and voluntary 'physical jerks' to the 1933 Syllabus. 'You may ask what reasons I have, as an educationist, for doubting the fundamental approach to Physical Education in the country – an approach which derives from the sort of history I have outlined and from the 1933 Syllabus.' The rigorous formal instruction, he pointed out, came from a necessity to have large numbers of pupils move around a school in an orderly way. That, plus the fact that the First World War army training had demanded immediate unthinking response. The last war, however, was different – much had to be explained to a civilian army, and the whole purpose of manoeuvres and objectives. The physical training of the soldier was consciously and deliberately directed towards training his mind as well as his body. He suggested his audience reviewed their games coaching and they would see that strict regimentation had gone.

'May I remind you that by and large youngsters do not indulge in gymnastics after they have left school any more than they do in history or geography. Neither will they – in my view – until the PE they get at school is treated much more as an art to be encouraged and fostered and less as a skill to be superimposed.'

'I believe that instead of elaborating a scheme of exercises designed to develop the muscular system, PE in the future will start from the child itself at its earliest age and by guiding and encouraging its earliest movements.'[15]

Alec Clegg suggested that this interpretation of PE is a long way from the obedience training of the turn of the century and between the wars, and from formalised competition. He thought it overcame 'the cardinal sin of putting so many youngsters in a position of inevitable failure.'

At a meeting of the British Association of Organisers and Lecturers in Physical Education Annual Conference Course in 1970 he declared, as always when talking with subject teachers that he was not a specialist, but

'what I propose to do is to try and set your subject in the context of the educational change which has been so much in our thoughts in this centennial year. I shall try and look at the changes in society which have taken place and then consider the ways in which education in general and your subject in particular has been modified to meet those changes. This will I hope lead us to a consideration of the changes which face us and the ways in which we are likely to meet or to fail to meet future change.'[16]

He traced with neat irony, some entertainment, but with sincere feeling for the inept, the progress of physical instruction from paramilitary army drill, through Morant's first syllabus for the Board of Education:

'. . . finally there is a commendable statement on their educational effect. 'The child unconsciously' (the syllabus said) 'acquires habits of discipline and order and learns to respond cheerfully and promptly to the word of command'. Later we are told it cultivates self-control, restraint, and indeed physical beauty and aesthetic sensitivity for the first time. But the method was essentially the same . . . Children standing on one spot and moving arms and legs to a command – arms raising sideways. Arms parting. Arms raising forward and upward, lowering sideways and downwards, and so on. The illustrations, the directions, the words of command, are all there. The teacher has no need to think.'

He continued by describing the setting aside of the old order due to the 1914–18 war . . . 'it accelerated the demand for more trained men and we entered the great era of examination and competition, the purpose of which was to elect a small élite from the labouring and middle-class youngsters who filled our elementary schools'. This paper, given four years before Alec Clegg's retirement and four years before the breaking-up of the West Riding Authority, indicates a certain amount of disillusion.

'The meaning behind secondary education for everyone was that we had to get the best out of every child. But we didn't mean it, of course. We still aimed at getting the best out of the best. We were then prepared to do what we could for the average. We offered compassion and support to the really weak, but it was devil take the next to the hindmost, and this after all was merely a reflection of society.'

The fast rate of change in society gave Alec Clegg cause to anticipate future trends: 'we could not get enough professionals and technicians and machines began to do the simple jobs of life'. He foresaw serious unemployment and with that condition, serious problems.

'It looks as if perhaps we ought if not as a matter of Christian principle as a matter of social expediency to be equally concerned for all our youngsters.'

This concern would, as a natural consequence, extend to health. Alec Clegg was interested in physical fitness, and 'an unfamiliar aspect of physical education'. 'Movement', a name adopted to describe one new interpretation of physical education took an opposite approach to that of physical 'training'.

It is not too fanciful to suggest that Alec Clegg's interest in physical education stemmed from his initial experience of the drill sergeant as a young boy and his later achievements at Bootham School. His own contribution to some of the physical education teaching at St Clement Danes School had a positive return in his language teaching in the classroom. He noticed how the teacher/pupil relationship changed imperceptibly when the teacher was *not* 'concerned with imparting a system of exercises based on the anatomy of the body and on techniques of acrobatics and games', 'going through the same graded routine'.

This was not pseudo-egalitarianism, he was vitally aware of individual

differences and concerned that each child should have his place and opportunity. Again he asked questions:

'How do we achieve this thing in physical education?'

'What are the signs that it can be done?'

'Can our physical education teachers tackle the expressive side of the
work?'

'Can they indeed be convinced that they should?'

'How can the profession gain a deeper understanding of child-centred
education and the Laban principles of physical education?'

'If physical education has real educational value is it not an educational
sin to concentrate on the adept and neglect the inept to the extent that
we do?'

'Is not our way of exploiting competition in a way that forces so many
children to fail a first class recipe for educational disaster?'

'What do we really do for each individual child when we make him
perform a stylised vault over a piece of apparatus whether he wants to or
not?'

'Games, like poetry, are to be enjoyed. Is it therefore not folly to force a
reluctant child to play games or to emphasise his failure if he plays them
badly?'

'Is not the practice of making youngsters in late adolescence go on doing
what they dislike a sure way of making them drop it for ever once they
leave school?'

'Is it not a fact that teachers of physical education because they themselves
have been gifted and adept are the least likely to be able to understand the
misery which their subject ill-taught can inflict on the clumsy?'

'How wise are we to think in terms of standards for children of a given
age?'

'If we challenge children arranged in a homogeneous intellectual group
with the same physical tasks, are these tasks not likely to be low enough
to be held in contempt by the gifted child and high enough to induce
despair in the unskilled?'[17]

Questions, again, for Aiglon:

'How wise are we to award marks and contrived standards? Athletic standards, for instance, are so often low enough to be held in contempt by the
adept and high enough to induce despair in the unskilled.'[18]

'I can understand half-a-dozen well-matched youngsters who already
delight in jumping or running wanting to compete against each other, but
for those who have not the delight is this a good means of achieving it?'

'I believe . . . that in the future education must be concerned not only with
what a man can do but with the sort of person he becomes as a result of
doing it . . . If I am right in these contentions then surely the world of

physical education will be an enormously powerful force in the future of education for it can do more to influence a man's attitudes and values, his relationship with others, his confidence, his sense of success or failure, his initiative, his determination, his endurance, and a whole lot of personal qualities than most other school activities. But of course if physical education is to do these things it will have to be very different from the obedience training of 70 years ago, or from the formalised competition of today. It will have to renounce its cardinal sin of putting so many young-sters in a position of inevitable failure and it will have to accept a pedagogical status of a higher order.'

'If I had my way I would so arrange things that every games player or gymnast who became a teacher should spend a fortnight of his course learning a classical ballet and at the end of it I would have him perform solos before his colleagues, and the object of this exercise would be to either realise an undiscovered gift in himself or to develop sympathy for those who were clumsy where he was gifted.'[19]

'I believe the subject to be at the crossroads – it can revert to muscle building or it can achieve an educational significance which, as far as I am aware, has not yet been fully realised and exploited in the schools of our Western civilisation.'[20]

'If education is to change . . . so that our weaklings receive the concern that they so urgently need and so that a child's personal qualities receive as much attention as his mental and physical qualities, then physical education in our secondary schools may well prove to be one of the most powerful weapons in the whole educational armoury.'[21]

The PE syllabus became less rigid, a pupil-centred approach became the norm, and 'movement' was introduced: 'an unfamiliar aspect of physical education'. Alec Clegg took interest in that the approach was through the individual child's efforts.[22] The concept of dance was new and children were introduced via skills, agilities, and games. The pupil-centred approach gave personal space, a sense of personal achievement and encouragement to surpass their own efforts. The complete set of Woolley Hall in-service programmes under Diana Jordan and Dorothy Phillips indicate a balance of theory and practice in a context of children's work, together with the contribution of PE advisers and teachers in schools.

The child was introduced to a vocabulary of movement. He was impelled into physical experience of all kinds which enabled him consciously and deliberately to use this effectively. He did it at his own pace; *nothing was taught as a trick*. There was the fullest opportunity for initiative, choice and creative effort by the pupil and a good deal more besides, such as purposeful co-operation in pairs and groups. The most moving educational experience I have ever witnessed was work of this kind and its effect on children was intense and unmistakable. But the main significance of it was the powerful effect on the mind and imagination. In work of this kind interaction of mind and body on mind is patently obvious.'[23]

'Of course it demands teaching of a very high order – to my way of thinking the very highest order – and it requires on the part of the teacher a very profound intellectual grasp of the finer points of pedagogy. It departs completely from the conception of muscular exercises which belong to the areas of multiplication, parsing and perspective drawing. It abandons imposed drill. It derives, as a great deal of art, language, music and arithmetic now do, from the guided experiences of the child. It is closely associated not only with games, agilities and athletics but equally with dance and drama and it calls very fully on the inner resources of the child to develop intensity and depth of understanding of the medium in which he is working.'

'. . . the study of movement in contrast to physical training for the teacher became the study of children as individuals and that a respect and acceptance of their different physical powers is implicit. *This is the first educational significance* . . . body/mind is an inseparable unity and that movement is a means towards this unity of the human being. *This is its second significance* . . . The ancient Greeks had a word for this unity which when cultivated through music, dance and poetry, meant *excellence* . . . I venture to think that we have lost the vision of this excellence but that we stand in some need of recovering it. It may be that the youth of today reflect this need, indeed sense its neglect. *This excellence is the third significant aspect of movement.*'

'. . . what about those areas in which men's activities are not directed towards visible achievement so much as their personal and social happiness and fulfillment.'[24]

At Dartington Hall in 1951 Alec Clegg gave the introductory lecture at the Modern Dance Holiday Course which summed up his approach to physical education in a quickly changing post-war world:

'Your education will consist in leading the child's play with things towards the adult games which are one of the finest pleasures that this country has given to humanity, in guiding the movement that a child enjoys for its own sake into athletic exercise and dancing and in developing the imaginative play so characteristic of the child into drama and acting. I think that PE thus concerned will rank with music and art as one of the fundamental creative outlets for the child; I think it will rightly encroach on English, art and music. I think that treated in this way it will form as valuable an aid to the mentally sick as it does to the physically defective, and if it does all these things, ladies and gentlemen, I as an educationist couldn't care less about the quality of the footwork.'[25]

The introduction to a vocabulary of movement through drama, agilities and games was brought together by his interest in a theory of dance exemplified by Rudolf Laban. Children, through natural behaviour, became aware of their movements and the ways in which these could communicate ideas and feelings. They learned that this was not pantomime but a fitting together of moves backed by reasons. They gained confidence in their use of space, and the space they occupied in relation to a group. Their dances in consequence became enactive, from themselves and from that point of departure they became aware of people and the outside world. They made this knowledge their own and had an added empathy when they studied drama, attempted a performance , or attended one. Alec Clegg defined this as internalising a process, the product at this stage was less important. A sequence could be enacted, images made through expressive movement.

The expression of feeling could, however, become self-indulgent, so the teacher guided, set problems, helped in developing ideas, did not abdicate. The end of the lesson would produce a complete re-enactment when what had been learned would be discussed, the meaning and use of speed and space, and the children left with ideas which would carry forward, and even contribute towards understanding other parts of home and school.

'Through movement all children should experience what it means to contribute, to share, to become a necessary part of a unified endeavour . . . Little wonder that this enables them to find a personal evaluation of this (endeavour) and of their companions and a sense of belonging, not in a passive way but in an active and meaningful way to the groups with which they associate.'[26]

'What movement can foster in children is also a requirement in other pursuits, most noticeable perhaps is the enjoyment and development of musical activity, speech, drama and of course dance.'

'. . . movement properly practised by teachers and children acts as a basic and fundamental agent in what we call education in its best sense. That it is to do with helping the child to maintain a unity of body, mind and feeling with consequent ability to grow as a receptive and self-disciplined and sensible person better prepared for his encounters with life and people because he has found pleasure, satisfaction and security as an active and creative member of a group and in his ability to grow in stature as an individual. This, however, pre-supposes a like of development from the metrics of movement to something beyond.'

Sadly, writing 'Notes on what has happened to education in recent years', Alec Clegg indicated some disillusion. This was in 1973 when he was due to retire in one year and where vast boundary changes were to take place across the country. He accepted change and growth, but on what had already been achieved, and anticipated destruction.[27]

'Laban himself had a personality of tolerance, kindness, reluctance to condemn, determination to make the best out of whatever he had to use in the way of human material. Dance was his main medium and to a lesser extent, drama. His contemporary, Hahn, was concerned with adventure training, canoeing, orienteering, climbing, and the like. We had in addition, games, swimming and gymnastics, especially gymnastics demanding the use of apparatus. We have seen an advance in adventure training, and a return to physical performance forced on those who do not necessarily want to compete. In my own county, adventure training has gone ahead, led by people with conviction – the Outward Bound folk – who can still draw inspiration from Hahn. And it is still moving; it has moved, for instance, into City Challenge.

But the Dance has regressed – it has lost leadership and is seeking comfort in notation, in what is called its philosophy, its history, most of which does very little for the child in his early years.

There has been a resurgence of Olympic gymnastics, floor work, beam work, bars at different levels – all excellent for those who want to do them, and of course there are still the major games.

But apart from the adventure training, movement in the primary school and dance at its best, what we have contrived is a means of setting apart the skilled from the unskilled.

Laban would not have tolerated this.'

Diana Jordan was appointed Warden of Woolley Hall in 1947, also a member of the Physical Education advisory team with special responsibility for the teaching of Dance in West Riding schools. She had trained initially at Bedford College of Physical Education. She had also taken classes before the War at the Mary Whigman School in Leipzig which specialised Rudolph Laban's Art of Movement and Dance. Laban, a Hungarian refugee from Nazi Germany, had opened a studio in Manchester and later moved to Goldsmith's College, London. He is known for his 'notation' system, and his theoretical work, and was also a dancer and choreographer. A personal record of people and events and of the development of Dance in the West Riding is given by those who contributed to that growth in 'Fifty Years of Dance, 1947 to 1997: A history of Yorkshire Movement and Dance,' published by Yorkshire Movement and Dance, a voluntary organisation. This group began as the West Riding Study Group which had its roots in a group formed in 1947, meeting in schools until 1952, when they made a base in the new Woolley Hall In-Service College. All the PE advisers contributed.

In 1974, a teacher from Norway wrote to Diana Jordan:

'First of all a group of inspectors and advisers, bound together in a friendly, firm and yet flexible team, where no personal ambition was allowed to spoil the common aim. Schools where the growth of each individual child meant more than marks or competition. Though I had not at the time met the Chief Education Officer, Mr Clegg, I strongly felt the existence of a true educationalist behind the team of workers.'

Alec Clegg consulted advisers and organisers frequently. One paper, unfortunately unsigned, focused attention on one aspect of dance and drama which gave 'an entry into the language of words'. There is something also to talk about which leads into stories and poetry and looking at paintings. They gain the love of words and use language with real pleasure. 'Children use words magnificently when feelings and experiences have lived.'[28]

Alec Clegg repeated many times how movement, music, art, drama interact; we divide them into manageable items for schools to think of one aspect in depth. Movement can induce speech spontaneously.

> 'What about drama? How often have I sat in a packed junior school hall and seen elves and fairies in their grease paint self-consciously performing their well-rehearsed steps and self-consciously uttering their speech-trained lines to their admiring parents . . . Again, how many times has one seen a brilliantly performed Shakespeare play put on by a grammar school when a member of staff takes a prominent part in the local amateur dramatic society and enjoys to the full putting on the School Certificate play and producing it so that every child is taught every movement and every inflection of the voice.'[29]

> 'There is as much that we know and don't use in connection with school drama. Make believe, imitation, imaginative play, the child's natural aids in the growing process. In early infancy there seems to be little difference for him between the results of fantasy and reality, and his enjoyment of and capacity for sustained imaginative play is one of the features of his junior years. We know all this and we know this fantasy and make believe are part of the growing process.'

Some children, through movement and drama, achieve a sense of accomplishment which they then express in words.

Alec Clegg preferred spontaneous play and acting out of children's imagined stories or interpretations of stories told to them, telling anecdotes, simulating actions and responses in attempts at interpreting favourite characters. The gifted take their fellows along. Understanding stage plays becomes more sharp and appreciation of an ability to cause them to suspend disbelief, to grasp other states of mind in time and space.

He placed special significance on pupils' ability to express or explain their ideas or perceptions in words or actions, and judged spontaneous dramatisation should precede a scripted play or 'the school play'. Active participation in movement, or mime, or dialogue gave some grounding. They begin from home and their society around them and gain insight into new interpretations in the construction of varying roles, through comedy and tragedy, and learn to accept and live with difference in people, with uncertainties, and to learn that the world does not conform to one person. They learn that they alone are finally responsible for their actions, the stands they take, their attitudes and convictions.

He thought drama could lead pupils to ideas of truth, loyalty, compassion: again and again these qualities are placed first in papers given to varied audiences – aspects of school learning which, he said, could not be measured on a scale of ten, but lacking them, scholarship was arid and even dangerous. The complexity of adult life needed people who would not follow the latest slogan most loudly shouted, or join a group which demanded mindless acquiescence, but who rather would give the other his space.

It is asking a lot of very young people as well as older pupils who are reading scripted plays and discussing writers' themes as well as specific stage presentations. Often it is the more silent or inarticulate pupils who feel most strongly. Superficial flow of chat is not the aim, rather the inconsistencies of human interaction – insight into beliefs, opinions, attitudes, fears, and their resolution through action.

Drama, therefore, Alec Clegg suggested, is movement, mime, talking, as well as text. The study of scripts, the presentation of 'school plays' follows, does not precede. Older pupils, with the smother of models society sets up, gain some balance and some ability to distinguish: they move from a stage of romance to one of healthy generalisation. They are able to take on scripts which are more than trivial 'plays for young people' and are at home with allusion, subtlety of language, and a well constructed dramatic event.

> 'It is my profound belief that in these junior and early secondary years, unless the child's drama gives him a profound personal experience, it can be of very little educational significance.'

This 'cross referencing' of other subjects would, hopefully, spill over into ease of reading and writing, using words vividly instead of producing obedient copies of 'correct' writing which is merely a pale echo of others' words. He emphasised the interconnectedness between the expressive arts and individual abilities. The key was language.

Language

A speech[30] given to the International Reading Association in New Orleans immediately on his retirement in 1974 makes clear the fount and precept of excellence from which Alec Clegg's teaching values are taken. It presents justification and base for work across the curriculum. Language, and how it is used, is his priority.

At the heart of his teaching was the acquisition of language integral to the children's lives. He quoted St John – 'In the beginning was the Word'. Reading and writing are skills, but being fallibly human, they are patterns of experience which become refined as they are practised. How each stage is learned affects future responses He sought teachers who would make children query, attempt to solve problems, find ways of explaining, which could convey a respect for truthfulness through situations and ideas, not people who merely inoculate with doses of information, inducing immunity to mental and spiritual autonomy.

> 'There will of course be no grading of children, no reading round the class, no activity which taunts the weak child with his incompetence and the whole process will be built on a profound principle which one school inspector described well over 100 years ago as 'that recognition which our natures crave and acknowledge with renewed endeavour and in this way self-esteem, security and enjoyment should accompany the beginning of the first two Rs'.'

> 'Reading is vitally important and it would be the utmost folly not to make improvements in its teaching which are consistent with the pleasure which ought to be derived from it. But we should take care, lest what we now do with mental development is what we tended to do in the '20s with a physical development, when we gave physical exercises to undernourished children in the hope of adding to their strength. It was then physical undernourishment which we dealt with. It is now spiritual and intellectual poverty which is our problem.'[31]

Alec Clegg's concern that many reading ploys were on the mental level of those early PE exercises – an automatic response, filling blanks, multiple choice tests, worksheets which merely produced tricks to complete more papers and did not enhance linguistic abilities. Strategies should come from working with authentic texts. The process is making meaning, the task must be meaningful. The children should read, be read to, have periods of uninterrupted silent reading.

He continued to affirm the central place of the teacher, and the crucial role infant teachers play in the teaching of reading. He reiterated that the method was the teacher's own, and the aim to have a child read with understanding, not one who barks at print. Early oral and written work sprang from the language of the individual child: when it is grasped that writing represents sounds, phonemes are recognised plus the alphabet, and sounds are learned as well as letters. They are then seen as expedients for making meaning in a text.

> 'In the end, the child has to derive for himself a basic set of rules about sound/symbol correspondence and also a knowledge of the grouping of sounds, and the grouping of symbols. On the basis of such rules, the individual is then free to create an endless variety of choices for himself. It is impossible directly to teach a 3 year old the rules of grammar, and it is just as difficult to teach a 6 year old the rules of the relationship between our sound system and visual system. He can be made aware of some of

them, and on the basis of this understanding he begins to read. It would be unfortunate if anxiety to help children were to reduce any efforts to increase motivation or interest to drills and practice, as it so often does.'

Books are read, then, with an appreciation of the language used, and writers' use of language. How the children begin, Clegg considered, was critical, and sincere methods were acceptable; a blanket dictatorial approach, whether children felt happy in it or not, did not get results. He noted one teacher's remark that she was afraid he would witness orthodox lessons; what he had recognised was the fact that she had solved the reading and writing problem for her class.

'We are never in any doubt why *we* want children to read, but in the end what is there in it for the child? What can books do for him that other things can't? We might say that we want children to read books so that they may listen to and, in a sense, converse with more voices than those they hear from the speakers around them. Books and printed words are embalmed voices, whereas a child, by the time he learns to read, can comprehend much of living speech addressed to him. To make as much of the language of books, he must work much harder. This is not merely a matter of deciphering but rather reinfusing the vitality of the spoken language into the deadness of print.'

It always comes, Alec Clegg reiterated, to the interaction of teacher and class, and his conclusion was that much had been imposed by publishers and the administrators in the way of materials and activities encapsulating the latest cliché: consumable workbooks, 'reading round the class', 'whole word', 'phonics', 'open education', 'mastery learning', 'learning styles', 'child centred', 'reading hysteria. . .'.

'One recognises it at once by its symptoms; reading lessons, reading teachers, reading consultants, reading structures, reading schemes going even into the high schools. In short, everything that one can think of which will ensure reading is seen by the pupils as a difficult and distasteful, albeit necessary, business.'

If provided material is used, in the manner of fitting pieces into a puzzle, assessments are obtained through tests, weekly checklists and the teachers are then assessed by validated lists of approved teaching behaviour. Alec Clegg again questioned: what are the costs of our actions? Who gains? Who loses? The teacher evaluates and uses all available resources and enquiry for class or individual to authenticate 'method', based on either 'conventional wisdom' or 'progressive'.

Teacher and children are mutually involved: only effective reading is enjoyed. Alec Clegg used a favourite comparison to bring out again the question of attitude. He pointed out that ninety per cent of his audience would have at some time liked or disliked a teacher; of those, only five per cent would have followed a disliked subject, mostly from necessity; but many, seventy-five per cent even, might have passed to an advanced stage a subject which they had enjoyed even with a disliked teacher. He gave again the example of the way to ensure an inevitable failure – the rigid vaulting horse. Ten pupils would be excellent – the teacher taking credit due to God Almighty, the rest would be passable, but the last five per cent deliberately shown up. That approach would not do in the teaching of an essential craft tool such as reading, to praise some and rebuke others. The point he made was that ninety per cent of any audience will have conceived a dislike of something. An educated audience would contain very few who disliked reading and writing, but there was a very real danger of creating a second-class curriculum for children with a poor background or no support from home.

> 'With an unfavourable home background and no school influence a child reaches the age of five with very little command of language, and this is a continuous handicap. Taken in conjunction with the work of Piaget, who amply illustrated the importance in its early years *of the dialogue between a child and its elders,* the evidence adds a powerful argument for nursery schools.'[32]

'Dialogue between the child and its elders' for Alec Clegg pointed the central place of language. Language is the medium through which we define and interpret participation in daily affairs, and our observations. Statements are something to work at; there cannot be just a bottomless store of second-hand comment. Thought has to be put into words which won't falsify or misrepresent. Alec Clegg said the teacher was there to lead, guide insightfulness towards quality. 'The Excitement of Writing' and 'Enjoying Writing' are the end product of children's struggles with forms and symbols, their thoughts, observations; and in older children's writing, a move towards cultural order found in their reading. They experience the need for disciplined expression, not maudlin self-indulgence, for ordering and reordering, saying what deeply matters to them in a manner acceptable to and understood by their readers so that they know they have conveyed something of what is in their minds. In their turn, as their reading extends and deepens they respond to what writers are telling them. They pick up allusion and reference and read with more than surface skimming. They listen to the writer's voice and message, and become articulate. This development was the inherent aim in teaching reading and writing.

He put a tall order to his teachers, looking for quality and comprehensive wholeness. Culture, as he interpreted it, was available to all children, their need and due. Grammar is not dispensed with and is part of the language, not in bits and pieces to fill in blanks in a notebook. They are introduced to the world of imagination, but also structure.

His concern for the humanity of all children took him from commitment to the Oxbridge Scheme, sincere acknowledgement of the values of the grammar schools which he felt were present in the best comprehensive and secondary modern schools, to expressed distress over the children who were losers. He told (at a grammar school Speech Day) the bright and advantaged that they had a responsibility which went along with privilege which was definitely an echo of his Quaker schooling. Service on the Newsom Committee gave him an abiding concern for those who were disadvantaged. He gave importance to those 'influences across all lives' which could reach children through schools and teaching at all levels. He emphasised at every level that reading, writing and talking were fundamental.

When Alec Clegg said his main interest was in 'Harrys, not Tom or Dick' he was not diminishing ability or persistence but drawing attention to those children who needed different ways and means to bring them to Dick's stage, and perhaps Tom's. The casualties:

'. . . My main interest, let me say at once, is in Harrys, not Tom or in Dick . . . we have interesting statistics about him. More of his kind die young, more suffer ill-health or have parents who are sick or more live in areas where there are relatively few doctors. They inhabit squalid and insanitary homes or attend old and derelict schools; more have parents who are unemployed. Harry is often short, underweight, his father is often an unskilled worker and he is likely to live in overcrowded conditions. More of his kind live in a polluted atmosphere . . . dereliction . . . irremediable squalor . . .'[33]

'. . . Tom and Dick will be read to at home.. They will have books. They may see how books give delight to their parents. Harry will hear no rhymes or stories and will have ten books, if any, in his home. Their enjoyment of books will be expected of Tom and Dick. There will be no such expectation of Harry, who, incidentally, because he is one of a large family will converse far less with adults.'

'Then the parents of Tom and Dick will be familiar with bookshops and will know their way round the educational system and will visit exhibitions and concerts. There will be none of this for Harry . . .'

'Harry will all too often come from the bottom 20% of the ability range and as no teachers were ever in that group none will know what it is like to be a member of it . . . And so it is that we tend to prize the gifted, to show compassion for the blind and the deaf and the seriously afflicted but to discard and reject the slow, and Harry either because of his poor native endowment or because of the difficulties he has to surmount is often, though by no means always, slow.'

'. . . And let us remember that *we are not talking of children who are exceptionally unfortunate.* We are talking of a fifth to a quarter of all children and we must remember that in any class anywhere on God's earth there are

circumstances likely to turn Harry into the sort of person he all too often
is. *In every class:*

> One child will be the least happy.
> One will be the least loved.
> One will be the least articulate.
> One will have the least support from home.
> One will like his teacher least.
> One will be the least liked by the teachers.
> One will be the least attractive . . .

. . . and so on. We could extend this list of hindrances to learning, any one
of which could have a far more crippling effect on Harry's education than
the recipes, methods, kits, packages, apparatus, or equipment that his
teacher might use or misuse.'

He qualified this statement, however:

'. . . there are bad schools and bad teachers, and whenever 100 teachers
are gathered together one will be the worst. But we have in my view no
idea of the potential of our youngsters, even of the most dull and disadvantaged if then *once the right chord is struck . . . let us remember we are
dealing with what cannot be measured as well as with what can.'*

'. . . as the teaching gets more and more sterile and routine more and more
teachers realise how little it does for the child's imagination, for his
aesthetic growth, for the nourishment of his spirit.'

'(These) visionary teachers realise what is happening and take exciting
steps to redress the balance by all means of novel and creative techniques.
This goes on for some time and weaker teachers who can't manage the
new skill climb on the bandwagon and can't play the instruments. The
new creative work becomes shoddy, sentimental and lacking in rigour,
and both loaves and hyacinths suffer. *Then comes the cry of back to the
basics* and the basics come back. After a time they get dull and sterile and
the cycle starts all over again.'

'At the present time in England we are reaching the stage when the
creative work that many teachers have been doing admirably for many
years is deteriorating and this deterioration has been speeded up by
creating many open plan buildings in an attempt to force by architecture
the type of teaching which many teachers find alien to all that they have
hitherto experienced. At worst it has been disastrous.'

His openly declared opinion was clearly underpinned by serious anxiety
for civilised living expressed with growing solicitude, not condemnation:

'. . . in many areas because a discarded and resentful group who all too
quickly amass the rapidly developing techniques of vandalism, violence

and villainy, my view is we create this group by maldistribution or even a withholding of our concern; we shall reap the whirlwind and deserve the millstone which we shall find round our necks.'

'What one suspects is happening in our civilisation at the present time is that more and more we are selling our educational souls to commerce and industry. Our attitude is 'suffer little children with an IQ of 130+ to come unto me for they shall add most to the gross national product'. Going lower down the ability range we provide a vocational outlet for the average, but the dull and slow we tend more and more to resent, they are a costly burden, at best they are slaves to the conveyor belt, many are unemployed and at worst they are violent and even criminal.'

'Yet our aim for them should be the same as for all other children; to get the best out of them. As Carlyle put it, the 'great aim of culture is that each should become all that he was created capable of being'.'

Alec Clegg suggested that the repeated phrase 'getting the best out of every child' '. . . means of course getting the best out of his mind, his body and his spirit'. He outlined in detail in several papers the progress made in improved medicine, clothing, housing, hygiene and general daily life. He was not 'too deeply concerned' about the intellectual side 'which attracts our perpetual attention'. He was deeply concerned about the spiritual side of school and home life.

'. . . The human spirit – a word which is apt to be contentious and unnerving but which I suggest will be of increasing importance in the near future.'

He quoted his favourite aunt's verse many times:

'If thou of fortune be bereft
And of this earthly store hath left
Two loaves, sell one, and with the dole,
Buy hyacinths to feed the soul.

He pointed out the need for both – the three Rs and the facts 'are valid subjects for an institution'. They are the building bricks. The mechanism of reading was essential, but the love of fine writing did not necessarily follow but pupils could be shown the best. Just as the facts of history must be learned, but visions of greatness and evil had to be apprehended. The facts of science were essential otherwise the imaginative vision which leads to scientific discovery is fantasy. Religious conviction is enhanced by the stories of the Bible. On a darker note, knowledge of the construction of an atom bomb could be used by a darker spirit. He definitely pointed out that intellect and spirit are identifiable separately, but one side could not be ignored at the expense of the other.

'. . . in my view handling the loaves is the technician's side of the teacher's job, nourishing the hyacinths calls for his professionalism.'

He applied the concept of loaves and hyacinths to written work. The presence of a necessary technical ability in legible handwriting, punctuation, spelling, and grounding in recording facts, proportionate with elegance of handwriting, balanced by love of words, ability to communicate from a personal angle, and evidence of children's personal aesthetic growth tacitly demonstrates professional skill. He found one of the poorest physical situations where he had been 'amazed by the standards of the work' and 'ways in which they manifested the immeasurable products of the human spirit'. He said also he had seen some situations 'where standards were low where there is no beauty, where work is ill-mounted and ill-displayed, where teachers mistake activity for learning and sentimentality for compassion. Schools where teachers provide more kits and gadgets and gimmicks than they or the children can cope with, where records of progress are ill-kept, where there is noise from lack of purpose, where writing and painting are artificially fancy'.

'. . . by this (English) I mean the ability to record facts, to express personal feelings, to write imaginative prose or poetry. When I speak of the teaching of English I do not mean the techniques of spelling and punctuation, *important as these are* . . . what I do mean is the teacher's ability to excite in the child delight in a word well chosen and well used, pride in the meaning clearly stated, and the sheer pleasure of creative effort. To this must, of course, be added the knowledge of *how* to stock the child's mind so that these things can happen.'[34]

'Creative writing' which was nothing more than repetitive comment about themselves, at length, unpunctuated and incoherent, was in his opinion 'personal' writing of a very poor order which diminished the efforts of those teachers of English who were aware they were working with classes at a hard intellectual level and at a difficult task of practice in the exact use of words and an ability to distinguish between genuine statement and specious pretence. As they grew older, children would discover they had to work equally at both technical demands and expressive ways of writing and speaking. English well used was not to be cast aside.

'. . . English which we divide into two parts labelled on the timetable Eng. Lang. And Eng. Lit . . . A child starts off by learning it at his own time and in his own way without being taught. He might even learn two separate varieties which he uses equally well, one with his playmates and one in his home, or one in his home and one in his classroom. Then he goes to school and learns to read and write and he is taught not to end sentences with a preposition. So that child may have at his command:

1   The language he uses on his friends which gives him a natural and
     robust form of expression.
2   His home speech which is perhaps a more useful though less vivid
     means of expression.
3   His written language which is extremely inhibited because it has to
     observe the conventions of spelling and of his teachers' idiosyncrasies
     about prepositions and the like.

And tied up with this is, of course, the need to learn to read . . . We are
beginning to sort these out. William Morris and his friends believed that
once everyone could read we should all be wise and good. We now know
that one of the first effects of universal literacy was to produce a demand
for the 'News of the World'. Furthermore, some teachers are realising that
if you really want a child to express himself in writing, he won't do it if his
attempt is also an exercise in writing, punctuation and spelling, and these
are things, therefore, which *must be taught in some other way or at some other
time.*'[35]

'the history of education reveals a constant swing from loaves to hyacinths
and hyacinths to loaves, and this I believe to be almost inevitable.'[36]

In 1963 the West Riding Education Committee published an anthology of
children's written work from a minority of schools. Ten years later
'Enjoying Writing' was compiled from work taken across a wide spectrum.
Many schools were producing their own anthologies. He recognised 'the
massive problem of teaching older children' and quoted George Sampson:
'English is not a school subject at all, it is a condition of school life'. There
was writing from a personal expressive starting point as well as concen-
trating on examinations. Alec Clegg said he 'fervently agreed with
Sampson's point of view', but added 'when children are studying specialist
subjects it is the duty of the teacher of that subject to ensure he receives
from his pupils the clarity, spelling, logic, reasoning and indeed the handwriting that the effective study of the subject demands'. He said
nevertheless, 'Let us remember we are dealing with what cannot be
measured as well as what can'. Ideas and attitudes have a central role,
which means reordering, rewriting, and some experiment, but he did not
say, 'Everyone should do as X, Y, Z have done,' but 'X, Y, Z have done
this – is there anything which can be taken for general use?' Teachers would
be working with individuals, thinking in words, using them to help thought
making meaning, and used across several disciplines. Teachers would be
identifying individual needs for competence, and children would not be
left writing rubbish or vapid commonplaces or self-centred unpunctuated
rambling. Punctuation should be used meaningfully, for emphasis.
Learning had to be within an examination mode, but examinations were
not an end in themselves. 'A well set language paper tests conceptual
maturity and linguistic adeptness.'[37]

Alec Clegg argued that the teacher at the instructional level utilises every useful method; at the professional level he reads to, works with, and uses every means of communication and persuasion for understanding. He reiterated that the pleasurable acquisition of reading and writing influences the entire curriculum. Alec Clegg approved a curriculum based on a developmental model of reading, the teachers involved in assessing children and teaching strategies. There would be emphasis on explicit comprehension – words well used.

> 'The child whose exploration with spoken language has been limited is going to have much greater difficulty with reading than one who has been encouraged to use language fully and freely, but the meeting between child and book is a new kind of encounter. Once a child becomes a reader in the sense that he can derive appropriate meanings from printed words, he becomes potentially a controller of his language experience. He can decide about input, he can begin to seek out the books he wants.'

> '. . . what will take children more deeply into the experience of the book is the question we should be asking, rather than by what means can I use this book as a launching pad into any one of a dozen endeavours.'

There should be authenticity, germane intention, genuine acts. The topic comes out of the reading, not stimulations around themes – 'themes' reduced to sociology, badly thought out judgements, 'deductions' and trivial 'solutions' to issues beyond their experience. 'Integrated studies' could be risky. Reading, writing, speaking and listening were interdependent and reality – teachers and children worked together. The teacher, Alec Clegg said, a most important point, knows how to get his class together 'to organise themselves . . . which stimulates their initiative and encourages their responsibility'. Aiglon was again in mind. There would be explicit teaching, not a complete retreat, 'discovery' would be made on some foundation, and they are involved intensely with the language through reading literature. Their own original writing would lead them to appreciate writers' language and style, and they would not be in danger of being trapped in their own vernacular. There would be, in this shared reading and writing, a balance of teacher's control and the child's assumption of independence and responsibility. Alec Clegg saw and recognised the beginning of a multicultural society and saw that encouragement to communicate solely in speech and writing in a local way[38] would impose a binding force as tight as any externally imposed, stilted accuracy. The requirements are crucially in precision, economy of style, and relevance to the situation disclosed in the splendidly individual qualities of each child – what children do with what they are given, what they discover and make something of their immediate world, taking from their lessons, tolerating each other, recognising each other's humanity. The aim to have wide reading of good literature on their own would go alongside their personal writing and aims, as they went through junior school and high school; analytical and objective writing would run alongside personal scripts.

'In the field of language, children now write almost before they can read, and the effort is again put into feeding the child the experiences which will impel him to communicate his ideas and his thoughts, rather than those which have been imposed upon him by his teacher. It is a realisation in the classroom of the Word, of the Gospel of St Luke. Many years ago, Thring foresaw this, and wrote 'Everyone can be taught to have the seeing eye, which is the beginning of all original composition'.[39]

'Bruner called language 'the calculus of thought'. This calculus can only be acquired in dialogue with an adult who already possesses it. One must be careful here. I don't want to offend the linguists. The child doesn't have to hear an adult say all the sentences he produces. He generates his own according to what he assimilates of the patterns in the speech he hears. But note two things about that: his progress will depend on the activity he shows in experimenting and creating – and this depends on the encouragement he gets. Secondly, many of his creations will be unacceptable in the adult grammar, though OK in the child's present grammar. Only through feedback from the adult does the child's grammar come to approximate that accepted by society. The two way exchange is what matters. The dialogue needs patience, plenty of time, some imagination, above all one of the partners must possess the language well.'

Two volumes of personal writing from children were published – 'The Excitement of Writing' and 'Enjoying Writing'. They contain a selection of writing from several schools across a wide age range. The latent intimation which these two volumes give is the empathy of teachers and classes. The writing could have been forced; as it was, what they were doing was reflecting, discriminating, in a two-way literary process with their teachers.

'I would now like to comment on the thing that happens with the gifted teaching of children which I have often found mystifying, but which I think I am beginning to understand. Time and again, I have seen teachers with no expertise themselves in painting or modelling or sensitive personal writing, who nevertheless secure wonderful work from the children whom they teach. There are, I think, a number of facts and qualities in these teachers which enable them to teach so superbly.'[40]

One lesson would not draw a line under what had been written – there would be discussions and class exchanges, learning to keep on talking and writing, reflecting, revising, an open-ended process. Their work is not adult, as their art is not, and as the teachers recognised. They learned the fun of words. Alec Clegg insisted that English, art, music and dance, and sport for sport science central to the quality of life, in one sense, are un-examinable, certainly not quantifiable. As with Aiglon, the children were asking and were being asked questions to get at meaning, a capacity to enjoy words, to use them sincerely in expressing ideas, to cope with the language of home, social life, school, and examinations. Alec Clegg under-stood that the teacher was drawing from the children, not using them as a springboard for self display, and, in understanding the message they have composed, corrects at the level of skills – spelling, punctuation, grammar. Not self reflexive, but unselfconscious statement from the younger ones would guide to the later outward-looking stage when argument, exposition, narrative, rules of evidence, reasoning, could be taken on board.

There was fine tuning. 'Meaningful encounters', another deplored cliché, left children at a loss. There was not to be abdication. The older children needed study skills, particularly those lacking home and district commitment; and literature-based experiences distinct from text used to re-use, to practise on, make into workbooks, or publishers' materials.

'. . . but there are two paths to be followed. The child must be able to record facts from direct observation, and the facts of history and geog-raphy and science as he has been taught them. Rigour must be demanded of the writing – its calligraphy, spelling and punctuation must be corrected, clearly logic and reasoning must be rewarded with praise and corrections must be meticulous, and made, if possible, in the child's presence. This kind of English will be used to introduce the child to the minimum of grammar that he may require . . .but the professional job must also be done. The hyacinths must be nourished and the child must also work from his feelings and imagination, inspired by experience which in his way may be contrived. He should see beautiful things in the class-room or on visits beyond the school, he must have fine English read to him at his level of understanding, he must learn to love words. The teacher must know how to build confidence on the child's success with words, but she must know how to guard against the fancy, the sentimental, and the sophisticated. Above all, she will act on the belief that children learn to write by writing, not by filling blanks, crossing out, underlining, and other vicious and useless practices.'

'A humanising curriculum'

The holistic, child-centred approach to reading and writing as a craft tool had success, yet, since the social/cultural environment is not static, Alec Clegg recognised that problems remained and different ones would appear within an expanding multicultural population. Those primary and post-primary children who do not find a self-propelling competence and confidence remain unmotivated and are left behind in a lower group, and there they remain. At the end of his service, he foresaw a press for standardisation which would produce a permanent group of losers. He saw the problem of general education as one which gave equal opportunities without discrimination. When equity is equated with conformity, paradoxically there are losers. The problem was to give the core skills, the 'tool kit', together with basic concepts and groundwork at the heart of school subjects; that is, some principles in common to give common ground. After that, he said, who could decide who was the better educated, the boy who had taken French and Greek, or the boy who has taken German and Latin? As time went on, he could have added technology and technical aspects of the curriculum.

Alec Clegg was sufficiently concerned, after giving evidence to the Bullock Committee on Reading, to circularise his advisers, assistant education officers and professional assistants: the Chairman was pre-occupied with 'standards'. Alec Clegg had responded

> 'we are running all manner of industries: telecommunications, aircraft, automobile, non-ferrous metals, man-made fibres, electronics, etc., most of which did not exist when I was at school, and I can't believe we are staffing them with illiterates.'
>
> 'Our book issues from the (West Riding) County Library to young readers have increased from 2.75 million to 8 million in the last four years (1968–72).'
>
> 'Puffin sales have gone up from 0.5 million to 5.5 million in the last ten years (1962–72).'[41]

In spite of real gains from 1944, he recognised the urgency of a situation which seemed inevitably to filter out those who found difficulty within quickening societal change and consequent changing expectations of schooling. He constantly reviewed the historical background – from needing to mark a name with more than a cross, 'learning by heart', to deciphering complicated diagrams and technical instructions, to reading for information, pleasure, understanding. At the end of his career, he pointed out the increasing expectations laid on schools. He said the losers would have to be catered for, or society would pay a heavy price; that more and more demands would be laid on the intellectually average. The problem, as Alec Clegg saw it, was to have education beyond bleak competence, but critical competence – 'conceptual literacy'.

It is possible to imagine Alec Clegg's reaction to the European dimension, when the inevitable interaction of more social groups whose levels of statement and description are/could be different from group to group, abroad in addition to home, and again different from tacit agreements in the home, renders translation a crucial matter and a more than superficial understanding. At the homely level of everyday interaction, he recognised one of the difficulties comprehensive schools would encounter would be the assumption on the part of those demanding equal opportunity that the pupils are a homogeneous group. They are not. They are not on a production line, either.

PART TWO

Accountability

'. . . an education service is not a factory which produces glass bottles or motor cars or radio sets or other inanimate devices. It produces people.'

'The force of commitment'

The Advisory Staff
The Colleges

ACCOUNTABILITY

The Chief Education Officer is accountable to the entire Education Committee. He also takes the majority party into account through the Chairman of the Education Committee. At crucial points in re-organisation, or recommendations, or suggestions for future development, or in representing the Committee's wishes in workable form, the CEO works with his Chairman on general principles. Alec Clegg said many times that he gave advice, reported, and left the Committee to decide: the County got its expressed wishes. The fact that all members of the Authority had, in theory (and, in the West Riding, in practice), direct access to its officers made for forceful discourse. There was a lively apprehension on the part of the Senior Clerks of responsibility to 'their' authority through its proliferation of committees. Alec Clegg said at the time of his retirement, which co-incided with the carve-up of the West Riding, that a heavy burden fell on the shoulders of officers such as Perraudin and Liversedge, who knew the Riding so well, and he was warm in his appreciation of the administrative contribution to the smoothness of the final massive operation, since detailed knowledge was indispensable. Replying to an enquiry of the Clerk to the County Council in 1974, Alec Clegg gave these men their standing, when he replied unequivocally in detailing the double task of the Education Department.[1]

> 'The first and most obvious task is that of supply . . . The bulk of the (first) of these tasks in my time has always fallen on the Chief Administrative Officer of the department – men like Wolfinden, Calvert, Tidswell and Roberts and now Chalkley. The load for them has been particularly heavy, as the job they perform is one that I, unlike some of my colleagues, have never seen as my main concern. In fact, I might say that, because of this, I have always sought men of high ability for this post.'

The various sections of the education service demanded an overview which was more than a mental aerial photograph. The whole was more than the sum of the parts, and each part affected the rest. The purpose of local committee decisions is the good of the entire community within parameters drawn by Parliamentary decree. All levels of administration have responsibility and respond: the CEO recognises this accountability through his officers. The Clerk to the County Council had enquired of Alec Clegg regarding his and the Deputy Education Officer's duties prior to the dissolution of the West Riding. Alec Clegg's concern for all grades of staff was made abundantly clear:

'The second task, which is at least as important as the first, but somewhat less easy to come to grips with, is to supply quality in education and to maintain the morale and vitality of some 320,000 pupils, 14,000 teachers, nearly 20,000 full-time students in higher education, and 100,000 part-time. In these matters, it is daily facing a multiplicity of problems raised by private individuals, and, less frequently, issues raised by a considerable number of powerful Unions.'

'You may, of course, be asked what I and other senior colleagues will be doing at this time. The answer to this will be the task for which we were appointed, additional tasks related to the carve up, and such minor matters as raising the school leaving age. But there will also fall upon us the major job of maintaining the morale of many people who are in the unhappy position of knowing that the employers to whom they have given a lifetime of service will disappear in two years time . . . My fear is lest those who decide these matters should not grasp the full significance of the development from a two-fold to a three-fold job, or that they may not see clearly that one cannot deal with people as one deals with invoices.'

The third 'major job' was, of course, that of dispersing the County among fourteen other Authorities. Alec Clegg was concerned for the load of the Chief Administrative Officer involved in negotiations.

This vast reorganisation came at the end of Alec Clegg's career, and it is a measure of his skill that it was accomplished in ways which avoided bringing discredit to the County. He voiced serious concern for some proposed sectors in full knowledge of their situation.

It had been due to this ability to balance central edicts with discerned local needs that an imaginative, on-going programme of development had been carried on through the years from 1947 until 1974. It is also a measure of Alec Clegg's skill that in their answerable relationships he maintained a balance between the many features of the educational scene when a dictatorship could have been established. Where the subjective lies is in the interpretation of such a remit by the type of person given it whether a bureaucracy flourishes or not: how people see their duty – in partnership, social service, moral obligations, or little Caesars. An essential feature of Alec Clegg's approach to the job was acceptance of the value of the other person. It is not too much to conjecture that Bootham School had made an impression. Behind succinct, factual, dry accounts set out in stark minuting of the setting up of governing bodies, appointment of staff, pro-vision for students, and his zeal in finding the right person for a post, lay this central value – concern for the human being.

At the centre of this concern also was the attention given to the status of the LEA. A memo dated March 1962[2] had been submitted to Alec Clegg, suggesting a response to public remarks in speeches and in the Press about the ability of LEAs in relation to the Ministry to engender innovation and influence educational thought and practice. Opinion had been given that

LEAs' latitude and discretion had been curtailed to the extent 'that the sole source of educational ideas was the Ministry of Education and that Local Authorities were little more than agents carrying out Ministerial policy.'

The memo listed some of the developments which had been initiated in the West Riding since World War II. The early events had become the substance of the first book on the West Riding which recorded the first ten years.

'Some of these developments have, of course, been the subject of debate and of controversy, but it would be justifiably argued that one of the points in favour of the existence of a Local Education Authority is that matters of this kind *are* subject to debate and controversy. It is often, for instance, as a direct result of discussion and debate and controversy that modifications and improvements are made to proposals.'

The detailed list, although not a complete one, illustrated the breadth of procedures undertaken and the rate of expansion attempted in the search for practical solutions to local educational problems.

Large scale investigations into the allocation of children into different types of secondary schools at 11+.
Parental choice of secondary school courses.
Junior colleges linked with secondary schools.
Training Colleges.
In-service training, Adult Education, Youth Work.
Care of Schools.
Special Schools.
Further Education Area Institutes, liaison with Schools Induction Courses.
Agricultural Education.
Youth Employment Service. Service to grammar schools, the organisation of residential courses for careers teachers, employers' contacts, vocational guidance techniques, vocational aptitude testing, careers conventions.
School building.
Remedial Centres.
School Museum Service – the circulation of works of art, musical facilities, for example orchestras.
External examinations.
Foreign exchanges: Arnsberg; Yorkshire/Lille.

The writers affirmed:

'As the Committee are, of course, aware, although some of their work has been carried out in co-operation with the Ministry, in fact almost all of it is due to the initiative of the West Riding Authority and almost all of it has been carried out with the Authority's own resources and has not in any sense been dependent upon pressures or suggestions from the Ministry of Education or any other body.'

It was then suggested that perhaps the document might be of interest outside the County. The Local Government Act of 1888 decentralised power to local authorities and made them responsible for detailed administration. By statute they were responsible for the running of the schools and the curriculum. Central authority retained general inspection. HMI contributed pamphlets, informally met with local authorities, took part in committee work at national and regional level, ran courses for teachers and gave opinion. The early years of Alec Clegg's administration had people of the highest calibre on County staff and at Government level who contributed advice and acted as moderators; there was a wide range of experience and ability on which to draw. Woolley Hall was a common meeting ground where status was left at the door.[3]

In a memo of 7th February 1958,[4] Alec Clegg responded to the Education Committee's wish to have explained duties and responsibilities of LEA Inspectors and Advisers, and also those of Her Majesty's Inspectors. He dealt candidly with popular misconceptions, and quoted the Ministry of Education report on 'Education in 1949' (p.91) which precisely stated that it was no part of HMIs' function to dictate but that teachers welcomed ideas and suggestions. He then went on to quote the Senior Chief Inspector, Sir Martin Roseveare's address to the Rothwell and Stanley Teachers' Association Refresher Course at Rothwell Grammar School in 1951, to the effect that HMIs' views were 'an offering into the pool'. He finally quoted the now classic letter which the Director of Education, Percival Sharp, sent to Head Teachers on 16th March 1931. Alec Clegg's point to the Committee was that conflicting evidence may come from all quarters – HMI, CCI, and Institutes of Education: teachers had to evaluate what was appropriate to their situation.[5]

Alec Clegg's point to the Committee in this memo was that local economic and educational circumstances had to be taken into account, and blanket diktat was not viable. HMIs had special knowledge and experience which usually included some teaching, and they had built up one hundred years' tradition. They were obliged to have regard for national interests and were not too closely identified with local interests. They were concerned with 'educational assessment and advice and, to a lesser extent, with administration'. A panel of inspectors would therefore carry out a 'full' inspection. He nevertheless pointed to the increase in HMI 'participation in administration, which had grown under war-time constraints, whereby direct responsibility was given to HMIs as a result of the development of methods which have proved convenient and expedient'. His conclusion (and concern) was that *no party* should believe 'it had acquired ultimate wisdom and bringing pressure to bear'. Although he was at that point discussing HMIs, he had in mind that arrogance which is found on occasion in several fields, and his concluding remark was of wariness of those 'folk who think they know all the answers' and 'I am sure you would watch this'.

'Because of the nature and source of the pressures to which the Ministry is exposed, because these pressures are exerted by those who are at best two stages removed from the classroom, because in them the trees of politics, finance, expediency, and even prejudice, on a nation-wide scale can so easily obscure the wood of true education, it is essential that information prepared by the expert and informed opinion of HM Inspectors in their daily contact with the schools should not only be available to the senior administrators of the Ministry but should be their professional life's blood. It is a good thing, a very good thing indeed, for the senior administrators to get about and see the institutions which the Local Education Authorities create within the framework which they devise, but only if they retain enough humility and have enough wisdom to realise that a valuable and secure knowledge can only be obtained from those who literally spend their lives in the schools, and on this matter I speak as an administrator who has often caught himself in this matter making hasty judgments on inadequate personal knowledge.'[6]

CHAPTER FOUR: THE ADVISORY STAFF

On 7th February 1958 Alec Clegg presented a review of duties and functions of the County Inspectorate and Advisory Staff in response to enquiries from members of the Education Committee.[7]

He gave an historical review and reminded the Committee of the length of time since the establishment of the first Inspector in 1891, and an Assistant Inspector a year or two later. The 1902 Act[8] gave the opportunity to make additional appointments, and by 1958 there were nine. Although the County Inspectors carried out full and routine inspections, they had a wide remit with important functions. They reported through the Director of the Committee independently of the County Divisions. The information in total thus presented to the Committee gave an overview on substantial essentials such as accommodation, staffing and equipment – a view of some breadth, which ensured equity within what was possible across the county. Individual reports were followed up, which balanced HMIs, and it was ensured that national demands were met. Teachers on probation were visited, advice given on the curriculum, timetables, school organisation, assistance with Divisional Education Officers' schedules, and estimates. In addition, together with the subject advisers, they assisted, supported and taught at in-service courses. There were also additional voluntary sessions and these, for example, in 1957–58 totalled one hundred and sixty-three.

Advisory staff were concerned with one subject across schools and institutions. Here again, concerns and issues outside their fields of study, where experience and professional training could add another dimension, were referred to them. Art and domestic science advisers were consulted on design, materials, colour schemes, plans for the loan of pictures, and an overview on the quality of purchases. They were concerned with school decoration, housecraft flats, and the Museum Service. Again, the advisers reported directly to the CEO and CCIs on matters which they thought should be given attention.

Alec Clegg added that the advisory service had a historical background also: the first domestic science inspector was appointed before 1890, a teacher of hygiene in 1902, an organising master for art in 1905, an organising inspector for rural districts in 1907, and an organiser for educational handwork in 1914.

The local Inspectorate and Advisory Group had a precedent to follow. W. Loring, Acting Senior Examiner at the Board of Education, held the appointment of First Head of the West Riding Education Department in 1903–4 for less than a year. On his leaving, inspectors already established for secondary, technical and elementary education were given the work of one Director of Education. Finally, in 1929, a Director of Education, J.H. Hallam, was appointed after serving ten years with the Riding. He was succeeded by A.L. Binns in 1939.[9] Suggestions on teaching methods began to be issued in pamphlet form, written by local inspectors. This followed the example of the earlier Technical Instruction Committee's local inspectors, who had suggested syllabuses, for example in domestic science and commercial subjects.

The Plowden Committee commented on the fact that fifty LEAs supported a local inspectorate. The total number of LEAs was one hundred and sixty-four. Alec Clegg valued and acknowledged the contribution of the West Riding Inspectorate and Advisory staff.[10] Each was responsible for around one hundred and fifty schools in the early 1950s, when there were seven inspectors. In addition, there were inspectors for technical colleges and institutions, and special schools. Their duties were broad, and they were guided by a senior inspector. Their pooled knowledge of schools in the Riding was considerable. Alec Clegg himself remarked that it would take him approximately four years, visiting daily, to visit each school once, and therefore his reliance, but not dependence, on their judgement was considerable. They shared the organisation and conduct of teachers' courses, advised in the schools, evaluated the needs of a wide range of institutions, their strengths, where support was needed, and future growth. Inspections of schools were made, and HMI reports followed up. There was a concern for the schools and rapport with school staff which came from willingness to teach, discuss ideas and difficulties, and genuinely advise. From Alec Clegg himself came the directive to CCIs and advisers to encourage and develop personal teaching skills, and to discover the problems of individual schools. In 1945 they found a wide range of 'uncertificated', college-trained, untrained and trained graduates, composing in total a teaching staff of itself well educated. It had taken twenty-five years to move from the pupil-teacher system to college training and one year graduate training. One of Alec Clegg's central concerns was for the teachers in schools in this immediate post-war period, and he worked towards the foundation of an in-service training college where teachers of all levels and status could meet on common ground. The local inspectorate and advisory staff gave attention and time to these informal meetings, and this strengthened goodwill and rapport with the schools. A large Authority could carry such an institution, and provide a client(le. From 1946 onwards, Alec Clegg had clear ideas as to the place and influence of those groups in working with schools and teachers, step by step, evaluating developing situations and districts in the course of post-war change. Skill lay in setting successful staging posts which took school, and child in school, along, which skill was not always apparent, or the progress of the school for that matter, to HMIs. On occasion, this meant sustained visiting over some time. The writer would wish to acknowledge the positive attitude of the physical education team, the adviser for domestic science, the art and science advisers, the music and religious education advisers to her school, and the support of the CCI.

Alec Clegg acknowledged his debt to the advisory staff. In a talk to advisers and organisers on 15th November 1948:

> '. . . we should all bear in mind that when folk stand on their dignity, they do so generally because that is all they have to stand on.'

> 'The fact remains that you, and you alone, have the right to say that in such and such an area of the county, such and such a subject needs attention . . . You can initiate improvements . . . and you can follow up. No other body can do that with the freedom you have. No other body has the potential you have.'

> 'I sense a certain diffidence when you deal with teachers. Is that because you don't want to tread on the toes of colleagues? Of one thing I am sure, it is you and your Branch who ought to be deciding on the kind of teachers you want, and the way you want them trained. At the moment I feel that decisions are being taken or forced by folk who place consideration of organisation, supply and administration before educational need.'[11]

The County Inspectorate was the centre of an administrative web since they linked with advisers, heads of schools, HMI, and reported directly to the Chief Education Officer. It was a system of checks and balances, sustained by informal relationships and goodwill.

> 'If these (informal relationships) are right, they can be one of the greatest joys of our profession.'[12]

> 'What I want to get over to you is that at their best, the informal relationships between an LEA staff and the schools are a reciprocal source of great creative power and effort; they are a reason for living, and personally the longer I live in my job, the more I am sustained and fortified by these relationships.'

Liaison was the keynote if each part was to work successfully. Alec Clegg again used a brief history to illustrate the contribution of the County Inspectorate. In 'The Local Authority and the School' he emphasised the importance of reasonable relationships in full appreciation of human nature.

> 'Perhaps I should start by pointing out that, in the last 20 years, the education service of this country has changed from an LEA service centrally supervised to a national education service locally administered. I mention this because it does, in fact, influence the relationship between schools and the LEA. Although the LEA is still the executive body which supplies schools, teachers, equipment, and encouragement, it now has to do this according to a national pattern, and has to respond to national requirements. We have two striking examples of this at the present time

– the *request* which could by a new Act be changed into a *requirement* that we establish comprehensive schools; and the Schools Council, which is making a lot of good and lively and interesting suggestions, but which could, if things went wrong, become a damaging imposition on our schools, which would relieve them of the necessity to think as effectively as the country's examination system does now.'

'Formal relationships at their highest are established by law. Each primary school has its 'instrument and articles of government'. The instrument sets out how the managers and governors are appointed, and the articles and rules set out what they do.'

'There is almost certain to be a section on organisation and curriculum, which should state clearly the head's position and responsibilities. Subject to the provisions of these articles, each head teacher shall control the internal organisation, management and discipline of the school, shall exercise supervision over the teaching and non-teaching staff, and shall have the power of suspending pupils from attendance, etc., etc.'

For Alec Clegg, it was the spirit in which administration was carried out that was the great matter. Niggling detail or 'mystique' had no place. Admin was there to make the daily life in schools advantageous to the children in them.

'. . . in the West Riding there are 10,000 teachers. It follows statistically that the few best are amongst the most remarkable people in the education service of this country, and it is a tremendous privilege to be able to see them operate and spend time with them.'

At the annual West Riding course held at Bretton Hall in 1965, Alec Clegg assessed his remit and the parameters within which he was constrained. He worked with a wide range of people from professional to amateur. As the appointed senior professional educationalist to the West Riding County Council Education Department responsible to the Education Committee, he was expected to produce advice and with equanimity take on board comment from a broad spectrum of political and social points of view.

He had found himself, after a few months' service in the county, Chief Officer of the largest education authority in the country at the beginning of a difficult post-war period when one of his first assignments was to guide educational planning through the county's 1946 Development Plan. He had witnessed the raising of the school leaving age to fifteen and foresaw the advent of comprehensivisation in the plans for multilateral schools at Otley and Tadcaster, which had been made during and immediately after World War II. Service in Worcestershire, when a fortuitous meeting with a forward-looking educationalist had influenced a practical outlook under-pinned by training and initial experience, had also fostered sympathy for those at the receiving end. Children and families were not bundles of

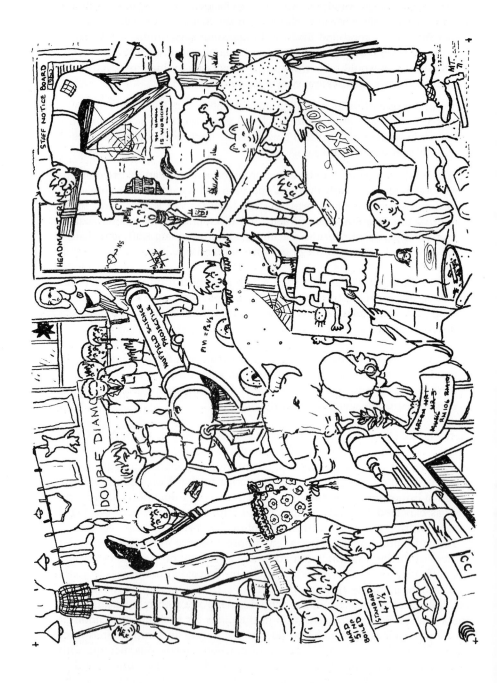

statistics neatly to be used for political ends, in records filed away gathering dust.

> 'What do I know? I probably know what is going on over the whole surface of West Riding education than most people, and at some points which interest me I do manage to get a little below the surface. Your stock-in-trade is children, mine is schools – and I think I know a little bit about schools.'

He quoted statistics which projected an increase in school population, and proposals to meet this contingency: 'in a perfect world we would have 100 new 3–form-entry schools; in a less perfect world we would need 40 schools, each of which would have to be larger than any existing school.' Many suggestions made to avert the emergency were not practicable and he countered arguments strongly which suggested dilution of the teaching service when staffing numbers were increased. He was decided in his views on teachers' influence, on the quality of leadership, on teaching methods. The 'two Rs' he hoped would be taught as the foundation, and in the way unique to the situation. At a conference for school heads at Woolley Hall in 1961:[13]

> 'It has been my great good fortune over the past twenty years to work with people who have seen clearly the nature of the educational process, and at certain levels at any rate put into practice what they have seen.'
>
> '. . . an education service is not a factory which produces glass bottles or motor cars or radio sets or other inanimate devices. It produces people.'

Care of these people implied knowledge of influences bearing on school life: Youth Employment, Further Education, Scholarship transfers, Schools Meals Service, Social Services, the Law, and awareness of responsibility to the Committee.

> 'It is for the teacher himself to decide what methods and practice *are best for him* and the only body that can require him to change them is the Committee that employs him, and they presumably would only issue an instruction to this end if his teaching were shown by its results to be ineffective.'[14]

He repeatedly commented on the use of 'modern methods' used 'without any understanding of their true significance' (p.174, 'The Changing Primary School'). Towards the end of his service, he became more vehement and perhaps disillusioned as to the use to which some had been put. The fact that he had a finger on the pulse of schools and teaching was illustrated in the brief list of what he termed the 'facts of life', recognising that a local authority the size of the West Riding would have wide variety in a heterogeneous community. '. . . but if the school is under good direction, it will surmount its difficulties'.

'It is a statistically established fact that the most powerful force in the education of a child, equal in potency to their own native intellectual endowment, is the aspiration which those nearest and dearest to him have for him. And an aspiration or expectation similar to this held for us by those with whom we work is a most notable and important incentive to work. It is the main motive force which any teacher uses in teaching a child, and it is undoubtedly a force which a head should consciously sincerely use on his staff. Time and time again it has become clear to me that these things succeed in a school which spring from the enthusiasm of a member of staff which is constantly re-fortified by the head's support.'[15]

In an interview with Martin Levitt for 'Javelin',[16] 'What it means to me', Alec Clegg clearly stated his appreciation of the professional teaching and advising he had found at every stage:

'I did not really know what education was about until it was my good fortune to work with a small group of men and women of outstanding distinction in the West Riding. It was with them that I learned how easy it is to prepare the bright child for examinations, and what a taxing, challenging job it is to see that justice is done by a youngster who is slow, or who has had a bad start. But I have, over 27 years in the West Riding, had the extraordinary privilege of being able to see the teaching genius at work at any time and the main fact that I have learned is that this genius which produced human qualities of the highest order has little to do with rules, records, tests, statistics, marks, grades, or examinations, *important as these may be*. The things that matter much more than the facts of the syllabus are the child's loves, hates, enthusiasms, hopes and fears, his imagination, his creative force, his initiative and a whole list of qualities which we can neither measure nor examine, and which, because of this, we tend grossly to undervalue.'

Alec Clegg built up a cohort of trained, experienced advisers and county inspectors who worked in the schools with heads and staff, who understood the physical and social environments, were knowledgeable about the breadth of ability and intelligence, and who knew their districts, who could interpret to HMI.

Alec Clegg's Bootham schooldays were influential in that Quaker influence on patterns of thought and conduct implied responsibility towards people as an unquestionable duty. Implicit in the verse which was often quoted, seemingly guilelessly, was consciousness of ways of knowing, of insightfulness which cannot be measured but is essential to mental health. Comprehension of people would be vitally important, and, for some, a religious sense would be the groundwork. Other patterns of thought would always be presented and if standards were not defined and implicit in home life, something in their place would be substituted outside the home. This was of primary concern when children had a deprived home life. The cultivation of a moral and ethical sense in children and adolescents then fell heavily on schools. The schools, Alec Clegg remarked, had to take into account the amount of education going on around them outside school which endorsed an education of material expectation.

'In the whole of the western world many children born in the late twenties and early thirties entered a world of deprivation caused by severe economic depression and unemployment, and the children of those days are now the fathers of the older teenagers. In the same way, children who were born into the agony of the war years and suffered a lack of a parent, evacuation and the fear of raids, are the parents of our younger teenagers. I think it is more likely that large numbers of such parents, deprived as they were of the disciplines of parenthood, have been unable to pass on what they themselves never experienced.'

'It has been a natural thing to blame the schools, even though between birth and 16 years according to my reckoning a child spends one hour in every eleven at school . . .'

The subtlety of the educational process Alec Clegg argued could be underestimated. Where RE can give values, moral aspects in the education of attitude, something positive is always presented. Children suffer in many ways: one by being given more freedom than they can properly use, loving permissively is not sufficient – left to themselves they will not develop as whole people knowing their own boundaries. The school cannot teach without taking into account outside personal contacts, family, friends, colleagues, parents.

'Religious education' is not closely related to 'religious knowledge', that is, teaching external events in the Bible, though children should know the Bible. Historical information and points of doctrine can be given without education in ethics and principles taking place. The real concern is what goes on in the mind, including themselves – quality of mind rather than commonplace.

Christian education is therefore more than instruction, a teacher's life is pastoral without wearing religion on the sleeve. The aim is a drawing together of all the different aspects of the child at home and school, to have a balanced, reasoning mind, controlled, critical perspective, not arrogantly unable to accept being told, a positive presentation of a way of life, showing one way, watching how much he can bear of responsibility, not too much as to leave him in despair. For the teacher this is more than propaganda which is exploitation of the immature, but guidance in a positive school context to help a child discover his strengths. Again came a question 'what shall we teach so that we shall best prepare children for contemporary society, at home in the world of things, people of some spirit, at peace with themselves?' Something of the children's minds and lives must be known, without intrusion; they are usually clear-sighted and often acute in their apprehension of adults as well as accepting the truth of each other. There had to be recognition of the value of people balanced to face today's unrest, self-regulating, not seeking external authority. A Quaker point of view balances Alec Clegg's own teacher training in educational platonic philosophy of the concept of an élite. His élitism was aimed at quality, not people, and leadership was a continuous effort to test 'the sense of the Meeting'.

From its establishment, the West Riding Education Committee had been concerned about religious education and introduced into its schools a syllabus of religious instruction as early as 1905. The nineteenth century had produced controversy between Church of England and Non-conformists which resulted in a Conscience Clause and the Cowper-Temple Clause ('no religious catechism or religious formulary which is distinctive of any particular denomination shall be taught in the school'). Voluntary schools placed on the rates brought prosecutions for non-payment of that part of the rate. The 1944 Act put upon local education authorities the duty of 'contributing towards the spiritual, moral, mental and physical development of the community by ensuring that sufficient education throughout those stages shall be available to meet the needs of the population of that area'. 'Voluntary schools' meeting half their costs of improvement were 'aided'. Where the LEA took over maintenance, they were 'controlled'. Religious instruction provided by the schools was based on an agreed syllabus. The scripture teaching of the earlier part of the twentieth century had been growing inadequate and it was recognised that grounding in the principles of Christian faith should be the aim since there was a basis of Christian belief common to all denominations. Religious instruction became open to inspection by the Act of 1870. This officially recognised its importance.

The Fifth Schedule of the Act of 1944 laid down procedures for bringing an agreed syllabus into operation and laid down that the day should begin with a collective act of worship 'not distinctive of any denomination'.

Training colleges, the universities, Ministry vacation courses added to in-service training to produce qualified status and parity of esteem. Local institutes of education gave special courses on their areas' agreed syllabuses. At the North of England Education Conference in Harrogate in 1956 Alec Clegg referred to the fact that no local authority had an adviser in religious education yet religious instruction was the only subject the schools had to teach by statute. Alderman Fuller Smith was Chairman of the West Riding Education Committee at the time and said that the West Riding should try to make such an appointment.

The Reverend Alan Loosemore was appointed in 1960, and ten years later Alec Clegg in a note to the West Riding Education Committee listed his commitments which indicated the growth and extent of a very wide remit:

1   Advising the Education Officer, e.g., on evidence submitted to the Newsom and Plowden Reports on RE.

2 Advising and on occasion attending the Education Committee when considering religious matters (eg., Agreed Syllabus affairs).

3 Attending interviews when theological awards are being considered by the Education Committee. These awards are made by the committee to students wishing to become clergymen, ministers and missionaries.

4 Visiting schools to discuss with heads and teachers RE and school assembly in their own schools. One important aspect of this is advising head teachers on the appointment of RE specialists in secondary schools. The adviser attends staffing interviews whenever possible when RE teachers are being appointed.

5 Arranging courses for teachers, e.g., at our Refresher Course College (Woolley Hall near Wakefield), at teachers' centres or in the schools. The following are typical – 'RE in Schools with Immigrant Children', 'RE and Joint Humanities Courses in Secondary Schools', 'Sixth Form Work', 'Religious Teaching and Young Children', 'Children's Expressive Work in RE and Related Subjects'.

6 Working in Further Education, e.g., advising area principals on religious topics in evening institutes, and organising courses at Grantley Hall Adult Education College (e.g., on such subjects as 'Christianity and the Arts', 'Christianity and Humanism', 'World Religions' and 'The New English Bible').

7 Keeping in touch with the five West Riding colleges of education. Visits are made and lectures are given from time to time. A study group for RE tutors in the colleges has been formed and meets once a term to discuss the needs and problems of schools generally, and to consider ways in which RE can make a vital contribution to school life.

8 Speaking at various groups – e.g., sixth form and other groups in school, PTAs, church organisations etc. One important aspect here is interpreting the changes in schools, curriculum, etc., to clergy, ministers and other church people, with the aim of encouraging good school-church relationships wherever possible.

9 Setting up a kind of RE advisory service. Keeping in touch with so many schools presents quite a problem – there are nearly 1,300 in the West Riding – but information is sent out regularly by the adviser, either separately or through the monthly Schools Bulletin. In addition, by co-operating with colleagues, the adviser is able to provide other services for teachers, e.g., together with the County Children's Librarian exhibitions of books have been arranged in Wakefield and in other parts of the county. There is also a flourishing School Museum Service and with the adviser's guidance teaching aids for RE have been added to the Service (e.g., films, slides, film strips, records, pictures, artefacts and exhibits which schools may borrow).

10 Acting in an advisory capacity to the Standing Advisory Council for Religious Education. When the conference for revising the Agreed Syllabus was set up in accordance with the 1944 Education Act, the adviser took an active part in the preparation of the new syllabus, which

was published in December 1966 under the title 'Suggestions for Religious Education'.

The summary is an indication of the value Alec Clegg placed on the entire advisory team. They were people who knew children and teachers, and the wide social and physical surroundings intimately:

'. . . The Adviser in Religious Education works as a member of a large advisory team (over 30 advisers) all of whom have general pastoral care of a group of schools in addition to their specialist role. As a team they are concerned with education as a person to person activity in which the needs of children are uppermost in their minds. Their concern is not chiefly the communication of knowledge or the acquisition of skills but the encouragement of right attitudes, especially towards learning, towards other people and towards life itself. In this important but difficult task the Adviser in Religious Education has a vital role to play.'

Chapter Five: The Colleges

When he took over from A.L. Binns in 1947, Alec Clegg was faced with a body of teachers who exemplified the progress of training methods from pupil teaching, bursaries, training colleges to a post-graduate year. From personal experience in the West Midlands, he understood the pressures of a war-time expenditure of effort in dealing with shortages and large classes. He insisted that a concept of career-long training should be behind immediate planning. Emphasis on 'life long learning' has come full circle. Without peremptorily dictating such a point of view, he neatly intimated that teacher, administrator, inspector, are all at some time in Aiglon's condition – no-one stops learning or involuntarily teaching at every professional level, and some learn to fly and some don't. He had a gift for seizing the moment in presenting his own attitude, without didactically presenting his thesis. He questioned, leaving his varied audiences to work out solutions. The extent of those solutions was documented in four Reports.[1] Concern for training, however, is demonstrated in the establishment of institutions which took in all contingencies as far as possible. He did not look for fixed canon law, but anticipated growth and change.

A practical educationalist, he translated beliefs into action. From 1947 to 1974, when he retired and the West Riding County Council ceased to exist, he had initiated educational foundations which affected practically all parts of the county's education plan. At the end of World War II, there was one training college at Bingley (1911). At the end of the county's life, there had been founded in addition:

Bretton Hall College for Music, Drama and Art (1949)
Lady Mabel College at Wentworth Woodhouse for Physical Education (1949)
Grantley Hall College for Adult Education (1949)
Ilkley College of Housecraft (1951)
Woolley Hall Training College for In-Service Training (1952)
Scawsby College of Education (formerly Swinton Day Training Centre) (1961)
Bramley Grange College for In-Service Further Education and Youth Service (1965)
Harrogate Training College, which met immediate post-war emergencies (1947)

Of these foundations, three remain. Bretton Hall is now a constituent college of the University of Leeds, Woolley Hall is administered by

Wakefield Metropolitan District Council, and Grantley Hall is under the North Riding County Council.

The 1968 Education Act required new Instruments of Government for the training colleges to be approved by the Department of Education and Science. Local politics, for the most part, met on a common ground. Alec Clegg outlined, in a letter of 13th January 1964, the difficulties embedded in a proposal in the Robbins Report to have university schools of education administer the colleges, rather than the LEAs:

> 'the answer is that if the unproductive administrative change demanded by Robbins came about, it would make the basic productive proposals of Crowther and Newsom completely unattainable.'

He successfully retained control of the colleges following the Robbins report, but seriously welcomed co-operation at university level. Leeds and Sheffield Universities' Institutes of Education staff became very familiar with Woolley Hall in particular, and were appreciated visitors.

The county finally had colleges accommodated in beautiful buildings bought, if compared with 1990s prices, for very little indeed – individual cost would not cover the price of the smallest cottage today. Both houses and grounds were enjoyed. Post-war building controls militated against new buildings, and the county was obliged to turn to the idea of conversion which it did to good effect. Several large mansions were surveyed before careful final decisions were made. The buildings were usually sited in grounds which were themselves attractive, and some beautiful as at Bretton. The art and needlecraft advisers were called in to advise on furniture and decoration. Immediately after the war there had to be adaptation and alteration, despite the immediate release of controlled materials, labour and furniture. The resulting imaginative, cultured ambience owes a great deal to the care and attention of the first people given the task, from the architects to the advisers. There was lively awareness of the social and cultural quality through the passage of time, 'when these buildings were being put to a use so fundamentally different from the now almost obsolete one for which they were designed'.

The moving principle behind Alec Clegg's interest in the specialist colleges was a conviction that specialist teaching should be more clearly defined, and future training of the specialist teacher should be planned in the light of the needs of children of the present time.[2] He was concerned that 'Group IV' subjects, as he termed them, should be given the value already given to academic studies. They were civilising and cultural sources, and should be accessible to more than a few, since they were an influential part of children's educational surroundings, adding to the quality of their daily experience.

> 'Sheer joy is the purpose of our teaching music, art, poetry, literature; the joy of learning should come from other subjects in the curriculum, and

this must not be killed at any stage. Once a child's enthusiasm is caught, and the purpose clear to him, he will tackle all the drill and routine a subject requires; but if you apply the wet blanket of drill and routine before the spark has been kindled, there will be no fire, no zest, no enthusiasm. Only the skills can survive bad teaching, and that is because most people have to read and have to count, and this exercise of their skills throughout life means that they are not forgotten. But if history or art or geography are badly taught, the mind will reject it as the body rejects a surfeit of sour fruit.'[3]

Bretton Hall [4]

The educational needs of the West Riding at the end of World War II were broad. Alec Clegg's inclination in regarding teacher training as preeminent gave weight to emphasis on quality in teaching the arts. Separate colleges for art, music and drama would not be financially viable, but a memo from HMI Priestley dated 12th January 1946 intimated that one college for the three subjects would meet the immediate emergency and future requirements. In addition, each subject would gain from the other two, and provide a broader vision. He also thought it could be advantageous to have a link with the new University Department of Education in Leeds, which would give a background in the principles of education. There could be training in teaching, supported by a general musical education, and wider interests.

Agendum 3A of a meeting of the sub-committee on post-war education[5] which met to discuss the provision of additional training colleges as set down by Circular 77 from the Ministry, noted that the Riding looked for permanent colleges. They minuted that, in their opinion, the 'catastrophe of the last six years' was mainly due to man's intellect outstripping his sensibilities. Clearly Alec Clegg's influence is seen in that continuing statement that civilising subjects such as art and music tend to be neglected in favour of what can be tested. Subjects such as art and music should have standards raised in the schools, and also status.

The memo continued with a comment on the traditional love of music-making in the Riding, regardless of social status. The suggestion was made that a college of music could include to advantage specialists in art and drama, to the end that a wide appreciation and understanding of the arts may influence children, and general awareness of all three subjects in all school activities. Clegg was appreciative of the kind of drama to be taught. He intimated that they were not teaching for the stage, but for children's responsiveness and discernment. In a memo to senior HMIs Haynes and Richardson, 16th February 1948, he stated that it could be recognised that training based on movement through dance and mime would link art and music. He went on to say with some pride that 'such people able to train from this source are few, and the ablest of them are already in the county'.

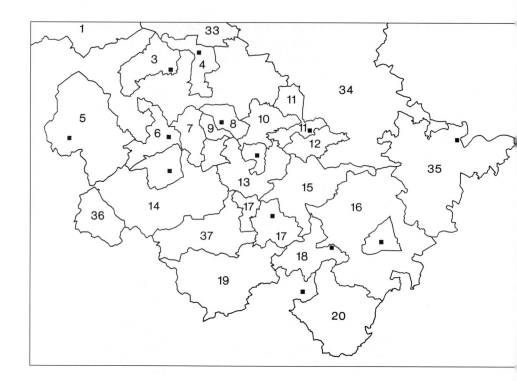

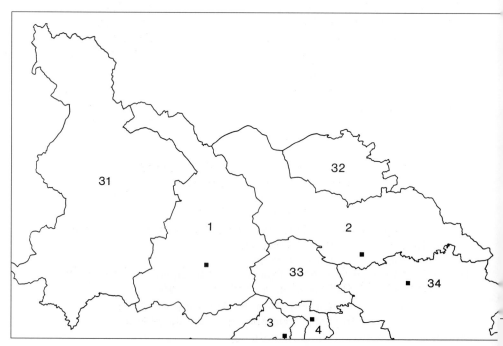

COUNTY of the WEST RIDING of YORKSHIRE

DIVISIONAL AREAS

'Outside' Divisional Executive		DIVISIONS	Site of local Administration
31	1	Skipton, Settle.	Skipton
32	2	Harrogate, Knaresborough.	Harrogate
	3	Bingley and Shipley.	Shipley
33	4	Pudsey, Ilkley, Otley.	Yeadon
	5	Todmorden, Sewerby Bridge.	Todmorden
	6	Brighouse, Elland.	Brighouse
	7	Mirfield, Spenborough, Heckmondwike.	
	8	Morley	Morley
	9	Batley	
	10	Rothwell, Stanley.	Wakefield
	11	Castleford	Castleford
	12	Pontefract	
	13	Ossett, Horbury.	Wakefield
36	14	Colne Valley, Kirkburton, Denby Dale.,	Huddersfield
	15	Cudworth, Royston, Hemsworth.	Wakefield
	16	Tickhill, Adwich, Bentley.	Doncaster
	17	Darfield, Darton. (+ 19, + 37.)	Barnsley
	18	Mexborough, Wath, Conisburgh.	Mexborough
37	19	Hoyland Nether, Stocksbridge.	Barnsley
	20	Maltby	Rotherham

'EXCEPTED' DISTRICT

34		Keighley	Keighley

KEY   1944 Division of 20 'DIVISIONS' and 'Rest'.
(Para. 1, p.1 of White Paper.)

Centre of Divisional Executive Administration.

County Boroughs – Wakefield, Dewsbury, Huddersfield, Halifax, Rotherham, Sheffield, Doncaster.

Boundary and number of Divisional Executive Districts, and districts outside the area of Divisional Executives.

(Source: The late W.J. Morrell, CCI.)
(Map: Courtesy of the old West Riding Castleford office.)

Further, in a letter dated 8th December 1949 to John Friend, the first Principal, he asked what was the purpose of drama in schools – not the school play, though this had a place. What were we training the teachers to do? He sought credence for what was hoped for; procedures that would bring together students who were able to deal with movement and drama at the schools' level, and with English. He suggested that they could be produced in a play by a leading teacher of drama, and he cited as examples Esme Church, John Allen, and Martin Brown. He saw the 'theatre' in schools as missing the point, but recognised that 'acting' was a valuable and traditional expressive part of children's play. He stressed the essential difference between encouragement and misplaced applause, recognising the psychological damage that can be done. He wondered when was the moment that children could be allowed to perform before their peers and before grown-ups. In making appointments, the College had to search very carefully, and heed the advice of people like those whom he had quoted, or earn the contempt of professional theatre; they must look for more than amateurs or incompetent professionals.

Art teaching came in for the same meticulous scrutiny. At the initial meeting with staff on 29th September 1949, he queried timing and extent in teaching technical knowledge. He did not dismiss it. How far did technical knowledge increase sensitivity, increase understanding; someone who is not an artist can appreciate artists' work. The question as to the extent of direction in teaching was control: how much, how little, and when. He said children could be made to do things, but when they are no longer obliged to do them, what remains? That was a root question, and the mature development of students was crucial to the maturation of their pupils. In art, 'sensibilities matured through visual and tactile experience of the world'. Clegg nevertheless realised that tools and skills and 'first absorption of factual knowledge' are necessary for the young child – that task tended to fill its mind and he asked his audience to think how sensitivity in the arts could be sustained. The search was for qualities and quality.

He sought for an appropriate way to teach arts subjects and compared the teaching of games, of which he had had some experience – stage by stage, point by point, until finally allowed to play a full game, all enthusiasm killed. He had evolved his own methods to encourage pleasure and enthusiasm. He had interviewed one art lecturer who had outlined a syllabus which would enable the art teacher to know exactly from the first day to the last what he would be doing at a given time. He then asked how often was music taught in that way – 'and consequently only the incurably musical survive'.

He wondered how, in the work of Bretton, it would be possible to make a start by attempting to foster qualities. Could not the experts get together without constructing a scheme as artificial in its way as his stereotype interviewee from whom he had quoted? Have them explain their interpretation of rhythm, form, lightness, strength, give illustrations to help their students apply this sensitivity in their own media – to get at the essence.

Bretton Hall was the first of the new training colleges. The Staff Inspector for Music had visited, and suggested that a training college for teachers of music could be appropriately sited in a county famed for its musical reputation. The addition of art and drama was discussed, which was in accord with Alec Clegg's thinking.

A special sub-committee had met to discuss proposals for post-war education in detail on 19th February 1946, when it was decided to found a college at Bretton Hall, which had come on the market. This college would specialise in the training of teachers of art, music and drama. At a further meeting on 16th December 1947, the Policy and Finance Sub-Committee agreed to purchase the Hall, and part of the adjoining grounds, from Lord Allendale. The Education Committee confirmed this decision on 23rd December 1947. The governing body was decided by the Further Education Sub-Committee on 6th September 1949, and the first meeting of governors was held on 14th November 1949 when the college first opened in September 1949. New Instruments of Government were required in accordance with the Education Act of 1968, for the approval of the Department of Education and Science, to take effect after April 1970. The last minutes of Bretton Hall Governors were dated 8th May 1970. Bretton Hall is now a constituent college of the University of Leeds.

Lady Mabel College for Physical Education : Wentworth Woodhouse [6]

At the start of his career at St Clement Danes, Alec Clegg took part in games teaching. He had a distinguished athletics record as a schoolboy at Bootham School which had followed an earlier, involuntary experience of military 'drill' at his father's school. When he was expected to discuss or talk about physical education, as always the lively interest in the history of curriculum subjects was evident, as was personal, vivid memory of past experience of his family and himself.

He noted particularly how fresh and novel was the idea of physical recreation for all manner of people rather than the prerogative of a select group. An increasingly affluent society had brought leisure and a wide interest in many sports which earlier had been the province of one or two groups. He also noted the passing of the Drill Sergeant and the enhanced status of PE teaching. Impetus had come through a new influence from abroad. Firstly, through re-ordered teaching approaches from Scandinavia before the First World War, and later through German refugees – Kurt Hahn who initiated the Outward Bound Movement, and Rudolf Laban who influenced a philosophy of physical education which he based on movement studies. The earlier concept of 'drill' for the incompetent and inferior was rejected. A radical point of view which accepted value in the individual and pleasure in personal ability with some influence on development of individual morale suggested an education which could encompass both team games and individual endeavour. It followed that a wide range of activities could be introduced and many could find an outlet in a wide personal choice instead of all experiencing the purgatory of going through every drill and activity. Physical education and games had become something far more than for the few who excelled upon whom total concentration had been expended. It is possible to surmise that Alec Clegg's attitude stemmed from personal experience of agonising drill, equipment planned for six-footers, and a pseudo-team spirit which coerced reluctant conformity. Respect for the individual in his chosen activity sphere met with Alec Clegg's approval. He quoted Newsom to the effect that a child's own esteem can be built up, permanently affecting character, when physical education is taught with insight and sensitivity.[7]

> 'The subject is an interesting one in that a revolution has taken place in it since the war and the older principles of drill and emphasis on science and remedial work has given way somewhat to the introduction of a more aesthetic handling of the training, which the girls' schools at any rate apparently welcomed.'

> 'But this matter of self-respect for others is surely the great province of the games field and the gymnasium and, let us face it, both can be brutalising in their effect. When dealing with whole classes I would minimise competition and encourage each child to compete against his own last effort. I would avoid the sort of teaching where 30 children are required to vault over a buck, so that half a dozen at least would be humiliated by their performance, and in its place would seek to provide situations which were just within each child's compass, so that each child would in fact succeed and, spurred on by his own success, would take the next step, and take it joyfully. I would encourage every form of outdoor pursuit as well as the normal team games, hiking, camping, canoeing, cycling, climbing, and so on, and would try to contrive situations in which the adept were encouraged to help the clumsy rather than make them more conscious of their clumsiness.'

> 'But the important thing in this as in other objectives I have stated is that all teachers, and particularly the PE teacher, should know precisely that the *development of self-respect* is the purpose of their teaching and that the physical skills are the tools which they use to this end.'

There was a particular shortage of women's places for physical training. Alec Clegg was concerned for appropriate and enjoyable PE for older girls, as was Miss Gordon, the Senior County Inspector. Miss Gordon had held the headship of a secondary grammar school of the same status in the north-east as that attended by Alec Clegg. The general health of school children was primary since a sick child did not get the best from enhanced PE. The marching, measuring distance, jumping over a buck just that fraction too high for most in a class, were dated and anathema. Although development of physical education was of primary concern, again it was not to be considered as an isolated subject but had a place in the more broad appreciation of physical activity generally, and was applicable to wider activities in, for example, Outward Bound situations and leisure time activities.

A physical education college was established at Wentworth Woodhouse, and opened in September 1949. The Policy and Finance Committee had approved in principle and at a meeting on 18th March 1947 had approved the lease of Hoober House in addition, from Earl Fitzwilliam. This house had been used as a hostel for maladjusted girls, and finally became part of the college's residential accommodation. There was a brief, initial period of two terms when the college was based in temporary accommodation in Harrogate. At a meeting of the Further Education Sub-Committee on 3rd January 1950 members of the governing sub-committee were appointed and held their first meeting on 10th February 1950. Under the Education Act of 1968, governing bodies for colleges of education were required and the Policy and Finance Sub-Committee met on 9th September and 9th December 1969 to reconstitute the governing body in accordance with the Instrument approved by the Department of Education and Science, taking effect from 1st April 1970. The last minutes were dated 27th May 1970. The college was named Lady Mabel College of Physical Education. Lady Mabel Smith was sister of Earl Fitzwilliam and a County Councillor who had strong interests in education.

The students took the Teacher's Certificate of Sheffield University. In addition to their main subject they were required to take English Language and a further subject chosen from art, music, biology or English literature. The syllabus was based on Rudolph Laban's principles of movement. Training was linked by a common theory applied to gymnastics, coaching games, a philosophy of movement. There were two complementary sections: one, the 'grammar' of physical education and the other regarded as the medium of the child's creative and aesthetic development. The course was basically of three years' duration; a one-year course was available for students coming from general subjects training colleges or for teachers with over three years' general teaching experience. A general base for admission was five 'O' Levels. The staff was closely linked with Bretton Hall and Sheffield Medical School.

Miss Hammond, Senior Inspector, summed up some aims of the college at the leaving ceremony of the first Principal. She looked for more than academic high fliers, a balanced outlook, quality of mind, a latent ability to make the unsure more self-accepting, a scheme of work which was more than a mere extension of school or athletic skills work. This scheme would include thoughtful active experiment in movement and include the relation of the spoken voice, music, movement linked with patterns and compositions, the way dramatic action merges. The first year out would be crucial.

An interesting annexe to Lady Mabel College was based at Castleford from 1967 to 1981. For the first five years the Tutor-in-Charge was Miss Margaret Dunn. The Principal Lecturer in Education, Miss Nancy Smith, became Tutor-in-Charge for the subsequent six years. It was the second college in the country to establish a four-year part-time teacher training course. Many students stayed on to complete the B.Ed. In 1974 when the West Riding was broken up, the Annexe became an outpost of Bretton Hall College. Again, as at Swindon, the quality of the mature students was up to standard. Qualifications were subject to the approval of the Institutes of Education of Leeds and Sheffield Universities. Students' previous occupations had been, again, clerks to office managers, banking, local government and civil service lower ranks.

Grantley Hall Adult College [8]

Further education did not develop as positively as did the rest of the educational planning. Rationalisation of FE work resulted in two area institutes, the Vermuyden Institute at Goole and the Rockingham Institute in the Wath-Swinton Division. The dream, however, was of a college along the lines of Ruskin College, Oxford. Looking at the success of Ruskin College, it was thought that numbers in the Riding would justify such an institution in the North. In the event, this aim was not practicable, but Grantley set an example in the provision of short-term courses, and could be regarded as a pioneer college in this respect.

Grantley Hall near Ripon came on the market in 1947, and was offered to the county. A scheme for a residential college for eighty adult students was approved at the Policy Sub-Committee's meeting of

16th September 1947. On 23rd September 1947 the Education Committee agreed the purchase for £13,500. The constitution of the governing body was determined at subsequent meetings – eight members of the Education Committee plus four co-opted members. Their first meeting was held on 22nd February 1947, and their last meeting on 29th March 1974. The North Riding Education Authority took the college when boundaries were changed.

Another beautiful Adam-style house, it was adapted around 1770 by Sir Fletcher Norton when he was Speaker of the House of Commons and later Lord Grantley. The thirty acres of well-planted grounds gave another perfect setting for courses of a weekend or ten days. Two kinds of courses became very popular as their value became realised: the first made places available to the general public and the second was organised in collaboration with professional, educational, governmental or industrial organisations for the exclusive use of their members. When the stables were converted during the 1963/64 session into an Art Room and a theatre workshop, there was an added attraction to the humanities curriculum. The courses were specifically provided for interest and not to further qualifications or promotion. The value of such courses came to be recognised in Further Education and Grantley gave an added dimension to those which developed at local technical colleges.

The industrial, professional and staff training courses catering for specialist audiences became very advanced as time went on and demanded a very high level of experience backed by vocational knowledge. Courses open to the general public were planned for people with a lively interest and enthusiasm rather than an academic background. Qualifications were not demanded, and there was freedom from tests and examinations. The tutors were experts in their field, often known nationally and internationally. Their skill lay in attention given to a mixed audience; and in putting across their theme to non-specialists. Practical work was popular. Age range and background of students was wide. In addition there was opportunity for private study.

Ilkley College [9]

The Policy Sub-Committee of the West Riding Education Committee met on 15th March 1949 to discuss particularly the suitability of buildings for the training of teachers of housecraft. Alderman Hyman had premises in Harrogate in mind, but at a later meeting of the Further Education Sub-Committee on 31st May 1949, a report was submitted on Wells House Hotel, Ilkley. Negotiations were completed for the acquisition of Wells House from Trustees of the Catholic Church. A special sub-committee to deal with the foundation of the college was appointed, and it was agreed to increase the number of the first students to be admitted from 150 to 180. The Education Committee met on 26th September 1950, when the purchase of the property was approved, and the date of opening decided – September 1951. The Further Education Sub-Committee determined the composition of the governing body on 31st May 1951, and the Governors held their first meeting on 3rd July 1951. The Policy Sub-Committee met on 9th September and 9th December 1969, to establish the requirements of the 1968 Education Act, to appoint new governing bodies in accordance with the Instruments as approved by the Department of Education and Science from April 1970. The last minutes of Ilkley College of Education Governing Sub-Committee, which were dated 28th April 1970, were approved by the West Riding Further Education Sub-Committee on 19th May 1970.

Peter Darvill[10] recounts in detail the acquisition of Wells House, and recounts the diplomacy required. Letters with Miss Bryant HMI had been exchanged, discussing its suitability, following a comparison of expenditure with Harlow Manor. The Chairman of the Education Committee favoured the Harrogate site, but it was pointed out that Wells House was the Ministry's choice, and the purchase was assured in the committee by a narrow margin. There was some acrimony over money, materials, and labour. Nevertheless, it was acquired for £40,000, the price of a small terraced cottage today.

There was a serious shortage of domestic science teachers. The aims of the college[11] encapsulated Alec Clegg's outlook on education, which he defined in a memorandum to the Policy and Finance Sub-Committee. It was well ahead of the orthodox domestic teaching, but did not break with tried approaches.

1 'That the college should be concerned with all branches of home-making, not merely cookery, needlework and laundry – a deliberate study made of the design and construction of all furnishings, fabrics and equipment of a house, as well as of the house itself, and the students, when trained, should be equipped to deal with all manner of minor repairs, such as are required in the home.'

2 'That, to this end, there should be well-developed art centre in the college, which would, however, lean to the conception of that subject which has come to be associated with the Council of Industrial Design, that is to say, the students would be encouraged to make a study of the design and quality of all manner of domestic furnishings and equipment. They would, of course, have an opportunity for the normal expressive aspect of this subject in needlework, painting, or even pottery.'

3 'That other subjects of the student's curriculum, such as history, might well be concerned with the development of homemaking in all its aspects, throughout history.'

4 'That the curriculum should be, if anything, somewhat less specialist than is customary in such colleges, and that particular emphasis should be laid on the development of a sound course in English language and literature. To this end, it was felt that a good and well-stocked library, which the students should learn to use as soon as possible, should be a major concern for the Authority in its initial equipment of the college.'

The curriculum followed that of Lady Mabel College, substituting domestic science and needlecraft for PE. The students took their main subject, also compulsory English; then there was a choice between art and design, physical education, religious knowledge, music, or social studies. On the specialist studies the college made a lengthy statement.

The specialist subjects were to be cookery, housecraft, needlework, and dressmaking. These, being 'part of the fabric of daily life, were crucial when much public taste was regrettably low'. It was consequently necessary to ensure that the students themselves should be capable of presenting their subject as one which 'gave opportunities for artistic and creative expression', and an integral part of their teaching. The significance of good design, and the place of artistic appreciation should be realised in the home. This was not to be work in isolation, but in context. The students should know of the historical background of their teaching situation as well as the history of their subject.

This implied that provision in the college should be made for the teaching of art. Above all, a well-stocked library would be essential. How to use books was a necessary skill. The result would be students who could meet present educational demands and have flexibility of mind to meet future developments.

Woolley Hall In-Service Training College [12]
The Policy Sub-Committee on 17th June 1947 resolved to lease Woolley
Hall and part of the grounds from N.W. Ewart Wentworth Esq. for twenty-
one years. At meetings held on 16th November 1948 and 18th January
1949, it was reported that the Hall was to be sold, and that difficulties
would be met in a purchase and in part of the grounds held on lease.
Negotiations overcame these difficulties, and at a meeting held on 12th
April 1949, it was confirmed that Woolley Hall and part of the park had
been bought from G. Goldham Knight Esq. of 130 Mount Street, London,
W1.

The Policy and Finance Sub-Committee met on 24th October 1950 to
deal with general organisation and administration, the constitution of a
governing body, and to appoint a Warden. The college opened in the
autumn of 1951. The first meeting of the Governing Sub-Committee was
held on 26th September 1951, and the last held on 26th February 1974.

On taking up his appointment as Chief Education Officer, Alec Clegg
reviewed the factual situation and in view of the aftermath of World War
II, the 1944 Education Act, and the demand from the Government for a
Development Plan, he regarded the predominant aim as one of maintaining quality in the schools. From this starting point, the condition of the
teachers was one immediate consideration, since the progress of the
children was the priority. The perennial debate on quality and quantity
seldom took account of the intellectual grounds on which children and
teachers met (Clegg's Question for Aiglon), that is, how they mentally
confronted; or of the teachers' knowledge of home atmosphere; or of the
teachers' personal wishes for broadened horizons. The teaching-learning
between child and teacher is present in spite of buildings, clerking, or social
class. Training would need constant appraisal in relation to the times. He
held firmly to the point of view that the children's best interest would
be served, since their development should be accepted as pre-eminent, by
giving teachers the opportunity to take part in the on-going countrywide
educational debate through in-service training.

At Woolley Hall, an undertaking was made to go well beyond sporadic
and 'refresher' courses; to make a centre which would become a meeting
place for open-ended discussions which would develop and integrate
educational ideas; to have a centre where serving teachers of all ranks could
meet on terms of equality and discuss queries, problems, situations, moves
ahead. Status was left at the door. He gave unequivocal reasons for the
establishment of Woolley Hall. [13]

1   'Teachers in their first years are often insecure and inexpert begin-
    ners, and may need help beyond that which their Heads can provide.'

2   'Older teachers may be so placed that they are unable to escape from
    the ruts cut deep by teacher routines repeated year after year (also
    personal circumstances).'

3 'Teachers can be very isolated. Seldom do heads of one school see the work of another, or secondary school heads see what is being done in primary schools, or even classroom teachers see what their neighbours are doing, and specialists can be the most isolated of all.'

4 'Heads and their staffs, as much as anyone else, need that recognition which our natures crave and acknowledge with renewed endeavour.'

His strong emphasis was on the fact that pupils are captive:

'It is, therefore, not only important that an Authority should try to help its weakest teachers, but even more so that its whole service should be illuminated by total and vigorous ideas which, in the main, will stem from the experimenters, the researchers, the visionaries, and even from the eccentrics, amongst its own teachers. It is from these that the orthodoxy of the next generation will come, and it is important that their present unorthodoxies should be known and exposed for the criticism of their colleagues.'

'This does not mean that in-service training should consist of meetings at which people who have reached some eminence in their profession should address the less elevated in an endeavour to pass on their superior wisdom. There is a place for this kind of thing, but much of it washes over those concerned leaving little deposit, as does much of the teaching in a 'formal' school.'

'Meaningful in-service training should be organised on the belief that teachers need to meet with their colleagues and others concerned in the service to check their own ideas, and learn new ones, to confirm their own doubts and aspirations, and to gain the confidence which comes from the support of others.'

'. . . What it does mean, of course, is that relative beginners should not attend residential courses; what it does mean is that there must be courses for teachers at all stages in their development which will vary from the hour's discussion group to the year's diploma course.'

The desire was to stimulate individual teachers in their own ideas, and progress was part of the basic philosophy behind Woolley Hall courses. It became a centre for continued debate on education well beyond the West Riding, and was the first of its kind in the country. The post-war Education Sub-Committee had met in October 1945, when the need for refresher courses was aired. After six years of war there was tiredness, a shortage of supplies, and surroundings inevitably run down. The demands of the new Act had to be met, and more teachers were needed. The qualitative side would be supervised by specialist advisers in their own main cultural subjects. The latest methods were required and a 'direct attack on the general sensibilities'. Alec Clegg wished Woolley Hall to become a forum where the 'best minds in the country' from the arts, sciences, commerce, and industry would meet. There was to be separate provision of staff for each course and attention paid to the selection of visiting lecturers. He considered that the West Riding was sufficiently large to undertake this exacting brief.

The hall was opened by Sir John Maud, Permanent Secretary to the Ministry of Education, in June 1951. The first Warden was Miss Diana Jordan, to whom the central philosophy informing the many and varied courses was due. Her Deputy was Miss Dorothy Phillips, later to be Warden at Bramley Grange, who returned to Woolley on Miss Jordan's retirement.

Initial questioning from the committee over in-service training taxed Alec Clegg's negotiating skills, but there was an ability to express aims in words suited to his many audiences. Detail was attended to, but any tendency to lose the larger vision was avoided. An ability to navigate the rocks and shallows of local government demanded acuity of a high order. A complete set of brochures of all the courses planned and held at Woolley Hall gives some indication of the breadth and depth in subjects, and the calibre of lecturers and directors of courses it attracted as the years passed. Alec Clegg had described his expectations:

'One type (of training) is obvious, teachers must be acquainted with the latest methods in the teaching of their subjects, arithmetic or dancing, Latin or field games. More important, however, is a direct attack on their general sensibilities and breadth of outlook. This can only be effected by bringing them into contact with the best minds in the country, either in industry or music, commerce or art, agriculture or theatre. These two aims can be combined into one course by the careful selection of speakers and lecturers.'

Scawsby College of Education [14]
By 1960 the national supply of teachers was in balance but parts of the West Riding, particularly in the south, had a shortage. Those areas which did not attract applicants needed immediate remedies since it was clear that the emergency could become a disaster, particularly with the introduction of the three-year college course in 1961. The Ministry favoured a day training plan to attract mature applicants rather than a temporary residential college, and approved the suggestion that mature students should apply, particularly mature women students whose families had reached a stage of self-sufficiency. Such a college had been set up in Leeds which had been successful in meeting required educational standards. In a period very different from the present time where change of profession or occupation is accepted and even expected, the prejudice had again been voiced that academic standards would be diminished and unsuitable applicants would be appointed. Those who lacked the required qualifications or were young enough still to obtain these through the usual routes were not accepted. The college, once founded after initial administrative

difficulties, and eventually with a preponderance of students on the three-year course, was successful to the extent that the Ministry was willing to consider a permanent foundation on a suitable site. In the event, the college closed after nine years. Scawsby College of Education, formerly Swinton Day Training College, opened in 1961 and closed in 1970. Alec Clegg commented that this training scheme points out 'how emergencies throw up talent' and 'these (students) were mature and understanding and the waves of fashion which affect most students blow over them leaving little deposit'.

The college was particularly helpful in providing links with Red House, a West Riding residential home for children in distress.

Premises intended for a secondary technical school were used as a temporary measure and the school accommodated in Mexborough Schofield Technical College buildings. Comprehensivisation was planned for local schools but a 'staged progress of moves' would mean a delay in comprehensivisation of no more than two years. There was some debate over the college and Councillor C.T. Broughton wrote to the South Yorkshire Times on 7th January 1961, answering criticisms.

The Education Committee met on 26th January 1960, when it approved the use of Swinton Technical High School as a Day Training College. A detailed scheme was demanded and a sub-committee was appointed to formulate a viable plan. The Policy and Finance Sub-Committee met on 5th April 1960, when it was resolved to establish a Day Training College at Swinton and to ask Ministry approval. This was confirmed at a meeting of the Further Education Sub-Committee on 24th May 1960. The Ministry approved the opening for January 1961. At this meeting the constitution of the governing body was determined and the first meeting of the Swinton Day Training College Governing Sub-Committee was held on 13th June 1960. At a meeting on 7th September 1965, the Governors decided that the college should be named Scawsby College of Education when it transferred to Scawsby. This transfer took place in the summer of 1967 and the first meeting of the Governing Sub-Committee of Scawsby College of Education was held on 27th September 1967. The Education Act of 1968 caused rearrangement of the Governors and the Policy and Finance Sub-Committee met on 9th September and 9th December 1969 to constitute a governing body in accordance with the Instruments approved by the Department of Education and Science, from 1st April 1970. The final minutes of Scawsby College of Education Governing Sub-Committee were dated 27th April 1970 and approved on 9th May 1970.

Bramley Grange [15]
Technical Education, Further Education, Informal Education,
A Community Centre.
The Deputy Education Officer.
Demand for places on Further Education and the Youth Service led to the opening of Bramley Grange, when Woolley Hall became heavily over-

subscribed. Miss Dorothy Phillips, Deputy Warden of Woolley Hall, was invited to open Bramley Grange, to be planned on similar lines. The college was equally successful, and its closure in 1974 was sincerely regretted. It was a serious loss, in that it imaginatively catered for an educational sector which was not always given priority.

Approval in principle was given at a meeting of the School Management Sub-Committee on 7th July 1964. The house, bought from the executors of Samuel Patchett, cost £27,000. The Policy and Finance Sub-Committee met on 9th February 1965 and for the last time on 26th March 1974.

War exigences in the West Riding had produced a surge of activity in technical education. In a letter to Alderman Collier in 1950, Alec Clegg urged that it could not be at all desirable to 'direct' young people into technical education following up the wartime temporary custom of 'direction of labour'. He considered that the wide intellectual range of technological and technical studies could not be pushed on to those children left behind by the 11+ examination. There had been a memo to the Policy Sub-Committee in 1948 on alternative courses in secondary (grammar) schools related to the major industries. Such courses withered due to the weight of the syllabus for School Certificate and Higher Scholarship 'in spite of the fact that much more highly intellectual ability was being demanded'.

In addition, further education was accepted as an extension of elementary education and rejected as equal or parallel to 'modern' or scientific studies at grammar school level. Gosden and Sharp give a lucid, matter-of-fact account of the development of technical education on which the country's prosperity depends. Technology is now at a peak, and there is a dearth of occupations for those lacking training, or are untrainable, or where predilections go in other directions. Alec Clegg foresaw this negative consequence of advanced technology and reiterated: what of those left behind? The sequel to their neglect could be dire in the extreme.

'Unskilled work is disappearing. The hewing of wood and the band-saw. But such unskilled work as there is, is even less interesting than it used to be because it is purposeless, its end cannot be seen.[16]

From his papers it is clear that Alec Clegg gave early thought to the concept of colleges of advanced technology and to the foundation of technical grammar schools which would have parallel reputation for rigour as the grammar schools. Secondary grammar schools after the 1918 Act had widened their curricula particularly in languages, art and music and he had attended one such school. He had enquired of business people of high standing in the Riding of ideas regarding a suitable education for commerce and industrial administration including other technological and advanced technical skills. To some surprise, vocational and technical *training* was placed second to a first-class general education for high echelons and middle range: professional training followed grammar school curriculum. Training for skilled technicians should have training following generous grounding in general subjects. Alec Clegg firmly believed that those who carried the graft of monotonous daily work should have opportunity for art, music, books and satisfying leisure activities which most take for granted as of right, and often don't use to the full.

> 'Sheer joy is the purpose of much of our teaching music, art, poetry, literature; the joy of learning should come from other subjects of the curriculum, and this must not be killed at any stage.'[17]

Given a curriculum in common, how the subjects are taught depends on the people in each class.

Technical education had come under the aegis of the officer with responsibility for higher education. Alec Clegg had from various reports seen that further education could be moved forward to meet growing post-war demands and he wished to see progress in this sector as in other sectors in content and presentation. He looked for a new system or plan for further education and persuaded the Education Committee to create a post specifically for this purpose when it was realised that the officer in charge of higher education, who would follow the retiring officer of many years, would have too heavy a remit in future.

J.M. Hogan was appointed in 1952 as Assistant Education Officer in full charge of further education after having had appointments as Inspector of Further Education in Somerset and Birmingham. Alec Clegg pointed out to HMI T.R. Weaver[18] that J.M. Hogan possibly could be the most senior officer in the county who had come up through the further education ranks. It was felt that he knew thoroughly the details and complications of such an appointment 'more than most in Local Government'. In 1955 Alec Clegg and Hogan presented a full Report on Technical Education to the Education Committee. Developments put demands on teaching staff, and Bramley Grange fulfilled one demand. In-service courses were a time-consuming commitment for Hogan. He regarded attendance at these weekends and occasionally mid-week as a major planning commitment in addition to routine work.

One extra task J.M. Hogan regarded as exacting was central to the development of higher technical and vocational education.[19] He was invited by the Department of Education and Science to serve on a working party which would eventually advise the Burnham Committee on staffing, taking into serious consideration the volume and grading of a wide variety and considerable amount of work of various kinds affecting the establishment and grading of staffs of further education institutions. It involved an inclusive review of vocational courses in technology, commerce and art, and an attempt to establish standards of comparability weighing academic, technical and crafts elements. Another invitation which he said was one of the most difficult jobs he had been asked to take over was the Chairmanship of the County Advisory Committee on Art Education.

J.M. Hogan became Deputy to Alec Clegg and R. Eyles took over Further Education and represented the Riding in the Yorkshire Council for Further Education. Hogan continued to be invited informally to attend meetings when his special interests were under discussion.

Towards the end of the life of the West Riding County Council J.M. Hogan summarised a statement of his interests which were indirectly the business of the County Council but which, in his opinion, supplemented the official remit to some advantage. He brought back into the Riding broad experience which gave an extra dimension to the daily round of administration. As Deputy Education Officer he was nominated from time to time to attend a number of ad hoc advisory or negotiating committees set up by the Yorkshire Association of Education Committees. He was also a member of the Executive Committee of the Association of Education Officers and served his year as President. In 1970 the Association of Chief Education Officers and Association of Education Officers merged, and in the autumn of 1970 the Society of Education Officers was established. It was during his year as President that the Association of Education Officers was asked to provide evidence for the Russell Committee[20] on the future of adult education. He also provided evidence for the Report of the Youth Service Development Council on Youth and Community Work in the 1970s.

An important development at the end of World War II was in careers guidance. Pre-war elementary school leavers gained work through the Labour Exchange; grammar schools were interested in those intending to teach or enter other professions, those leaving at sixteen mostly fending for themselves, but generally other opportunities for young people were limited unlike the present time, particularly for the girls. The experiences of the Second World War brought Registration and 'direction of labour'. War-time conditions and emergencies forced into the open some discontinuity in the provision of informal and leisure education for young people uncommitted to the professions. The Board of Education asked local education authorities to set up Youth Committees. The West Riding complied and certain members of the Education Committee met with representatives of several youth organisations. Registration for all young people was the early age of sixteen, and official weight was exerted to some extent to see that most were in a suitable youth group or class. There was a youth group explosion, the authority found it had large numbers to deal with, and standards varied.

It fell to Hogan to integrate youth work with further education and youth employment when he arrived after the war. By this time there was a Youth Committee. He was a member of the Regional Youth Service Advisory Committee. There were six Area Youth Committees served by an Area Youth Officer. The Albermarle Report of 1960 encouraged the professional development of youth workers and the West Riding responded by running courses at Bramley Grange and appointing a Youth Officer.

Hogan's wider interests contributed substantially to the quality of informal educational provision in the Riding. In connection with his Youth Service remit he was a member of a working party of the Council of the Duke of Edinburgh's Award, assisted in producing a report which contributed suggestions about its further development. A similar invitation came from a working party established by the National Association of Youth Clubs.

He was a member of the Council and Grants Committee of King George's Jubilee Trust. He was particularly concerned with applications to carry out experimental work generally in the Youth Service, in particular those youth organisations developing work in social and community services. He considered the Jubilee Trust as a body which was forward-looking in its approaches and well-grounded in its pioneering work.

Hogan was particularly interested in the Outward Bound Trust as a member of the Council and the Management Committee. In addition he was the Chairman of the City Challenge Committee which acted as the Governing Body for City Challenge Courses which were held countrywide. He was also a Director of the Mountain Schools at Eskdale and Ullswater.

His experience was sought by the Outward Bound Trust when educational documents needed interpretation, when such documents could be interpreted in several ways, depending on points of view, official office, association with local education authorities, or the Department of Education and Science. Hogan thought highly of Outward Bound and was sure of the benefit gained by the Authority through this link with expert practice in meticulous training in outdoor pursuits. He also considered the metamorphosis of Bewerley Park from a field studies centre into an expert centre an achievement, and appreciated his contact with Outward Bound staff. He thought they had influenced his strong emphasis on safety pre-cautions throughout the county. In addition to the purchase of Bewerley Park Field Centre near Pateley Bridge, the acquisition of Buckden House, Bingley, was approved by the Education Committee and Department of Education and Science. A former Methodist Guild Holiday Home, it was planned as a second outdoor pursuits centre following the inspection and recommendations of a special Sub-Committee. Purchase was agreed on 24th September 1968. The Policy and Finance Sub-Committee appointed members to the Buckden House Management Committee which met first on 8th August 1969 and finally on 14th March 1974. Buckden House became associated with Bingley Training College until the closure of that college in 1970. In 1974 it was taken over by Bradford Education Committee.

The youth clubs and agencies which were supported by the youth service opened up ideas and opportunities for a wide range of young people. Alec Clegg intimated time and again in his speeches that the widest school interests should be kindled in as many young people as possible and did not like the exclusive concentration on the few who were outstanding in one physical skill. Perhaps from his own experience he condemned the diminishing and occasional personal humiliation of many. He felt that self-control, self-discipline, individual effort in addition to team spirit were attributes to be desired, and sought this end when he taught at St Clement Danes.

At the back of all his work on behalf of the many average young people in school and out of school and beyond, supporting and encouraging, was the wide variety of professional courses at Bramley Grange which became in its turn a focal point, complementing Woolley Hall.

A Community Centre

With the raising of school-leaving age, concerns over problems of the final year and a growing interest in what was termed 'informal education' in the youth clubs, focused attention on older pupils' welfare. New ideas about school buildings were being aired, 'open-plan' became fashionable and ideas for sixth form centres. Suggestions came from the Architects' Branch of the Ministry of Education. The Newsom Committee had suggested an extended and varied school day which took in early evening activities. These would be informal and leisure activities as in youth clubs. Alec Clegg considered a 'community college' to be particularly relevant to the mining areas which would serve the entire age range. The idea was vague, definition imprecise, and a philosophy behind it unstated. It had to work out its aims and objectives as it went along. Some facilities were to be open to the public and the concept of 'community' underlined the fact that the institution was intended for the people living in one locality.

A 'High School and Community Centre' was suggested to serve South Kirby and South Elmsall, to be located at South Kirby / Moorthorpe, where previously a school had been proposed for pupils aged thirteen to eighteen.[21] The Carnegie Trust made £30,000 available, and the extension was named the Carnegie Centre. Minsthorpe High School and Community College opened in February 1969.

After a few years Alec Clegg and those responsible for the Centre reviewed their aims. From the school/centre base it was possible to offer services of education, assistance, guidance and opportunity to people on the basis of human relationships after they have left school, and '. . . to offer a continuing service to the community, related to the needs of people as these present themselves, to serve as *one* of the centres of the community's participation in its own education and recreation, and to offer continuing support and assistance in partnership with social service agencies for those people or groups of people who continue to have particular needs.'

Harrogate Training College [22]

The end of World War II brought a serious state of affairs, in that there was an exceptionally acute shortage of teachers. Many had been lost to war service; fewer people were leaving the training colleges by the early stages of the war and, together with earlier cuts in college admissions which had left a temporary surplus quickly absorbed, the position in 1945 was difficult and exceptional.

The Board of Education faced the problem of fully staffing the schools as quickly as possible to meet the coming emergency at the end of the war. The final plan agreed by a special committee of the Board of Education was to set up around fifty institutions, run by the LEAs and funded by the Government.

The emergency scheme consisted of one working year of forty-eight weeks – that is, the two-year course compressed and minus the long breaks. A full one-third of the time was spent in school. The follow-up was rigorous – two years' supervision which included part-time courses, more reading and written work, and supervision in schools from advisers and head teacher who submitted reports. West Riding County Council inspectors were made responsible for all probationers in their area. In addition, when the institutes of education were established in the universities, there were day, weekend and vacation courses run by their lecturers who, from Leeds and Sheffield universities, also contributed to the in-service work at Woolley Hall. Local technical colleges and colleges of art were also a source of valuable support. Students, on two years' probation, were assigned to one particular member of the advisory/local inspectorate, who were generous in advice and guidance in classroom work.

The Minister of Education agreed to the establishment of emergency training colleges at Harrogate and Wakefield. At a meeting of the Further Education Sub-Committee on 3rd September 1946, the Committee appointed members to a panel to select a principal and staff. At a meeting of the Policy Sub-Committee on 17th June 1947, it was decided that a committee of management would be appropriate for each training college, and the members designated governors. The first committees of management were appointed at a meeting of the Further Education Sub-Committee on 7th October 1947. The first meeting of the Harrogate Training College Governing Sub-Committee was convened on 5th October 1947, and the college opened at the beginning of that term. The Policy and Finance Sub-Committee met on 16th October 1948, when the life of the college was extended to March 1951. The Governing Sub-Committee met for the last time on 25th November 1950.

Harrogate College was residential, taking male students at first. The college at Wakefield had only one year's life, and was a day college taking men and women. Altogether 590 qualified teachers were trained at Harrogate and Wakefield.

CONCLUSION: 'MUCH IN MY MIND'

Sir Alec Clegg became one of the leading chief education officers of his time, but more, in that he carried through mandated reorganisation unique to the immediate post-war period and later during his career, in a particularly individual style. As time went on his comments took on the character of 'sayings', often quoted, but unfortunately also misinterpreted or used out of context.

In exercising a gift for giving the other person space, he himself supplied the essential factor which held inter-relationships in balance and brought about an educational administration greater than the sum of its parts. A practical visionary, he presented to his employers, colleagues, and the wider public, measures to contain the exigencies of his remit but with persistence paid heed to what could be.[1] Not an intellectual, but able to enthuse a considerable range of people.

The terms of his appointment demanded going down many planning avenues in the course of a long, professional career; lectures, talks and publications were consistent in their reiteration of ideas shaped throughout his tenure, again supplying the essential factor which would perhaps make sense of varied prescriptions. Three unifying ideas threaded through his planning, concepts of knowing, becoming, thinking. The source of these would seem to come from interpretation of his experience of family, school, and sharp observation across his professional life; but also from a practical stance in pointing out that studies should be conducted on what could be brought about through action based on sound theory and philosophy rather than 'little researches' where children were used to promote the researcher. Ideas and attitudes could be many and various; that change was inevitable was accepted, but Alec Clegg pointed out that danger lay in going along one path only, a bleak road to dictatorship. One brilliantly illuminated facet of common practice should not render all else negative, so he said he deliberately talked with those with whom he disagreed to learn their mental point of departure or what made them dispute. Assimilated Quaker principles gave the base in valuing the other person. Interpretation of the evidence he collected or had collected for him, plus his accumulated experience of the past through three generations of his family, gave an informed foundation for action on behalf of the children.

These ideas put children at the centre. What have we done, are doing, to individual children? How do they 'know'? 'Logos' is the active principle. How did the young slave boy 'know'? He is told, learns what he is told, goes beyond repetition and 'knows that he knows', demonstrated in how he uses his learnt knowledge. He ceases to imitate, and becomes himself. To get a child to make this personal move, to think for himself, Alec Clegg demonstrated in his own interaction with professionals and the public, and he said is at the heart of teaching. The start is crucial, he emphasised, and put speaking, reading and writing first, from the very first attempts at making the mental link between the sound and the phoneme on paper. The diverse human beings in any class will go in their personal directions, but their common experience is that they have learnt a fundamental principle. The more central the learned idea, the greater will be the applicability to new problems. Then, he thought, for what objective, completion, or perfection, or does the horizon ever recede, and 'process' is therefore as important as 'product' in that it is open-ended. Accepting the concept of a questioning mind, interested in ideas and the world, Alec Clegg put examinations in perspective – staging posts, not termini.

He insisted that how the children learnt to read was central, and the 'Two Rs' were a priority. How the children grew, what they became as adults, would depend on how they built their own knowledge structures. They interacted at three levels, home, peers and school, and they were in school for a brief time compared with interaction between home and environment. Language would be used on levels of abstraction, meaning, and understanding the abstractions of other people. These levels of abstraction would be a concern of the schools' teaching when communicating thought patterns of the subjects. Children's personal impressions would need to be understood when implicit intellectual patterns of the subject had necessarily to be taught. The curriculum is not static: Alec Clegg envisaged a world of increasing technological complexity on the horizon and these core skills would become increasingly important in enabling definition and redefinition of ideas about a difficult world demanding understanding of complex processes. If the groundwork – how to read and interpret – was not well settled in, then those missing out would be permanently intellectually crippled. Cramming facts was not good enough; planning of work to release skill, mentally to organise assimilated material for themselves with independence of mind, with pleasure in the topic itself, would rest on initial groundwork in school, seriously influenced by the background of home and peer group. From this crucial fact, Alec Clegg's concern for the children who were deprived, neglected or maltreated was practical.[2] Their start was shaky, their command of language less sure, only the most strongly motivated would have the resilience and strength of will to persevere.

Alec Clegg recognised the difficulty of the primary task in having the children think clearly. He quoted Whitehead that 'each subject is a facet of a unitary way of life'. There is a 'grammar' of a subject and bridges across subjects. Some children seek facts and others reasons, and reasoning will take a child across subject boundaries. Imaginatively there can be play with an idea from several aspects which could involve a group. Behavioural significance lies in the children's responses. A curriculum of separate subjects could leave space for several angles, not necessarily 'integrated studies'. His brief poem suggested a synthesis of sensation and cognition associated with the arts since his predilection lay in the direction of

language, art, dance and music. At the back of it all was a principle of exactness in expressing perceptions, attention to detail, metaphor and analogy.
The children's writing did not 'happen'. There was careful teaching,[3] and
a relationship with music, movement and painting which gave the children
opportunity to communicate at several levels. The creative process is an
essential part of thinking at the highest level and an exacting exercise. If
only 'loaves' are given, he reiterated, there is overload; much is forgotten
if not parroted or rejected. How much advanced maths, he wondered, does
the average person remember since he does not need that level in everyday
life? Insight, intuition and imagination are of first importance. Learning
could possibly be unproductive where there is no playfulness or divergent
thinking. Together, he added, with precise critical thinking; distinguishing
between technical statement, generalisation and analysing principles. To
know, sense, understand, demonstrate, formulate, record, analyse, select,
is 'pot-filling' – at its best a process of discovery and an activity of the
creative imagination; at its worst, cramming, most of which would be
forgotten.[4]

> 'I would like to put before you one quotation from George Sampson's
> 'English for the English' written well over half a century ago. It is a look
> into the future and had turned out to be only too true. 'Budding psychol-
> ogists will walk the schools and medical students will walk the hospitals
> and children will be as useful to the educationalists as dogs to the vivi-
> sectionist. They will be inoculated with tasks of knowledge and tested for
> reactions, their minds will be calibrated periodically with exactness and
> their abilities reduced to tables and curves. The psychologist will rejoice
> and so will the routine-loving official whose cardiac register leaps up when
> he beholds statistics from on high and the sensitive mind will be docketed
> and disposed of and education comfortably removed from the trouble-
> some world of fantasy'.'

Alec Clegg added:[5]

> 'But there are two kinds of education: the education of the mind by
> imparting facts and teaching skills, and the education of the spirit, and the
> material to be worked on here is the child's loves and hates, his hopes and
> fears, or in other terms his courage, his integrity, his compassion and other
> great human qualities.'

★   ★   ★   ★   ★

Alec Clegg, concerned for all children, asked what has been done to the
individual child, since children are the material cause of the teaching remit?
   Reading and writing gave skills to enjoy a common ground. With
Whitehead, the ground of 'authority of the subject, plus freedom to associate knowledge with the known of other subjects'. He questioned how does

the pupil use history or geography to endorse his own mental ordering and his motivations: a question of drives and values. They deserved more than becoming 'pots with the lid on' or being served the bland offering of 'Nuffield porridge or CSE cornflakes'. In being taught they create their own order, grasp transforming principles to get at quality rather than the false coin of an over-stuffed mind.[6]

He faced the fact, reiterated many times since his day, that the forming power of required common grounding cannot be retained for an exclusive minority, but is the due and right of an entire community. A jigsaw puzzle of plans would not suffice for the future since the need would be for a skilled, intelligent population well beyond the concept of a labour force. In a stratified society where leisure is most pushed on to people who could least cope with it he said:[7]

> 'What I do not accept is that education should be made a weapon of each successive aspiring segment. In my view education should be concerned first and foremost with doing the best for and getting the best out of each individual and only incidentally should it be concerned with the gross national product and material advance.'

He saw ahead. The information explosion of the nineties would have supplied evidence for his stance that we are educating the whole person. The knowledge revolution of the present time with access to literature on the Internet, an effect as far-reaching as the printing press in 1450 when scholars could have a personal library for the first time, means that knowledge is accessible and not exclusive. Alec Clegg in his day wanted children to read and to realise that the store of knowledge *is* accessible, to be used and not just memorised. His questions – What do we know? How do we know? – were central. To rely on the store only, which is 'pot-filling' and not on how it is used, leaves deficiencies open to trivialisation and manipulation by routine-loving officialdom trapped in its turn. 'We are living in an illiterate society in spite of a deal of formalised, complex education.'

★   ★   ★   ★   ★

It followed, therefore, that the first and continuing skill of the teacher would be diagnosis: a professional role from a general review to particular class situations and particular children well beyond the instructional role which was nevertheless in the remit. Alec Clegg did not rule out instruction. Children had to be told since they are ignorant of the existence of what has to be learned. There were, he said, habits of thought to inculcate daily, insights from unconscious processes, re-ordering of ideas and to build on school experiences. This training he said is professional expertise. He continually put forward the creative part played by the arts, a culture of quality and insightfulness which extended well outside the classroom

'. . .within the rigid schedule of course requirements, examination require-ments, examination deadlines, make time for talking' – an ongoing remit which taught the give and take of life-space and social ease in meeting people. Good practice, he insisted, was knowing the reason for the methods used. He desired the children to be independent in thought, use their personal gifts and judgement. Dismay came when he saw successful, highly personal techniques in school turned into universal dogma.

How the curriculum is presented was skilfully conveyed to his audiences through his own experiences in mathematics and physical education. He was influenced through early personal misery and encouraged the planning at Wentworth Woodhouse as well as the advisers. He saw children as volatile human energy fields to be encouraged to live with that sufficient tension that gives a spur to the next step. His experience of the school curriculum at the receiving end came from his grandfather's and father's points of view in addition to his own. His service coincided with height-ened professional interest in educational psychology and philosophy, in the psychology of childhood and adolescence, in group psychology. He sought the definition of 'abilities' and was insightful that the many ways of knowl-edge and experience implied an open-minded attitude towards life-long learning; the process went on. Education should be more than instruction, and open-ended. Those strata of school administration which had grown through expediency should be re-ordered when necessary to the best advantage. The early years as a trained teacher and administrative assist-ant during the second half of World War II and in the immediate peace gave a reservoir of practical experience.

The necessity for diagnosis gave the opportunity again to question. Administrative devices on behalf of the children led Alec Clegg to investi-gate two aspects of planning. The first was a challenge which queried immutability of the IQ. Does it, in fact, vary? If so, by how much and in response to what kind of stimuli? The second challenge logically followed – a criticism of the fixed conclusions of examinations.

He commented on ideas embedded in technology, on the risk of 'quanti-fying', quoting Farish at Cambridge who, in 1792, 'conceived the idea of giving a number to a piece of writing'. What of the criteria? Levels of sensi-tivity? Creativity? Facts? The numbers gave a form, a bias view, too biased? The marking was at a moment in time. What of the communication between writer and marker?

The practical consequences of this questioning were pilot schemes affecting the transfer of pupils at the crucial ages of eleven plus and eight-een plus, when entire future lives could be at stake since at this period educational divisions as well as social strata were rigid. Where a child went at eleven determined his future life, and to a certain extent, which univer-sity a student entered at eighteen. The Thorne Selection Scheme and the Oxbridge Scheme were, during their time, successful, and would seem to support Alec Clegg's criticism of sorting procedures. Attention, he thought, should be given to a 'borderland' rather than having an arbitrary line drawn below an arbitrary, agreed point on a list of marks, which might not be the same point on another list.

At a Woolley Hall course in 1956[8] he said plainly he put the children at the centre:

'How can we best identify the main problem? Whether you regard the educational process as stuffing a pot with knowledge or the releasing of potential in one form or another, the job in both cases is to get the lid off. It's no use holding a kettle under a tap if the lid's on. It's no good starting an engine unless the gears engage the car and set it in motion. It is perfectly possible for a child to spend hundreds of hours on a subject which in retrospect is sterile and arid. I don't myself know one single algebraic equation though I once got 63% in the subject. The problem is how can we, with classes of 40 and teachers of average ability, make a child receptive? If the child is genuinely receptive it would use what it gets, or, if you like it the other way round, it would give out what there is within it.'

Their common experience is that something has been learned, perceived by an individual in his unique way, reflected upon, then knowing he has some inkling how to use the knowledge. Alec Clegg's persistent questions were phrased to cause reflection on different modes of learning, to attempt to move his audiences from their habitual mental set, and in moving outside to imagine other facets of a subject or that one subject could be reflected in several fields of enquiry. In considering the arts as paramount he was involving his adult audiences in a two-way exchange on the nature of communication in full awareness of the intellectual and social complexities of his day and with foreboding as to the future. In talking with sixth forms he engaged young adults in thinking about their 'subjects' as the common factor in wider reading, their subjects being the roots of their authority beyond the level of memory. He implied he wanted them to have the wisdom which comes from knowledge – 'a well-informed person is no better than a well-fed person'.

'There is one final point which to me is of supreme importance. Education is a public service to which all are subjected. It is very, very new. My own grandfather was among the first men ever to be employed in it, and it is, therefore, not yet three generations old. It is now mass produced. We have produced a system of education which is in essence very simple. In order to get on in the world children must learn certain skills, and in order to understand what is going on around them they must know certain facts. The purpose of the school is to teach these skills and impart these facts. You and I don't necessarily believe that this is the whole truth, but it is on this conception that our educational system is based and it is because of the tendency of the human mind to run in channels cut by wheels of its own routine that this system has become rigid and petrified and most difficult to alter. All that we do at 11+ tends to preserve the idea that the acquisition of knowledge and education are one and the same thing, and the same may be said even more truthfully about the General Certificate of Education. We tend to magnify the importance of what we can mark out of ten and overlook what we can't. We produce innumerable books and theories as to how to teach a child to read, but there is very little published on how to make him *want* to read. It is as if we are put before a great organ with three keyboards and a full range of stops and all we do is play a five-finger exercise using one stop labelled 'examinations'. Yet the folly of identifying knowledge with education has been recognised by all educationists from Plato onwards. I once heard Lord Samuel say that learning is the enemy of initiative. Ruskin said, 'the spirit needs several sorts of good, of which knowledge is only one'. 'All the learning in the world is not judgement' said Goethe. Of science, Henri Poincaré, the mathematician, once said 'Science is built up of facts as a house is built up of stones, but an accumulation of facts is no more science than a heap of stones is a house'.'

The use children make of what they retain from their being taught is the great matter, that they are genuinely receptive and make something of the ideas an informed mind produces – the sign and symbols of the subject and their relations is a world of ideas *through childish eyes.* Supporting this stance again was his emphasis on exactness, and precision in statement – he was looking at the process rather than the result although he enjoyed children's productions in writing and art. He had faith in ordinary children and therefore a logical reaction against the difficulties set up for some and worked for their condition to be improved. He became an expert on deprivation, and recognised solutions were difficult. The key question was how much support to give and what kind of action would balance any deficiency or disaster in social conditions. He accepted that feeling and beauty come only when basic physical needs for living had been met. The children's need culturally, he pointed out, is reading, writing, speaking, to express thought, that is, to cope with the 'groundwork'. The 'basics' are the skills, the necessary tools of lettering and numbering, (and now the computer), in order to express the groundwork. The question that Alec Clegg posed was how the *groundwork* in school subjects was to be presented, and enquired into different methods of teaching these. The basic skills, he said, of letters and number should be taught by any method which proved suitable for the children, to ensure they were equipped. They need the taught skills of their letters and numbers which will give meaning to the configurations and patterns of the different school subjects which is their grounding. He emphasised the central role of aesthetic experience as a force which moves the child to use his reading and writing to effect. He seriously believed that more children than the top 20% could be brought into a range of complex experiences in some appreciation of art, music, literature, movement, drama, simply to add quality to their lives. He was aware that what he wanted for the children would not necessarily give them

material wealth but his belief was firm that average people *could* achieve,
'all-rounders' who would balance 'the specialists'.⁹

> 'The success of an educational system may perhaps be measured by the
> security and self-confidence of growing children and their ability to face
> normal situations with confidence.'

> 'The variety of school situations around the country is to be welcomed –
> uniformity would be viewed with suspicion and distaste.'

Education was seen to reach out, 'from pre-school play-group to university of the air and a range of ancillary services'.

The central aim for quality was, consequently, not a didactically stated
belief in progress as material advancement, but in personal growth. Vivid
presentation of past and present school procedures through accounts of his
grandfather's, father's and aunts' teaching demonstrate ideas of gradual
change, the past encapsulated in the present, central ideas transformed
across a progression of techniques; in social conventions as well as working
institutions, which society used to balance tradition and innovation. An
accusation of 'progressive' gimmickry was unfounded. He wished thought
to be given to tasks, adjustment could balance innovation, and the debate
on innovation/preservation taken seriously. Again he raised questions: of
innovation, grading or degrading, attaining or losing, humanistic advance
or diminishing returns, the professional who works with colleagues, or the
amateur who uses ideas for his hobby. The teachers would be encouraging
discrimination. It was necessary to go into new situations not with eyes
closed ('could not play the tune') but to prove questions. What is given?
What is left behind, or taken away? How is the idea applied? Problems raise
more problems and he thought professional methods were on the whole a
co-operative effort which gave one individual the 'eureka' moment:
surprise favours a prepared mind, quoting Whitehead. The application,
however, depends on the personal skill of the individual teacher.

He therefore affirmed the key importance of teachers. As Chief
Education Officer this was the point where he started: that the children
were foremost and teachers in school one crucial factor. Education was
part of the cultural development of groups, and at the turning point of the
immediate post-war period, education was part of unavoidable social
reconstruction. Education was part of the formative process of an educative
society on the move.

He searched for a science of teaching, not gimmickry, and said he was
'taking *teaching* seriously'. This starting point took him into schools to see
what was actually being done, in a spirit of inquiry. What were they doing?
How were the problems of an entire range assessed – from clever to
retarded, from social advantage to social deprivation? Over-indulgence in
research findings could lead to rejection of useful, practical measures. A
'fresh approach' can be from a variety of starting points and open new

dimensions. Teaching in context, he found, was not linear from 'traditional' to 'experimental', but in most schools a mixture of viewpoints and
appropriate methods, according to situations – good practice is an end in
itself. An innovation could be far-reaching and complex, or suited to only
one situation. Methods in one school might not be useful in another. Social
and personal attitudes are involved, and any method needs the full and
informed co-operation of concerned people. He accepted the necessity to
compromise but always affirmed a civilising programme for schools and he
maintained many times that part of his remit was to give average children
their English cultural inheritance. Radical social changes ahead in work
and leisure made more urgent the effort in mental discernment each had
to make for himself. The children were there to be taught. Out of this belief
arose his concern for the lost. There is no doubt that, as the Chief
Education Officer, the broad vista of humanity in a large Authority gave
him pause for thought. He could have stayed behind a barricade of administrative parlance, a collector of statistics, children marks on a graph.
Instead, without any sentimentality, he gave a commitment to the northern
children.

The groundwork for Aiglon would be 'mastery of fundamental ideas'.
Alec Clegg used the Socratic method in the light of his own schooling and
training, and set questions time and again which obliged his audiences to
seek answers. There was lively debate, listeners were invited to seek their
own solutions, putting in effort applicable to their condition and leaving
the discussion open-ended. One implied question repeatedly presented to
his listeners – how do we prepare such groundwork that every child has a
substantial, supportive foundation? Life is not static, what source of
renewal for mind and spirit can we provide? How to have them continue
thinking flexibly, creatively? He insisted on groundwork, the use of sufficient structure to aid memory, when and what to leave behind, judge when
'advanced' becomes 'elementary', irrelevant or dated. His skill lay in the
ability to put educational ideas over in both professional and layman's
language without being too simplistic, talking down, or patronising. There
was debate, not verbal confrontation. His audiences were not springboards
for self display. The speech given to the International Reading Association
Conference at New Orleans in 1974[10] immediately on retirement
condenses his philosophy of education through his vision of children and
his ideas about teaching – 'my obsession about teaching'.

The classroom needed an innate order, structure but not rigidity,
direction accompanied by reflection and questioning which would accommodate change and rearrangement. The pattern of working would be
peculiar to the individual teacher, but 'better an old-fashioned teacher than
one who thinks he is modern because he has changed the labels'. A few
necessary common goals, but schemes, places, lessons were impossible to
duplicate for a mass market. The romantic point of view of children-in-
nature is distinctly an adult stance and the theory which, in stressing to the
extreme the individuality of each child to learn in his own way which slides

into anti-social do-as-you-please is doing that child a disservice. 'Modern' methods, he complained towards the end of his time, had been trivialised or misapplied. He said change would be inevitable and foresaw an extreme reaction towards demands of the market place which began with the Industrial Revolution when craftsmen became 'hands', 'skills' for the workers, and 'education' for the selected few. Selection and approval should be in the interests of the community and the individual. In making very young children a priority he was not sentimentalising infancy. He recognised the importance of primary school teaching and his efforts in the direction of middle schools came from genuine respect for the teaching he found for himself, whether innovative or orthodox. He acknowledged that methods could not be lifted or applied indiscriminately and was aware of the brief life of an idea helped on its way by uncritical publicity. The collection of films, tapes, children's art, at Bretton Hall College is a testimony to heads and staffs and the support of the Director and County Advisers. He sought quality in the generalist as well as the specialist, arguing that one balanced the other and that the generalist was a most necessary member of the public.

Alec Clegg was faced with a wide variety of schools and inevitable comprehensivisation. He attempted a Herculean task when he envisaged all human life as an educative society since he included influences of family life, social structure, workplace, and leisure interests. The wide range of topics covered in his speeches and papers indicate the stimulation and fascination which the breadth of culture and social class of his hearers had for him. From the comfort of a close, middle-class family he had feeling for children brought up in quite different circumstances. He retained a strong link with Bootham School[11] as a Governor until his death. The Quaker concept of responsibility was plain and evidenced in a concern for average teachers in ordinary schools demonstrated by his consistent visiting across twenty-seven years. As one senior clerk said, 'He's slipped t'leash'. Many times. At the same time, with dispassionate clarity he saw that reorganisation, realignment of the curriculum would be ahead – he hoped with vision, understanding, and margins for manoeuvre.

A tribute paid at the opening of the Sir Alec Clegg Library, Bretton Hall College, was that he 'was noted for firmness of purpose mixed with informality and approachability'. A professional, using theory to support practice, driven and visionary yet detached, at the same time a skilled politician used to the cut and thrust of debate, despairing on occasions, but falling back on Socratic questioning, goading his hearers to rethink entrenched attitudes. He wished for quality in daily life. Emphatic on the 'fallacies of the IQ', with Viscount Hilton, he aimed for 'a wider appreciation more than a single skill'.[12]

*   *   *   *   *

Alec Clegg's terms of reference were broad. He took over a large region with a heterogenous population contained in distinctive historical, geographical, social and ideological backgrounds within which context the schools' preoccupations, anxieties and terms of reference were set.

This remit carried him well outside the accepted stereotype of the administrator in an ivory tower substituting paperwork for the real world. He went out to see for himself, to judge for himself the nature of the schools and schoolchildren, teachers and parents in, for him, a new part of the country. With practical experience behind him, in a short time it was possible to think broadly of educational demands from 'higher' to 'special needs'. Fluid, complex, sometimes ambiguous situations would be handled from a still centre, a definite philosophy.

This philosophy was supported by a lively sense of history reflected through events which had directly affected his family. He was aware of immediate incidents which had their source in past social change and from records of family members which precluded any impersonal, chronological account of bare facts. This and that had happened to known people at such a time, and his listeners tacitly appreciated the historical context. He entered a situation which still held vestiges of policy and social attitudes from the nineteenth century which had set down the elementary system. Political, religious and educational controversies had contributed to involved relationships, and the first Directive from both Authority and the Government was to carry out a post-war Development Plan. Many consultations and deputations resulted.

The Taunton Commission of 1868 had assisted the grammar schools, but elementary education remained the fate of the greater part of the population and was administered by local clerks later designated divisional education officers. Alec Clegg himself commented at the time when an adviser for further education was a point at issue, on the evident high ability of early students and local government officers, many of whom at a later date would have been undoubtedly at grammar school and in university. These people had been grounded when the higher grade schools were blocked in their development towards secondary level. The 1902 Act gave the public secondary grammar schools of the type of which Samuel Clegg was Headmaster; the 1918 Act followed, establishing more secondary grammar schools, and the 1944 Act gave secondary education to all children.

It was at this point in educational development that Alec Clegg entered the education service and several years later when appointed to the West Riding almost immediately was given charge of the County's education, with the local social and psychological background past legislation had produced, but, in addition, with those euphoric hopes and ambitions latent in the immediate post-war climate. There were high expectations. He took over elementary schools (eleven to fourteen age group), central schools, technical schools, secondary schools and grammar schools, a training college; also links with public and independent schools and two universities. There were also traces of the English tradition of care for young people by landowners, for example, Miss Pilkington's school, and three schools established by the Milnes Gaskell family. In this ambience universal elementary education gave priority to moral standards and 'keeping one's place'. The 1944 Act established a three-tier system based on IQ and tests. In speeches and papers Alec Clegg made clear that all children were the accepted responsibility. The size of the West Riding gave scope and a rare opportunity.

He worked, as a consequence, with his committees, to put the children's welfare before them in careful presentation of facts; listened to local inspectors, advisers, teachers; gave time to national committees, studied educational systems abroad; in all for the sake of pooled experience and information which would add value to the schools in his charge. He was the channel through which techniques, new knowledge, tried ways, passed. In taking this stance he gathered around him at the peak of his service a group of colleagues of high calibre and breadth of skill. In the office there was impatience of dead routine but attention to necessary detail: he streamlined his committee work and delegated to colleagues to give experience and to give to staff meetings a common base of informed comment which added to the value of their educational debate. The vast store of information which accumulated contributed to social concern well beyond political parties.

Alec Clegg's personal writing makes clear his decisive point of view towards the education of young people which gave firm ground from which he could carry through committee plans. He brought to the post a lively awareness that the paperwork masked the human aspect of his charge. The post of Director of Education had grown from 1889 to a position of some authority. Alec Clegg had breadth of view and discernment which tempered any romanticism with hard-headed acceptance of the immediate situation. 'I give the facts and advice . . . let them decide.' He was the servant of his local authority, within that remit there was wide scope. He looked at what was, what could be, and accomplished much. His legacy, a liberal view of education in a growing technological age, remains.

In 1947, standing at that point in time, looking back, he could review the slow and tortuous process by which a public system of education had been built. At the end of the Second World War there was a deep wish for personal space, a great deal of hope and some optimism for things to come. It was not nostalgia, an ache for 'good old days', an ache for an England that never was which ran counter to some of his accumulated evidence. He saw some failures of accountability, the utter waste of lively minds, the grind of 'basics' which were neither 'foundation' nor 'groundwork', but routines to provide work-hands and so many Mr Pooters, the learning-by-rote of which ninety per cent was immediately lost, the 'drills' which deadened thinking. He was aware of the paradox of stability only through change, and was afraid of reaction, not change, which would harden.

Alec Clegg was acutely aware of tensions caused by social class and educational disparity: from the middle-class Taunton Report which left town endowments with the reformed grammar schools, leaving later 1902 and 1918 foundations with few civic scholarships, to the social concerns of the Crowther and Newsom Reports. He identified the marginalised, the visionaries, the talented. Insulated as far as family background, and detached to that extent, the discovery from membership of the Crowther and Newsom committees that things could be otherwise was startling. A naturally born observer from his place in the family and from professional appointments which set him apart, the watcher became committed.

Educational problems Alec Clegg found locally reflected the wider problems of a modern state which had lived through World War I, a twenty years' truce, and World War II. The immediate post-war period's problem was the breadth of provision and re-planning required. In the forefront of change after World War II were new world-wide societies in their incipient stages of growth towards multi-racialism with a diversity of religious and ethical values. There were problems of practical compassionate help and rehabilitation and also problems of comparison with other countries' plans. Alec Clegg's reports to his committee towards the end of his career following visits to Canada, the United States of America and Australia disclosed differences as well as similarities. He had welcomed exchanges with France and Germany and there was consideration of one with Russia. He set on one side technical problems of administration, economics and politics in his insistence on again getting at the active principle, this time behind the variety of signs and symbols peculiar to the people of different countries, that is, a semantic and cultural interpretation of aspects of learning since these fundamental qualities leach through every level of occupation and profession. He was interested in the lives of the people and recognised that many countries were at a turning point.

He took the West Riding appointment at a crucial point in English educational history. Times of change and expansion have been from 1868 to 1899; the 1940s and 1950s which were the early part of his remit and again in the 1990s. Alec Clegg was sufficiently far-seeing to warn seriously that all children must be catered for. He had a lively grasp of educational history as it affected the individual, and of administration. His grandfather, father and he himself worked through an administrative arrangement which moved from promoted clerks to professionally qualified men. By the time he arrived in the West Riding he had experienced the pervasive atmosphere of anticipated post-war reconstruction. There was determination in a new educational realism in the face of acceptance of loss, responsibility for those returning who had had their immediate pre-war education blocked at eighteen, and at twenty-eight had to be accommodated again into the mainstream of civilian life, and, crucially, to enhance the education of a generation of children taught under wartime shortages. He did not suggest putting the clock back but was alert to open-ended solutions. Reform and rehabilitation should leave room for advance. Far-sighted enough to see that the second half of the twentieth century would move towards a vastly different life from that of the first half, he was realist enough to recognise that the Development Plan devised by the Government would only be the beginning. His protest was that the

Authority was given too little time to plan with some foresight and cited Authorities which refused to meet the deadline. He pointed in his talks and lectures, however, at this unique time, to the desire for an educative society which would be self-determining.

He was aware of the deeper significance of reform. In several papers he traced the course of educational aims and theories, pointed out that decisions had been made politically. This, he said, he did not dispute, since the people decided. Reform would have to be more than false egalitarianism, 'opportunity for all' meant more than levelling down to drab mediocrity. Practically he was faced with a society which is neither homogeneous nor a conurbation. Apart from the unique, acute post-war question of absorbing people returning to civilian life, the aims have a modern ring.

He was almost immediately presented with the task of implementing the 1946 Development Plan – a requirement of Government. Little time had been given. He followed a tradition of service to education in the Riding of people of the calibre of A.H.D. Acland (who had himself produced a plan for secondary education for the Riding at the turn of the century similar to his plan for Wales), and C.G.L. Milnes Gaskell of Thornes House, the first long-serving Chairman of the West Riding County Council who had gained much autonomy for the county using his experience as a barrister. Alec Clegg grew dispirited when 'the idealism and the hopes of the immediate post-war years were treated with cynicism as time went on'.

Alec Clegg therefore came into the West Riding at a turning point in its educational growth. It was a challenge and his good fortune, since much had to be tidied following the war. Final restrictions were not lifted until 1952. The situation had to be assessed, short-term action taken and long-term goals identified. In the light of the Development Plan Alec Clegg had a few months to get acquainted with a large county, and, with the Birmingham and Worcestershire influence new in his mind, was alert to many inhibiting situations which the children could suffer. The work he gave himself was demanding. He became, as time went on, expert on deprivation and delinquency, the needs of the less able, the 'second quartile' and the able blocked by circumstance. He began with the infant schools which he said were the most vulnerable and at the same time most crucial since theirs was the decisive stage in the children's lives when a mental disposition was set. His use of the 'loaves and hyacinths' analogy was not pseudo-Victorian sentimentality. In taking a quotation which would catch attention he was implying that outer and inner worlds should be in balance: the intellect, which deals with outer reality alone, imposes and does not liberate the imagination. Learning to read was not just a few words at the beginning, then added words, but many new ones all at once, all presenting a new idea. Talking, the children become fluent, even making their own words. Imagination plays on the child's reasoning and reasoning plays on their imagining, so not total learning by rote, but a balance. Hence his strong insistence on the importance of home and necessary enrichment in school. His ideas were not always fashionable, sometimes misinterpreted from misappropriated or misapplied vocabulary, but his gift in expressing difficult concepts in plain language caught the attention of his hearers and caused discussion. He asked his hearers to think about what they were doing. He spoke very plainly, and as well as misinterpretation suffered some excessive over-praise; but in perspective, reduced the burden of unproductive routine.

Evaluation of teaching method across the field of education, from infant to adviser, to college and university, always in relation to the schools. This led to evaluation of different types of leadership in schools and in administration. He discussed the role of advisers and inspectors. A detached observer, he looked at West Riding people with interest, at their intergroup behaviour in a large region where social distinctions were an intricate weave of overlapping related parts. A second result coming from the interest in teaching method was the move to make centres of excellence in training, and the colleges were the result of careful thought and received professional advice.

He worked for change in educational terms, and looked at humane and scientific points of view which would support democratic progress. From his first junior appointment in a situation where rules were interpreted literally he moved to an interpretation of administration as service to the community. Practically this implied contact with all sections in the education department including the physical context of education. Care of schools and upkeep of buildings was as important as architects' planning. The art advisers were brought in to pay attention to the quality and design of furnishings as well as schools' decoration. Caretaking was regarded as a major contribution to the atmosphere of a school.

Alec Clegg chose to look at the contemporary classroom at work, at the human beings, children and adults, and did not commit to one path in philosophy, psychology or politics, but selected theory which would increase discernment. That there must be order and system was recognised, but not at the expense of the schools' integrity. At the same time he did not prescribe in detail to twenty highly idiosyncratic Divisions plus Part III Authorities, but paid attention to balance – centrally and locally. He was obliged to look at unfinished business, differentiation, diversity of aspiration, perspectives, and forward planning. A realist, he accepted reality and recognised social barriers and life spaces thus affected, so deplored rigidity in outlook and noted the effect of group influence and decisions on individuals. Through Alec Clegg's writing runs the perception of things as they were in his time, but also the vision of what could be. He was subtly hard on his audiences and strove to make them think for themselves. Plain expression disguised scholarship.

He had moved forward from an inconsequential rather than careless boyhood through detached junior administrator to committed purpose in later years. The language is plain, forceful, without hyperbole, but with neat irony at times. In discussing examples of didactic teaching of grammar

and isolated exercises expected of very young children, he then used his
own remark on 'illocutionary'[13] statements, neatly enclosing his argument
in such a statement – no doubt with quiet amusement – and also saw to it
that there was a message for Aiglon in the second part of his sentences.

Apparently simple prose marked central principles. His heroes were
Thring and Charles Hoole.[14] There was plain dislike of sham, of a ploy
passing as innovation. He publicly admitted in one lecture that 'universal'
education had produced one response – towards cheap values, false hearti-
ness, poor speech which replaced local idiom. To give all schools what most
public schools and most grammar schools (these last he said 'the finest
education in the first half of the century') had to offer would, he said, at
the practical level imply a very long, full, school day, and the result would
not come about overnight.

The central argument in his writing reflected ideas of equality, morality
and individual autonomy. He visited abroad and sought a practical application of educational philosophy in action in the United States of America,
Canada and Australia. He hoped for understanding of other cultures and
sought a careful balance which gives unity in diversity and seemed to return
to England confirmed in the British way. His wide remit enabled him to
disseminate knowledge of the schools to a large audience. He lectured to all
levels, professional, social, and the general public, with clarity, balance and
economy. Difficult ideas and issues were propounded in plain, unequivocal language, illustrated with apt quotations.

There was also appreciation of the span of history, not as a historian,
but as a member of an extended family. He noted significant detailed historical events in the history of education in relation to their influence on
his immediate forebears. It was the unpretentious ephemera of family classroom experience, evoking memories, which gave substance to ideas on a
liberal education in a technological age. He encompassed a broad sweep
of nineteenth and early twentieth-century events using to good account
telling details pertinent to the point he wished to make – pertinent references rather than bland generality. Alec Clegg's personal world was rich:
home, a range of teaching experience to draw upon from an extended
family, friends and acquaintances across the educational spectrum. He
turned all advice into his own reality. He deplored the diminishing returns
of gifted teaching reduced to trendiness and was dismayed by the lack of
reading and writing competence when he found it. His appreciation of style
and spontaneity was vividly demonstrated in 'The Excitement of Writing'
but fully grasped the skill of the teachers behind the published books of
children's work.

Many papers concerning the less fortunately placed children reveal
compassion for and recognition of the ills and cross accidents one part of
the community suffers. 'Crossed with Adversity' was the product of a
lengthy, personal investigation into the social conditions of some families.
Privacy and confidentiality were completely respected. At a less tragic level,
where the liberal emphasis on quality in cultural life was blocked by those

groups whose social mores presented an inescapable structure that could not take on board a concept of individual difference, he understood how group weight could have also a far-reaching inhibiting effect. A group's strong egalitarian predilection boded ill for the odd man out who desired a different life. This recognised situation brought about the Oxbridge experiment. Alec Clegg was accurate in his survey of retardation when he presented to unbelieving educationists the thought that some pupils were held back by factors other than a low I.Q.

Practical coaching of games as well as teaching French, plus his own first humiliating experience of PE, gave feeling for the average pupil, and the 'second quartile'. First administrative appointments gave the shock that human beings could be marks on a graph, or that allocation to school depended on the arbitrary drawing of a tidy line which could affect a child's entire future. The warmth of the Worcestershire experience gave some insight into a different attitude of mind.

Through his writing and the accumulation of recorded experience there are intimations of early influences. The recurrent use of the word 'concern' as implied in Quaker philosophy – responsibility, solicitude rather than disquiet, heedfulness which was not busybodying. Quaker emphasis on the value of the person, the human being, brought ease of meeting people, king or coalman, with equal courtesy, not Jack's-as-good-as-his-master, but allowing the other his space. There is no better defence than elaborate courtesy. What is apparent in his papers is that training and a classical education plus the discipline of two degrees gave intellectual breadth as experience grew. What is clear is his belief that those who have received most have duties and responsibilities. He was referred to by a CEO colleague as 'the conscience of their association'. Alec Clegg warned seriously of the consequences of neglecting the inveterate losers. Planning for the community should be recognised as common sense. His training at Borough Road College gave him a philosophy of education which was realism shot through with idealism, but gave him the firm conviction of the value of training.

What he brought to the post were the roots of beliefs from family, friends, school, university, to support that training. What Alec Clegg found could have been dealt with from a bureaucratic position. Across his life there were critical moments. Being the only boy, plus the critical place in the family as the only boy and the youngest member, would give him an observant eye, in addition to being left to his own devices to the extent that Edwardian children were left. Perhaps it was recollection of his early cheerful inconsequence that led him to say in later years 'Never write off a cynical student, something they need or do unexpectedly leads into new insights'. The incident of the Christmas rose and later an encounter with the PE instructor were clearly two early moments when he would learn how actions affect others. A letter to his father in 1921 shows anxiety to do what he could.

The West Riding benefited from self-containment grounded in family values and a Quaker schooling. Bootham days were influential in that

Quaker influence on patterns of thought and conduct implied responsibility towards people as an unquestionable duty. A classical curriculum alongside ideas of service and the value of the other person evinced spoken 'concern' for the needs of West Riding children. His training at Borough Road is reflected in an ongoing exposition of difficult philosophical concepts in plain language – a formidable background used to effect and carried lightly. A child of his upbringing and period, with a classical education, and training in the liberal philosophical educators, he had the good fortune to find himself early in his career in an administration that was compatible in that it was possible to aim at general cultural interests as part of its schools' remit during the immediate post-war period of reconstruction. Together, the Birmingham and Worcestershire experiences were two positive critical contributive times.

The centre of a wide circle of friends, colleagues and professional acquaintances in the field of education, he was sufficiently sure of himself that he could give immediate staff that margin which ensured a return through individual skills, and at school level leave room for a variety of teaching methods. There was a common appreciation of ranging ideas and differences of opinion as well as agreement. It is said that a chief is as good as his staff; occasionally the man, colleagues and occasion come together for a brief period. It is in the nature of things to change, but in Alec Clegg's thirty years all aspects of the educational remit were touched upon and a mark left.

Awareness of ways of knowing is implied in the use of 'loaves and hyacinths' analogy, of insightfulness which cannot be quantified but is essential for mental health in a climate of material expectation. He included knowledge of persons, and for some a religious sense would underpin patterns of thought. Other patterns of thought would be presented, but if standards were not implicit, then something in their place would be learned outside the home. That a good standard should be in place underpinned his concern for the children whose home background was deficient or deprived. The interpretation of a moral and ethical sense in such cases then fell heavily on the schools. It was not a religious critical point but a belief in the centrality ethic – children do not come particularly trailing clouds of glory but are small people containing much in embryo and learning at critical moments responsibility for themselves and acceptance of other people. They could not be left to themselves.

He balanced moral purpose with a strong attention towards art, music and reading, the pleasure that these subjects could give and the perspectives that they could accommodate. He let his writing convey his beliefs implicitly in his argument and so ensured the message was taken: the apparently simple approach is many-layered. If the tasks were daunting, determination came through – his concern for the quality of exactness and the level of understanding, in their turn a consequence of his training in language which would give him appreciation of interpretation and translation – to convey and encourage the difficult wrestle with words. The training in language studies would give an illuminating vision of language acquisition from cradle to adulthood; from childhood implicit knowledge (appreciation of the excitement of writing) to the point when revision and rewriting occurs (clear in the older children's work and in later practice using discourse across the curriculum). He felt that this skill was the need and due of all children in all walks of life, to be at ease in their speaking, reading and writing, and was sincere in his conviction that examinations could never quantify some internalised qualities.

What Alec Clegg brought to the job also was an ability to give space to colleagues and as far as possible make use of the talents of all he encountered. Much of what he gathered together was the result of team-work which was acknowledged. The size of the West Riding precluded one person planning all aspects in educational administration. Skilled in acquiring people to whom some aspects of administration could be assigned, he had colleagues deputise on committees and give reports. Alec Clegg regularly attended two – the Education Committee, and the Policy and Finance Sub-Committee. He used data to share a planned vision of educational progress to get at the meaning behind the events. Interpretation of reports as well as the mass of local and central literature which arrived weekly was shared with professional colleagues. There is evidence of consultation as notes on papers disclose. There was questioning to gain perspectives and margins for discussion, yet a personal voice came through in the nature of his questions and apparent waywardness of definitions: colleagues were provoked to respond, and he lifted apparent orders or diktat beyond the plane of flat demands. Major values were consistently identified beyond politics or ephemera. The prevailing social climate was put in place at the same time demonstrating the irony present in freedom of action which neatly binds, when the apparent removal of boundaries masks insidious control. He identified heavy social pressures on children and how their personal culture was controlled, and reminded his colleagues that they had in total an overview of the county and could identify what needed attention as no other group could. He put them in Aiglon's shoes, his imagined human being who must learn to fly that is, asked for insights, continual reflection, alternative perspectives, questioned how 'liberating' were some points of view when 'monitoring' resulted in prescription and the stifling of initiative. Both sides were fortunate in the other, and one early group was sufficiently together in post before moving on began, to make a foundation which persisted through development until 1974, when what was about to be destroyed was realised.[15]

References and Bibliography

The main sources for this book are found in the personal papers of Sir Alec Clegg, in the National Arts Education Archive at Bretton Hall College of the University of Leeds; the Brotherton Library, Special Collections Section, A.B. Clegg papers; and the West Yorkshire Archive Service Headquarters, Wakefield, A.B. Clegg papers. I am sincerely indebted to Lady Clegg for permission to quote extensively. Some authoritative background texts have been put in to attest to the statutory context in which local government for education was conducted. A silent message of continuity and change is presented in lists of committee papers, reports, and Acts of Parliament. Sir Alec Clegg's papers reflect the local impact. Earlier manuscripts and publications concerning Sir Alec Clegg have taken a definite approach to his work. This book attempts to trace, through his own words, the reflection of his training and experience translated into a practical philosophy of education and the workable interpretation of this as far as possible in the light of his remit. References are counterpoint to the text, numbered for each part, and central legislation is noted where that effectively set parameters, but which inevitably received a local, idiosyncratic response.

All references AC/PL/. . ., AC/BK/. . ., refer to the National Arts Education Archive at Bretton Hall College of the University of Leeds.

References

INTRODUCTION

1   AC/PL/410 'Topics for Aiglon.' Undated notes.
     Also AC/PL/519 'A Cultural Democracy', Claire Brown.
2   WYAS A.B. Clegg and other educational papers, A398.
     The West Riding Development Plan 1947, Box 45.
3   Norwood Committee on Examinations and Curriculum 1941–1943.
     PRO ED/12/478–480; ED 138/16; ED 136/107.
4   Hadow Report, 1926: 'The Education of the Adolescent'. PRO ED/97; ED/10/47; ED/24/1265.
5   Spens Report: 'To report on secondary schools other than elementary schools with particular regard to the education of pupils who do not remain at school after the age of 16.'
6   WYAS A.B. Clegg papers, Box 15.
7   Spens Report: pp. 359, 352, 372, 373 & 374.

8   AC/PL/557 'Notes on a few things which concern me.' No date.
9   WYAS The West Riding Development Plan, 1947, Box 45.
10   AC/PL/29 Address to Headmasters of Division XIII, IAHM, Leeds 1947.
11   AC/PL/262 'The Newsom Report and its aftermath.' Talk at the North of England Education Conference at Liverpool, 1968.
12   AC/PL/235 'What comprehensive schools cannot do.' Talk at Derby Local Education Authority course, Buxton, 1966.
13   With B.E. Megson, 'Children in Distress,' (1968/1973, London, Penguin) p.75.
14   Circular 10/65 Direction towards comprehensivisation. Raising of the school leaving age announced in 1964.
15   AC/PL/12 'What it means to me: education.'
16   AC/PL/559 'Note of a conversation held with a distinguished educationist.'
17   AC/PL/557 'A few things which concern me.'
18   AC/PL/236 'Formation of character through education.' Talk at Charlotte Mason College.
19   AC/PL/410 'Topics for Aiglon.' Undated notes.

Introduction: Additional Papers

The Brotherton Library, the University of Leeds, Special Collections Section, Index MS731. WRCC. A.B. Clegg papers.

Box 07   First World War and Post First World War Reconstruction.
Box 41   Hadow Reorganisation, 1926–1939.
Box 44   Post Second World War Reconstruction.
Box 45   The Development Plan.
Box 48   Proposed new secondary schools, 1902–1939.
Box 54   Post-war Education, memos; Index to Post-war Education Minutes.
Box 55   Copies of Area Surveys, Meetings of Deputations re Development Plan.
Box 57   Secondary Education, 1902–1939.
Boxes 17, 18, 19 & 20:
          Secondary Education, 1944 to March 1974.

National Arts Education Archive, Bretton Hall College of the University of Leeds, Sir Alec Clegg papers.

AC/PL/22   Talk to Headmasters of Grammar Schools.
AC/PL/29   The West Riding Development Plan, 1947.

West Yorkshire Archive Service Headquarters, Wakefield, A.B. Clegg papers, A398.

Box 13   1948 file re Multi-lateralism.
Box 15   1946–1959 Educational Development – The Future Development in Secondary Schools.

Box 16   1961 & 1974 Comprehensive Schools Scheme.
Box 20   Secondary Curriculum Development.
Box 3   The British Way and Purpose. Booklet, 1963.
Box 35   The Boundary Commission, 1965.

CHAPTER ONE

1   The Crowther Report: 'Education 15–18'. PRO ED146/29–44.
2   The Beloe Report: 'Secondary School Examinations other than GCE'. PRO ED147/303–313.
3   The Robbins Report on Higher Education. PRO ED46/945–949; D116; ED117; ED118; HC 1962–3 xi–xix.
4   The Newsom Report: '13–16'. PRO ED146/45–63.
5   AC/PL/121 'Selection at 11+.' Talk given in Australia, 1975.
6   AC/PL/87 'The Thorne Shadow Scheme.' Talk given at a National Union of Teachers Council Meeting at the Museum, Leeds, 1955.
7   AC/PL/131 'Exams at Secondary School.' Talk given to Headmasters of the Skipton area schools.
8   AC/PL/108 Speech Day, Ilkley Grammar School.
9   AC/PL/91 Speech Day, Prince Henry's Grammar School, Otley.
10   Continued theme at Ilkley and Otley Grammar School Speech Days.
11   List of relevant papers at end of Chapter.
     Results – Oxford: 1 First, 28 Seconds, 4 Thirds.
               Cambridge: 1 First, 9 Upper Seconds, 12 Lower Seconds, 5 Thirds.
               Over the period, 1 failure and 1 withdrawal.
12   AC/PL/174 'Education and the Working Class.' BBC Third Programme.
13   The Franks Committee. Written evidence, Part XI, p.27, memo to Policy and Finance Committee, March 1970.
14   AC/PL/122 'Filling Pots and Lighting Fires.' Talk given in Australia.
15   AC/PL/240 'The Raising of the School Leaving Age.' Annual Conference of the Conservative and Unionist Teachers' Association, London, 1966.
16   Annual Conference of South East Lindsey Schools, Horncastle, 1964.
17   AC/PL/210 An Open Meeting of the National Froebel Foundation at the College of Preceptors, London. 'What is the Newsom child like? What is his home and his school like?'
18   See 15 above.
19   AC/PL/210 'Half Our Future.' Open Meeting of the National Froebel Foundation at the College of Preceptors, London.
20   AC/PL/44 Course for Teachers of Backward Children, Grantley Hall.
21   AC/PL/204 'The Less Able.' Ackworth School, 1964.
22   AC/PL/291 Talk to Staff of Delamere Forest School, 1971.
23   AC/PL/207 'Secondary Eduction: Average and Below Average Pupils.' Institute of Youth Employment Officers Annual Conference, 1964.
24   AC/PL/266 'Child Distress and the Schools.' Talk at DES course: 'The Education of Socially Deprived Children,' Froebel College, Roehampton.

25 WYAS Sir Alec Clegg papers A398, Boxes 28 and 29.
26 AC/PL/241 'Educational Problems Solved and Unsolved.' UDC Association Annual Conference, 1966.
27 AC/PL/344 'Child Distress in Schools.' Talk at Barnsley and District Liaison Committee Conference.
28 See 24 above.
29 AC/PL/332 Rotherham College of Technology, Prize Giving, 1973.
30 See 15 above.

Chapter One: Additional Papers

National Arts Education Archive, Bretton Hall College of the University of Leeds, Sir Alec Clegg papers.

AC/PL/105 Summer Meeting of the Association of Education Officers, 1956. Talk on 15–18 Year Olds. (Essential pertinent questions.)
AC/PL/006 Some of the more important facts mentioned in the Crowther Report.
AC/PL/196 'Newsom.' Summary. Notes.
AC/PL/210 'Half Our Future.' What is the Newsom child like?
AC/PL/161 The Crowther Report. Talk at Nottingham Institute of Education.
AC/PL/262 The Newsom Report and its Aftermath. Address at the North of England Education Conference, Liverpool.
AC/PL/207 'Secondary Education: average and below average pupils.' Talk to North Yorkshire Education Officers' Conference, Scarborough.
AC/PL/295 'Education in Society.' Talk at West Riding Vacation Course.
AC/PL/298 'How Equal is Opportunity?' Children's Bureau, Beveridge Hall.
AC/PL/507 'Social Workers in the Schools.'
AC/PL/310 'Recipe for Failure.' Talk at the National Children's Homes Conference, Swanwick.
AC/PL/112 'Secondary School Examinations at 15/16.' Talk given at the annual meeting of Chief Education Officers' Association.
AC/PL/131 'Exams at Secondary Schools.' Talk given to headmasters at Skipton.
AC/PL/183 'Beloe' examinations. Talk given to the West Riding Association NUT, Leeds, 1962.

Home and School:

The Brotherton Library, the University of Leeds, Special Collections Section, Index MS731. WRCC. A.B. Clegg papers.

Box 09   Social Education – general.

Box 10   School Health Service, Mentally and Physically Handicapped
            Children.
Box 11   School Meals and Milk.
Box 12   Minsthorpe, Immigrant Children and the EPA project.
Box 14   Discarded and difficult children and Dartington Hall.

West Yorkshire Archive Service Headquarters, Wakefield. A.B. Clegg
papers, A398. These are essential papers – but not for publication in detail.
They endorse the argument that some children are blocked by circumstances, not inability.

Boxes 4, 22, 24, 28, 34.
Box 25   RoSLA. Alternative School Experiment, 1974.
Box 15   File papers by Mr Woolfe (Research Officer).
Box 27   The Newsom Report and its Aftermath, 1968–71.

The Oxbridge Scheme:

The Brotherton Library, the University of Leeds, Special Collections
Section, Index MS731. WRCC. A.B. Clegg papers.

Box 23   Scholarships and Grants.
Box 23A The Oxbridge Scheme.
Boxes 28 & 29 For comparison: Higher Education Finance, 1902–1939.

West Yorkshire Archive Service Headquarters, Wakefield, A.B. Clegg
papers, A398.

Boxes 10, 14, 26, 30, 31.
Box 11   Files re 1964, 1966–1969; 1950s-1960s; 1968–1969; 1065–1971;
            1965–1972.

The Thorne Scheme. Examinations:

The Brotherton Library, the University of Leeds, Special Collections
Section, Index MS731. WRCC. A.B. Clegg papers.

Box 21   The Thorne Scheme – Selection for Secondary Education.
Box 22   Examinations 1944–1974.

CHAPTER TWO

1   AC/PL/599, AC/PL/00008 Obituary.
2   AC/PL/210 'Half Our Future.' Open meeting at the College of Preceptors,
    London, 1965.
3   AC/PL/122 'Filling pots and lighting fires.' Talk given in Australia.
4   AC/PL.225 Opening talk at Annual Conference of National Association

of School Inspectors, Nottingham.

5　AC/PL/392 'Some observations on English primary schools.' Notes.

6　AC/PL/23 'Educational activities.' Talk given to Huddersfield teachers.

7　AC/PL/225 See 4 above.

8　AC/PL/40 Introductory lecture, Bingley Vacation Course, 1950.

9　AC/PL/57 Talk given at final session, Bingley Vacation Course, 1952.

10　AC/PL/40 See 8 above.

11　AC/PL/425 'Team Work and Beauty.' Review of Sir Alec Clegg's career spanning thirty years.

12　AC/PL/268 'The First Two Rs.' Speech to International Reading Association, New Orleans, USA.

13　The Times Educational Supplement, 4th October 1974.

14　AC/PL/40 See 8 above.

15　AC/PL/317A Notes. No date.

16　AC/PL/210 'Half Our Future.' Open meeting on the Newsom Report at the National Froebel Foundation, 1965.

17　AC/PL/103 'The College – the first seven years.' Talk given at Bretton Hall.

18　AC/PL/49 'My idea of a teacher of the arts.' Talk at Bretton Hall.

19　AC/PL/235 'What Comprehensive Schools Cannot Do.' Talk at Derby LEA Course, Buxton, 1966.

20　AC/PL/430 Expansion of knowledge and reform of the curriculum.'

21　AC/PL/118 'Civilised Values and Further Education.' Talk given in Australia.

22　AC/PL/430 'Expansion of knowledge and reform of the curriculum.'

23　AC/PL/235 See 19 above.

24　AC/PL/224 Talk given at West Riding Vacation Course, Bretton Hall.

25　AC/PL/235 See 19 above.

26　AC/PL/225 See 4 above.

27　AC/PL/609 'National Priorities: Neglect of the Early Years.' Contribution to a series of talks on Education in the 1970s (no date). (Quoted Hadow, 1931; J.S. Bruner, 1965, The Process of Education.)

28　AC/PL/109 'Art in our Society.' Talk at a refresher course for FE teachers, Ilminster.

29　AC/PL/124 'Technical Education.' Talk given in Australia.

30　AC/PL/118 See 21 above.

31　AC/PL/143 'Present Trends in Technological Education.' Talk at the 1959 Convocation of the Textile Institute.

32　AC/PL/87 'The Thorne Shadow Scheme.' Talk given at NUT Council Meeting at Leeds.

33　AC/PL/118 See 21 above.

34　AC/PL/143 See 31 above.

35　The Letters of Matthew Arnold, 2 vols., Macmillan, 1895.

36　AC/PL/163 Conference for Secondary School Heads, Woolley Hall. Opening talk.

37　AC/PL/156 'Problems of the Final Year.' Talk given at the London Institute of Education, Goldsmiths College, 1960.

38　AC/PL/535 Notes on the formation of comprehensive schools in the West

Riding for the Chairman of the West Riding Education Committee.

39   AC/PL/278 Address to the British Association of Organisers and Lecturers in Physical Education, Annual Conference, 1970.

40   AC/PL/41 The Post-war Development Plan.

41   AC/PL/235 'What Comprehensive Schools Cannot Do.' Talk at Derbyshire LEA Conference, Buxton, 1966.

42   AC/PL/535 See 38 above.

43   P.H.J.H. Gosden and P.R. Sharp, 1978, The Development of an Education Service: the West Riding 1889–1974, p.189.

44   AC/PL/535 See 38 above.

45   AC/PL/439 Mexborough Grammar School Sixth Form College. Notes prepared for the Director of Education by the Headmaster.

46   AC/PL/535 See 38 above.

47   AC/PL/439 See 45 above.

48   AC/PL/500 'Minsthorpe: Problems and Possibilities – Aims, Objectives and Philosophy of a Community College.' From the Headmaster, with Staff considerations. Account taken of a Conference at Woolley Hall in 1967. Document undated.

p.48 The nursery/primary ambience.
      A full review has been written by: Marsh, L.G., 1987, A case-study of the process of change in Primary Education within Oxfordshire and the West Riding of Yorkshire from 1944 to 1972. (Unpublished D.Phil., The University of York.)

Chapter Two: Additional Papers

The Brotherton Library, the University of Leeds, Special Collections Section, Index MS731. WRCC. A.B. Clegg papers.

>   Box 15   Primary Education, 1944–1974.
>   Box 16   Middle Schools.
>   Box 31   Further Education and Youth Services
>   Box 32   Agricultural Education 1902–1974. Youth employment inter-war.
>   Box 49   Evening and Technical Schools. Regulations and General Issues, 1902–1939.

West Yorkshire Archive Service Headquarters, Wakefield. A.B. Clegg papers, A398.

>   Box 03   1972 The Changing Primary School. Alec Clegg.
>   Box 15   1944–1959 Educational Development in Secondary Schools. Development Plan.
>   Box 03   1935–1955 Earlier papers re elementary schools.
>   Box 02   1953–1957 The Modern School file.
>   Box 10   1952–1956 Sub-committee to consider the supply and training of special teachers.
>   Box 11   1962 Supply and training of specialist teachers. Sub-committee.

Box 13   1963–1966 File re primary education.
Box 09   1961–1962 Conferences with Heads of Schools.
Box 16   Multilateral schools booklets, letters, articles.
          Comprehensive schools scheme.
          Papers re Educational Advisory Council.
Box 14   File re reorganisation of education.
Box 22   Minsthorpe High School.
Box 36   Batley Community Project.
Box 38   1962–1969 Robbins Report Correspondence.
Box 13   Trends in Education.
Box 32   1955–1960. Papers re Rural Studies.

CHAPTER THREE

1   AC/PL/49 'My idea of a teacher of the arts.' Talk at Bretton Hall, 1951.
2   AC/PL/103 'The College – the first seven years.' Speech given at Bretton Hall, 1956.
3   AC/PL/27 Speech given to 'Art Academy'. No date, no indication of institution.
4   AC/PL/33 Bretton Hall, 26th October 1949.
5   AC/PL/49 See 1 above.
6   AC/PL/79 Notes to the Director, 1954. WYAS Box 9, A.B. Clegg papers, A398.
7   AC/PL/17 Notes on 'The teaching of the arts.' 'What, in order of importance, are the purposes of teaching an art?' 1956.
8   WYAS Box 28, A.B. Clegg papers, A398.
9   AC/PL/278 Annual Conference Address: British Association of Organisers and Lecturers in PE, 1970.
10   AC/PL/106 'PE and its contribution to the development of children.' Talk at Woolley Hall, 1956.
11   AC/PL/278 See 9 above.
12   WYAS A.B. Clegg papers, A398, Boxes.
13   AC/PL/106 See 10 above.
14   AC/PL/278 See 9 above.
15   AC/PL/36 Annual Conference, National Association of Organisers and Lecturers in PE, 1950. Opening Address.
16   AC/PL/278 See 9 above.
17   AC/PL/278 See 9 above.
18   AC/PL/218 Outward Bound Conference, Harrogate. Notes for a talk on 'Outward Bound in Education'.
19   AC/PL/221 British Association of Organisers and Lecturers in PE. Annual Conference, 1965. Talk on 'Physical Education in its relation to examinations and to the general subjects of the curriculum.'
20   AC/PL/175 Talk at Ministry of Education Conference, Woolley Hall, for PE lecturers, 1962.

21   AC/PL/278 See 9 above.
22   AC/PL/394 'Movement.' Talk given at Grantley Hall. No date. (Also 556.)
23   AC/PL/278 See 9 above.
24   AC/PL/394, 556. See 22 above.
25   AC/PL/36 See 15 above.
26   AC/PL/394, 556 See 22 above.
27   WYAS A.B. Clegg papers, A398, Box 28: 'Notes on what has happened to education in recent years', 1973.
28   WYAS A.B. Clegg papers, A398, Box 2, c.1972.
29   AC/PL/49 See 1 above.
30   AC/PL/368 'The First Two Rs.' Speech to the International Reading Association, New Orleans. Own handwriting, 1974.
31   WYAS A.B Clegg papers, A392, Box 2. 'Reading Hysteria' and 'Reading'.
32   WYAS A.B. Clegg papers, A392, Boxes 2 and 28.
33   AC/PL/368 See 30 above.
34   AC/PL/202 'Continuity in Teaching English.' Talk given at NATE Conference, Leeds.
35   AC/PL/49 See 1 above.
36   AC/PL/368 See 30 above.
37   WYAS A.B. Clegg papers, A398, Box 2. Notes on Reading.
38   Conversation overheard in a shop in Sawley between two small boys.
39   AC/PL/184 Physical Education Association, New Year Conference, 1963. 'Is PE an Art or a Science?' Methods across the curriculum.
40   AC/PL/368 See 30 above.
41   WYAS A.B. Clegg papers, A398, Box 2, 1972.

Chapter Three: Additional Papers

National Arts Education Archive, Bretton Hall College of the University of Leeds, Sir Alec Clegg papers.

AC/PL/134	'Physical Education for Senior Girls.' Woolley Hall, 1953. Also Notes for a lecture, 1958.
AC/PL/221	British Association of Organisers in Physical Education Annual Conference, Liverpool, 1965.
AC/PL/163	Conference for Secondary School Heads, Woolley Hall, 1961.
AC/PL/416	Questions on PE, movement (1973) and nursery education (undated).
AC/PL/300	An informal, extempore address by Sir Alec Clegg to the student body, Toronto Teachers' College, 1971.

West Yorkshire Archive Service Headquarters, Wakefield,. A.B.Clegg Papers, Boxes 1 to 39, A398.

Box 10	1952–1956 Sub-Committee to consider the supply and training of special teachers.

Box 32   1955–1960 Papers re Arts and Handicrafts, Music Reports, PE
           Reports, Rural Studies.
           1955–1962, 1965, 1960 and 1968. Papers re Science, Special
           Schools.
Box 35   1940–1946 Best work 4A English.
           1963–1970 'The Excitement of Writing', children's work, books
           of poetry.
Box 38   1964–1973 'The Excitement of Writing', 'Enjoying Writing'.
Box 39   1963–1964 'The Excitement of Writing.'
Box 27   Students' poetry and stories.
Box 29   Enjoying writing poems, examples of handwriting.
Box 03   1972 Essays, poems by primary school children.

CHAPTER FOUR

1   West Yorkshire Archive Service Headquarters, Wakefield. A.B. Clegg papers,
     A398, Box 14.
2   WYAS Box 14.
3   Through ABC papers there is appreciation of the interaction of HMI with all
     local levels. See also 'The Local Authority and the School', AC/PL/238, 1966.
4   WYAS A.B. Clegg papers, A398, Box 9.
5   AC/PL/238
6   AC/PL/135 Public Lecture, the Institute of Education, University of London,
     1958. 'The powers, duties, and changing attitudes of HMIs, the part they play
     in the formation of national educational policy, their relationship with central
     and local government.
     Attached: 'Functions of HM and CC Inspectors'.
7   WYAS A.B. Clegg papers, A398, Box 9.
8   WRCC minutes, Education Committee, 20.10.1902. The WR campaigned
     nationally for County Councils to be reorganised as the local education
     authorities for secondary schooling.
9   Gosden & Sharp, 1978, The Development of an Education Service
     1889–1974, Martin Robertson, pp. 20ff, 122–124; 271–273.
10   WYAS A.B. Clegg papers, A398, Box 3.
11   WYAS Box 14.
12   AC/PL/238 'The Local Authority and the School.' Course for newly-
     appointed Heads of Secondary Schools, Oxford University Department of
     Education.
13   AC/PL/163 Opening talk at Conference for Secondary School Heads at
     Woolley Hall, 1961.
14   WYAS A.B. Clegg papers, A398, Box 9.
15   AC/PL/238 See 12 above.
16   AC/PL/12 'What it means to me : education.'

Chapter Four: Additional Papers

The Brotherton Library, the University of Leeds, Special Collections Section, Index MS731. WRCC. A.B. Clegg papers.

Box 44   Post-Second World War.
Box 52   Policy and Finance Indexes, 1952–1954.
Box 53   Administration.
Box 56   Changes in the Education Services in the county over the last six years.
Box 58   1902 Act, 1906–1908 Bills. Establishment of the Education Committee, devolution of power.
Boxes 17–20 Secondary Education, 1944–1974.
Boxes 28–29 Higher Education Finance 1902–1939.
Box 30   Finance, General, 1902–1974.
Box 34   Extracts from West Riding Education Committee Annual Reports, 1905–1939.
Box 37   First World War and Post-First World War Reconstruction.
Box 42   School Premises, Building Programmes, Elementary and Secondary, 1902–1939.
Box 46   Extracts from West Riding Education Authority Annual Reports, Secondary.
Box 47   Secondary Education, 1902–1939. (Curriculum, Grants to Secondary Schools, General, Regulations.)
Box 48   Proposed new secondary schools, 1902–1939.
Box 51   Miscellaneous Statistics, 1944–1974.
Box 54   Index to Post-war Education Minutes and Memos.
Box 38   Half-time system and exemptions, 1902–1932.
Boxes 7, 8 and 8A
            West Riding Education Committee Annual Reports: 1904–1915; 1914–1939; and Triennial Statements in Education.
Box 27   '. . . inspectors, advisers . . .'

National Arts Education Archive, Bretton Hall College of the University of Leeds, Sir Alec Clegg papers.

AC/PL/157   'Functions of the Local Authority in relation to the Ministry on the one hand and to Schools and Parents on the other.' Course for Administrative Officers, 1960, West Midlands Advisory Council.
AC/PL/102   'Some relics of the 1944 Act and of the Development Plan.' Conference of CC Inspectors, Advisers, and Administrative Staff. No date.
AC/PL/38   Conference of CC Inspectors and Advisers, Beechwood, Harrogate, 1950.
AC/PL/135   'The powers, duties, and changing attitudes of HMIs, the part they play in the formation of national educational policy, their

relationship with central and local government.' Public lecture, the Institute of Education, University of London, 1958.

West Yorkshire Archive Service Headquarters, Wakefield. A.B. Clegg papers, A398.

Box 9   Conference of Inspectors and Advisers.
Dr A.G. Hughes: 'What a good adviser should do.' the idea of an education staff college gave a blueprint for Woolley Hall College.

Box 15   1946–1959 'Educational Development – The Future Development in Secondary Schools.'

RC/13/45–462
Policy and Finance Sub-Committee Minutes. Resignations and promotions. Depletion of CCIs and Advisory Staff.

CHAPTER FIVE

1   Four Reports: WYAS A.B. Clegg papers, A398, Box 15.
    1953 Ten Years of Change
    1964 Changes and Delusions in Education
    1964 Education 1954–1964
    1974 The Final Ten Years

2   AC/PL/82 'The Training of the Specialist Teacher.' Talk at the Conference of the Incorporated Association of Headmasters, Woolley Hall, 1954.

3   AC/PL/156 'Problems of the final year.' Talk given at Goldsmiths College, the Institute of Education, London University, 1960.

4   **Bretton Hall** WYAS, WRCC Further Education Sub-Committee, Index RC/13/336–341, 1949–1970.
University of Leeds Special Collections, ABC Archive, Index MS731 and Box 26A 1945–1972.

5   WYAS Special Sub-Committee appointed to review Post-War Education: Agendum 3A, 19.2.46. WRCC Education Committee.
See Gosden and Sharp, 1978, The Development of an Education Service: The West Riding, 1889–1974, Martin Robertson, pp.25, 113, 120, 159, 165; and Reconstruction Committee, pp.161, 162.
Circular 77, Ministry of Education on the provision of additional training colleges.

6   **Lady Mabel College** WYAS, WRCC Further Education Sub-Committee and Policy & Finance Sub-Committee. Index RC/13/342–347, 1949–1970.
University of Leeds Special Collections, The Brotherton Library, Index MS731, Box 26.

7   AC/PL/156 'Problems of the final year.' Talk given at Goldsmiths College, The Institute of Education, London University.

8   **Grantley Hall Adult College** WYAS, WRCC Further Education

Sub-Committee and Policy & Finance Sub-Committee. Index RC/13/348–353, 1951–1970.
WYAS A.B. Clegg papers, A398, Box 13.
University of Leeds, Special Collections, The Brotherton Library, Index MS731, Box 32.
Gosden and Sharp, 1978, The Development of an Education Service: The West Riding, 1889–1974, Martin Robertson, pp.204–207.

9   **Ilkley College** WYAS, WRCC Education Committee minutes and Further Education Sub-Committee minutes. Index RC/13/348–353, 1951–1970.
WYAS, A.B. Clegg papers, A398, Box 9.
AC/PL/173. Talk at the tenth Annual Commemoration Service.

10   AC/BK/17 Darvill, P., Parts I, II & III. A.B. Clegg papers. Bretton Hall.

11   University of Leeds, Special Collections, The Brotherton Library, Index MS731, Box 26.

12   **Woolley Hall** WYAS WRCC, Education Committee, Further Education Sub-Committee, and Wakefield Metropolitan District Education Committee, Index RC/13/354–359, 1951–1970.
A.B. Clegg papers, A398, Boxes 1, 6, 13, 17, 27.

13   AC/PL/238 'The Local Authority and the School.' Course for newly appointed Heads of Secondary Schools, Oxford University Department of Education, 1966. Attached note on in-service training.

14   **Scawsby College** WYAS WRCC, Education Committee, Index RC/13/367–368, 1964–1970.
University of Leeds, Special Collections, The Brotherton Library, Index MS731, A.B. Clegg papers, Box 26.

15   **Bramley Grange** WYAS WRCC, Education Committee, Further Education Sub-Committee, Index RC/13/369.
University of Leeds, Special Collections, The Brotherton Library, Index MS731, A.B. Clegg papers, Boxes 7, 8, 9, 32.
Gosden and Sharp, 1978. The Development of an Education Service: The West Riding, 1889–1974, Martin Robertson, pp.1–13 (1890s); 83, 93–98 (1902–1944); 201–204 (1944–1974).

16   AC/PL/88 Talk at the opening of the Horticultural Section of the Bingley Vacation Course, 1955.

17   AC/PL/156 'Problems of the Final Year.' Talk given at Goldsmiths College, London University, Institute of Education, 1960.

18   The Weaver Report on Colleges of Higher Education (F.E.), 1966.

19   WYAS A.B. Clegg papers, A398, Box 14. Letter 10.3.1970. Hogan to Clegg.

20   Morton, Ann, 1997. Education and the State from 1833, PRO Publications, p.74 on the Russell Committee.

21   AC/PL/500 'Minsthorpe: Problems and Possibilities.'

22   **Harrogate Training College** WYAS WRCC, Education Committee, Further Education Sub-Committee, Policy and Finance Sub-Committee, Index RC/13/329, 1947–1950.
Gosden and Sharp, 1978, The Development of an Education Service: The West Riding, 1889–1974, p.246.

Chapter Five: Additional Papers

The Brotherton Library, the University of Leeds, Special Collections Section, Index MS731. WRCC. A.B. Clegg papers.

Box 26   Bingley, Emergency Training Colleges, Bretton Hall, Lady Mabel, Woolley Hall, Scawsby and Ilkley.

Box 32   Agricultural Education 1902–1974, Grantley Hall and Bramley Grange.

West Yorkshire Archive Service Headquarters, Wakefield. A.B. Clegg papers, A398.

Box 17   The history of courses at Woolley Hall, 1960s, 1970s.

Box 27   Woolley Hall courses from 1945 to 1952.

Box 36   Dormant training colleges, 1950. Education of teachers and future of training colleges.

CONCLUSION

1   AC/PL/201 'Change and Delusion in Education.' Bretton Hall Foundation Lecture, p.14, 1964.

2   Clegg, A.B. and Megson, B.E., 1968, Children in Distress. London: Penguin. AC/PL/204 Talk given at Ackworth School Open Day.

3   See The Use of English, 1995, Vol.47, No.1, pp.7–17. 'Poetry and Painting', Jill Pirrie. The Use of English, 1994, Vol.46, No.1, pp.36–52. 'Catching a Mind: Jill Pirrie's English Teaching', J. Pye.

4   AC/PL/368 'The First Two Rs.' Speech to the International Reading Association, New Orleans, 1974.

5   AC/PL/323 Centenary Dinner, Hull National Union of Teachers.

6   AC/PL/171 'Attitudes.' Talk given at the North of England Education Conference, Southport, 1962.

7   AC/PL/323 See 5 above.

8   AC/PL/106 'Physical Education and its contribution to the development of children.' Woolley Hall, 1956.

9   WYAS A.B. Clegg papers, A398, Box 13.

10   AC/PL/368 See 4 above.

11   WYAS A.B. Clegg papers, A398, Box 12.

12   Viscount Milton, MP for Wakefield, at the Annual Prizegiving of the Industrial and Fine Art Institution, Wakefield, December 1896.

13   Searle, J.R., 1969. Speech Acts: An Essay in the Philosophy of Language, Cambridge University Press, p.14.

14   Thring, E., Headmaster, Uppingham School. Theory and Practice of Teaching.
     Hoole, Charles, Headmaster, Rotherham Grammar School.

15   WYAS A.B. Clegg papers, A398. The Boundary Commission, Box 35.

Conclusion: Additional References

National Arts Education Archive, Bretton Hall College of the University
of Leeds, Sir Alec Clegg papers.

AC/PL/012 'What it means to me: education.'
and
AC/PL/325, 326   'Education, mind and spirit.' Conferences at Reading
                  (1973), York University, and Canada.
AC/PL/236 'Formation of character through education.' Talk at Charlotte
          Mason College, 1966.
AC/PL/272 'Principles and Priorities.' Cambridge Union Society 'teach-in',
          1969.
AC/PL/597 'We have much to worry us.' Times Educational Supplement,
          11.10.1974.
AC/PL/378 Talk to European Council of International Schools. No date.
AC/PL/377 'Loaves and Hyacinths.' No date.

Bibliography

ORIGINAL SOURCES

Boxes 1–59 'Alexander Bradshaw Clegg Papers', Special Collections Section, the
    Brotherton Library, University of Leeds. ('Personal' files in Boxes 2 and 3.)
MS731, Index to the above papers: West Riding County Council, Leeds
    University.
Boxes containing Papers, Lectures and Addresses by Sir Alec Clegg, numbered 57
    to 727, National Arts Education Archive at Bretton Hall College of the
    University of Leeds, Bretton Hall near Wakefield.
Boxes 1–39/A398,West Riding Education Department: Alec Clegg and other
    Education Papers, West Yorkshire Archive Service Headquarters, Newstead
    Road, Wakefield.

At Bretton Hall:
Crouch, Christopher, 1987. National Arts Education Archive Research Project:
    The Contribution of Sir Alec Clegg to the Arts in Schools. Published work
    by and relating to Sir Alec Clegg.
The Lawrence Batley Centre for the National Arts Education Archive (Trust) at
    Bretton Hall College of the University of Leeds: Bramley Occasional Papers
    Volume 4, 1991. The Sir Alec Clegg Memorial Volume marking the Opening
    of the Trust's Interpretation and Research Centre.
Woodward, Eric, Editor, 1991. Sir Alec Clegg: His Own Words. National Arts
    Education Archive, Bretton Hall College of the University of Leeds.

Darvill, Peter. Sir Alec Clegg: the man, his ideas, and his schools. (AC/BK/17–1, 2 & 3), National Arts Education Archive, Bretton Hall College of the University of Leeds.

Mace, David, M.A. Art and Education in the West Riding, 1945–1974.

'The Development of Art and Craft Education in the West Riding Education Authority during the period of Sir Alec Clegg's service as Chief Education Officer, 1945–74, with particular reference to Art in the National Curriculum' (DM/BK/323/2, Bretton Hall College).

Sir Alec Clegg and the Arts in Schools, 1945–74 (DM/BK/322).

The Exhibition, N.A.E.A. 1990– (DM/BK/320).

Art Education in the West Riding, Reference Material (DM/BK/323/1).

Art Education in the West Riding, Supporting Material (DM/BK/323/2).

Flower Paintings from South Kirkby Primary School: Collection of Sir Alec Clegg. N.A.E.A., Bretton.

Tapes, Paintings. The National Arts Education Archive, Bretton Hall College of the University of Leeds, Sir Alec Clegg collection.

SIR ALEC CLEGG'S PUBLICATIONS

The Excitement of Writing.	1964	London: Chatto & Windus.
Enjoying Writing.	1973	London: Chatto & Windus.
The Years of Change.	1953	West Riding Education Committee.
Education 1954–64.	1964	A report on the development of the Education Service in the West Riding. West Riding Education Committee.
The First Ten Years, 1964–74.	1974	West Riding Education Committee.
Children in Distress.	1968,	1973 (with B.E. Megson) London: Penguin.
The Changing Primary School: its problems and priorities, a statement by teachers.	1972	London: Chatto & Windus.
About Our Schools.	1980, 1981	London: Blackwell.

Particular A.B. Clegg Personal References

Arnold, Matthew	1895	Letters. Macmillan.
Thring, E.	1883	Theory and Practice of Teaching.
Whitehead, A.N.	1932	The Aims of Education, London: Williams and Norbert.
Shuttleworth, Sir James Kaye	1862	Four periods of Public Education as reviewed in 1832, 1834, 1846, 1862.
AC/PL/414, 415		Quotations (Bretton)

1947–74 (SIR ALEC CLEGG'S PERIOD OF OFFICE)

Abercrombie, M.L. 1960, The Anatomy of Judgement. London: Hutchinson.

Berger, Peter 1970, A Rumour of Angels (USA, 1969). London: Penguin Press.

Bishop, A.S. 1971, The Rise of a Central Authority in Education. Cambridge University Press.

Bruner, J. 1964, On Knowing: Essays for the Left Hand. Cambridge MA, Harvard University Press.

Bruner, J. 1965, The Process of Education. Cambridge MA, Harvard University Press.

Buber, M. 1947, Between Man and Man: Essay on Education. Fontana Books.

Castle, E.B. 1954, People in School. Heinemann.

Clegg, S. 1918, Drawing and Design: a school course in composition. London: Pitman.

Collingwood, R.G. 1951, An Autobiography. Oxford University Press (Reprint of 1939 edition).

Dent, H.C. 1943, A landmark in English education: a commentary on the White Paper on educational reconstruction. London: University of London Press.

Education, Board of 1931, Handbook for the consideration of teachers and others concerned in the work of public elementary schools. HMSO.

Education, Board of 1943, Educational Reconstruction. Command Paper 6458. HMSO.

Friends, Society of, Books of Friends' Faith and Practice.

Gregory, R.L. 1970, The Intelligent Eye. London: Weidenfeld & Nicolson.

Hodgkin, R.A. 1970, Reconnaissance on an Educational Frontier. Oxford University Press.

Hogan, J.M. 1970, Beyond the Classroom. Reading: Educational Explorers.

Holmes, E. 1911, What is and what might be. London: Constable.

Hudson, L. 1966, Contrary Imaginations. London: Methuen.

Jordan, D. 1966, Childhood and Movement. Oxford: Blackwell.

Koestler, A. 1959, The Sleepwalkers. London: Hutchinson.

Koestler, A. 1964, The Act of Creation. London: Hutchinson.

Kuhn, T.S. 1965, The Structure of Scientific Revolutions. University of Chicago Press.

Long Eaton Advertiser 1930, Obituary of Samuel Clegg (A.B. Clegg's father) 21st March, Long Eaton, Derbyshire.

Newsome, David 1974, Two Classes of Men: Platonism and English Romantic Thought. London: John Murray.

Niblett, W.R. (Ed.) 1963, Moral Education in a Changing Society.

Raine, K. 1967, Defending Ancient Springs. Oxford University Press.

Read, H. 1945, Education through Art. London: Faber.

Sadler, M.E. 1905, Report on the secondary and higher education in Derbyshire. Education Committee of the County of Derbyshire.

Schon, D.A. 1963, Displacement of Concepts. London: Tavistock.

Vygotsky, L.S. 1962, Thought and Language. Massachusetts Institute of Technology.

Wilson, P. 1961, Views and Prospects from Curzon Street (Senior Chief HMI). Oxford: Blackwell.

AUTHORITATIVE TEXTS

Barber B.J. and Beresford, M.W. 1974, The West Riding County Council. WRCC.
Bishop, A.S. 1971, The Rise of Central Authority for English Education. Cambridge University Press. (A detailed history).
Gosden, P.H.J.H. and Sharp, P.R. 1978, The Development of an Education Service: The West Riding.
Martin Robertson. (Essential reference).
Greenhalgh, V. 1974, Local Education Administrators, 1870–1974. University of Leeds (unpublished Ph.D.) (Essential reference).
Leese, J. 1950, Personalities and Power in English Education. Leeds: E.J. Arnold and Son, Ltd.
Morton, A. 1997, Education and the State. Public Records Office, Reader's Guide No. 18 PRO Publications. (Essential reference)
Musgrove, F. 1990, The North of England. Oxford: Blackwell (particularly the last two chapters).
Reader, W.J. 1966, Professional Men: The Rise of the Professional Classes in Nineteenth Century England. London: Weidenfeld & Nicolson.

★   ★   ★   ★   ★   ★   ★

Halsbury's Statutes, Vol. 4, No. 15, 1918–44. Leeds Public Library.
Statistics of Education. Information on Schools, Finances, Teaching. HMSO.
Education Committees Yearbook. Councils and Education Press.
Education Authorities Directory. Councils and Education Press.
British Education Index. Guide to articles on educational topics which have appeared in periodicals and journals.

GENERAL BIBLIOGRAPHY

Archambault, R.A. 1965, Philosophical Analysis and Education. Routledge and Kegan Paul.
Benton, Michael 1978, The First Two Rs. University of Southampton..
Castle, E.B. 1970, The Teacher. Oxford University Press.
Clegg, A.B. 1976, 'Rigour and Inspiration', Times Educational Supplement, 9th July 3188.
Dean, J. 1975, 'The local advisory service and the professional development of teachers.' Journal of the National Association of Inspectors and Educational Advisers, Vol.2, pp.9–13.
Dewey, J. 1916, Democracy and Education.

Eisner, E. Instructional and Expressive Objectives. AERA Monograph No. 3.

Eisner, E. 1991, The Enlightened Eye: A Qualitative Enquiry and the Enhancement of Educational Practice. N.Y.: Longman.

Gosden, P.H.J.H. 1983, The Education System since 1944. Oxford: Martin Robertson.

Gosden, P.H.J.H. 1976, Education in the Second World War: A study in Policy and Administration. Oxford: Martin Robertson.

Gregory, R.L. 1970, The Intelligent Eye. London: Weidenfeld & Nicolson.

Higginson, J.H. 1979, Selections from Michael Sadler: Studies in World Citizenship. Dejalle & Meyorre Publishers Ltd.

Hirst, P.H. and Peters, R.S. 1970, The Logic of Education. Routledge and Kegan Paul.

'Kingman Report' 1988, Report of the Committee of Inquiry into the Teaching of the English Language. Sir John Kingman, FRS.

Knox, W.W. 1980, British Apprenticeships 1800–1914. University of Edinburgh. (unpublished Ph.D.) (Authoritative text)

Kogan, M. and Van Der Eyken, W. 1973, County Hall: the role of the Chief Education Officer. Penguin.

Linnett, C.P. 1986, Secondary Technical Schools in England and Wales: a study of Curriculum and Administration Policies, 1889–1965. University of London (unpublished Ph.D.) (Authoritative text)

Maclure, J.S. 1984, Educational Development and School Building: aspects of public policy, 1945–1973. London: Longman.

Marsden, W.E. 1987, Unequal Education in England and Wales: The Nineteenth Century Roots. London: The Woburn Press.

Marsden, W.E. 1991, Educating the Respectable: a study of Fleet Road Board School, Hampstead, 1879–1903. London: The Woburn Press.

Marsh, L.G. 1987, A Case Study of the Process of Change in Primary Education within Oxfordshire and the West Riding of Yorkshire from 1944 to 1972 University of York (unpublished Ph.D.).

Moffet, J. 1968, Teaching the Universe of Discourse. N.Y.: Houghton Mifflin Co.

Open University 1979, Language Development, ref. P232. Open University Press.

Protherough, R. and Atkinson, J. 1991 The Making of English Teachers. Open University Press.

Sanderson, M. 1994, The Missing Stratum: Technical Education in England, 1900–90. London: The Athlone Press.

Sandstrom, C.J. 1966, Psychology of Childhood and Adolescence. Penguin.

Summerfield, P. and Evans, E.J. 1990, Technical Education and the State since 1850. Manchester University Press.

Weaver, Sir Toby 1979, 'Education, retrospect and prospect: an administrative testimony.' Cambridge Journal of Education, Vol.9, pp.2–17.

NATIONAL COMMITTEES AND REPORTS

1920   Cmnd 968.xv.385. Departmental Committee on Scholarships and Free Places. (PRO.ED.12/434).

1921 National Expenditure (Geddes). (PRO.ED.24/1301–11).

1923 Cmnd 737.xii.308. A non-parliamentary committee appointed by the Prime Minister. Classics in Education.

1924 Report of a Consultative Committee for the Non-Parliamentary Board of Education. Hadow in Chair. Psychological Tests of Educable Capacity.

1925 Cmnd 2409.xii.203. Departmental Committee on the Training of Teachers for Elementary Schools (Burnham).

1926 A Non-Parliamentary Committee of the Board of Education and the Ministry of Labour: Education and Industry in England and Wales.

1926 The Education of the Adolescent (Hadow). (PRO.ED.97; ED.10/47; ED.24/1265).

1926 Board of Education Survey of Technical and Further Education in England and Wales.

1926–8 Malcolm Report of the Committee on Education and Industry in England and Wales, Parts I and II.

1928 A Departmental Committee of the Board of Education: Examinations for part-time students.

1928 Consultative Committee, Board of Education, Hadow in Chair: Books in Public Elementary Schools.

1928 Emmott Committee of Enquiry with the Relations of Technical Education to other forms of Education, Industry, and Commerce.

1938 Spen's Report on Secondary Education with special reference to Grammar Schools and Technical High Schools. 'To report on secondary schools other than elementary schools with particular regard to the education of pupils who do not remain at school after the age of 16.'

1941–3 Norwood Committee on Examinations and Curricula (PRO ED.12/478–480; ED.138/16; ED.136/681).

1942 Fleming Committee on the Public Schools and the General Education System (PRO ED.136/597–607; ED.136/607).

1942–4 McNair Report on the Supply, Training and Recruitment of Teachers and Youth Leaders (PRO ED.86/94–109).

1943 Norwood Report on Examinations (PRO ED.142/56).

1942–4 School Planning Committee under Sir Robert Wood – Buildings. (PRO ED.10/285; ED.136–336; ED.338–380).

1943 Government White Paper on Reconstruction. HMSO.

1943 Fleming Advisory Committee on Post-war Teachers (PRO ED.143/32; ED.136–687).

1945 Percy Report on Higher Technological Education (PRO ED.46/295–296).

1946 Cmnd 6824 Barlow Committee appointed by the Lord President of the Council, Report on Scientific Manpower (PRO HC.1924–5.xii; 1201, 1814, 1818).

1947 Report of the Local Government Boundary Commission. HMSO.

1952 Federation of British Industries: Report of the Universities and Industry Conferences, London.

1957–9 Willis-Jackson Report on the Supply and Training of Teachers for Technical Colleges. CATS Designated. (PRO ED.46/972–977).

1958 White Paper: Secondary Education for All: a New Drive (Gosden, 1983, p31).

1959–60 The Crowther Report: 15–18 (PRO ED.146/29–44).

1960 Beloe Report on Secondary Schools Examinations other than GCE (PRO ED.147/303–313).

1960 Albemarle Report: The Youth Service (Gosden, 1983, p43).

1962 National Committee for the Certificate in Office Studies (PRO ED.46/869–870; ED.200).

1963 The Newsom Report: 13–16 (PRO ED.146/45–63).

1963 Lockwood Report on Curriculum and Examinations (PRO ED.147/812–816).

1963 Robbins Report on Higher Education (PRO ED.46/945–949; ED.116; ED.117; ED.118; HC.1962–3 xi-xix).

1964 Henniker-Heaton Report on Day Release (PRO ED.204/4).

1964 Local Government Commission for England: Report No. 7: Report Proposals for West Yorkshire Special Review Area; Research Study No. 7: Aspects of Education in a Large Authority.

1965 Brynmor Jones Report on Audio Visual Aids in Higher Scientific Education. HMSO. (PRO ED.181, EA1, EA2).

1966–7 Royal Commission on Local Government in England. Volumes I, II & III. Redcliffe Maud.

1966 Weaver Report on Colleges of Higher Education, (FE). (PRO ED.86/359–361).

1967 Plowden Report on Children and their Primary Schools (PRO ED.146/64–93; ED.207/1–14).

1968 DES Sub-committee on Management Education (PRO ED.201).

1969 Willey Committee on Teacher Training. House of Commons Select Committee for B.Ed.

1970 Maud Report of the Committee of Management of Local Government.

1970 Donnison Commission on the Public Schools (Gosden, 1983, p45).

1970 DES and National Advisory Council on Education for Industry and Commerce (NACEIC). (PRO ED.46/699–750; ED.205).

1970 James Committee on Teacher Training (PRO ED.145).

1970 Weaver Group on Working of HMI in FE: Report from the Select Committee on Education and Science (PRO HC.1967–81, Cmnd 3860).

1972 The New Local Authorities – Management and Structure: Report on Local Authority Management Structures, Department of Environment, HMSO.

1972 DES – Education: A Framework for Expansion. Cmnd 5174.

1973 Russell Report on Adult Education: A Plan for Development (PRO ED.175/25).

1973 Ogilvie – Schools Council Paper on gifted children in the primary school.

1978 Warnock Report on the Education of Handicapped Children and Young People (PRO HC.1977–8, Cmnd 7212).

1978   Waddell Report on Secondary School Examinations and Syllabuses (PRO HC.1977/81 iix, Cmnd 7281).
1981   Macfarlane Report. Education Post 16.

LEGISLATION

1880   Education Act (Mundella).
1899   Board of Education Act (1899–1944).
1902   Education Act (Balfour). Abolished School Boards, and LEAs could 'provide education other than elementary'.
1918   Secondary (Grammar) Schools (Fisher).
1921   School leaving age raised to 14.
1944   Butler Act. Tripartite System – schools branch, FE branch, special educational provisions (PRO ED.31/500–548; ED.136/377–541; ED.142).
1948/53 Special educational provision modified.
1953   Voluntary Schools grants.
1959   Grants on buildings and new aided denominational schools.
1962   Awards to students.
1965   Circular 10/65. Direction towards comprehensivisation. Raising of school leaving age announced in 1964.
1967   Grant payable to new aided schools increased.
1970   Short's Bill to enforce comprehensivisation, circular 10/70 issued and circular 10/65 withdrawn.
1973   School leaving age raised to 16.
1975   Grant payable to aided schools again increased.
        A duty laid on LEAs for handicapped children in schools.
1979   Removed compulsion to re-organise on comprehensive lines.
1980   Assisted places scheme.
        Power of LEAs to provide meals and milk.
1981   Special educational provisions (Warnock).
1988   Education Reform Act.

ADMINISTRATION

1833–1899   Committee of the Privy Council on Education.
1856–1899   Education Department.
1899–1944   Board of Education.
1944–1964   Ministry of Education.
1964–1992   Department of Education and Science
1992–1995   Department for Education
1995 ——   Department for Education and Employment